Funeral of the CITY WATCH BOXES

I SPY BLUE

I SPY BLUE

The Police and Crime
in the City of London from
Elizabeth I to Victoria

DONALD RUMBELOW

I Spy Blue, I Spy Black,
I Spy a Peeler in a shiny hat.

MACMILLAN
ST MARTIN'S PRESS

SBN boards: 333 10652 0
Library of Congress Catalog Card No. 70-171584

First published 1971 by
MACMILLAN LONDON LTD
London and Basingstoke
Associated companies in New York Toronto
Dublin Melbourne Johannesburg and Madras

Printed in Great Britain by
ROBERT MACLEHOSE AND CO LTD
The University Press, Glasgow

To Polly
with love

Contents

Plates

ACKNOWLEDGEMENTS

British Museum, Department of Prints and Drawings: 3, 4

City Police: 8, 9, 10, 12

Guildhall Library: 1, 5, 6, 7, 13

London Museum: 2, 15

The Times: 11

Rev. H. Johnson: 14

A2

Illustrations in the Text

ACKNOWLEDGEMENTS

Gerald Howson: 5, 6, 7

City Police: 12

Guildhall Library: the remainder

Acknowledgements

To the Commissioner of the City of London Police Sir Arthur Young, C.M.G., C.V.O., K.P.M., for making the whole thing possible; to Chief Superintendent W. Burley for his frequent help and encouragement; and to those of my colleagues who helped in so many other ways.

To Mr P. E. Jones, O.B.E., the former Assistant Keeper of Records at the City of London Guildhall, and the present Assistant Keeper, Miss Betty Masters, I owe a particularly heavy debt. Not only did they tolerate with the utmost good humour – though at times this must have been strained – my permanent occupation, as well as my daily disruption, of the Records Office, but helped me as well in so many other ways too numerous to mention. I shall always think fondly of the many kindnesses I had from them. I should also like to thank Stan Mayles and John Martin for helping to make my stay so pleasant, and to John in particular for showing me how simple it is partly to demolish a corridor wall with a trolley-load of Police Committee boxes.

To the staffs of the Guildhall Library and the Commissioners' Library, New Scotland Yard, to Mr Ringrose of Lincoln's Inn Library, to Dr J. J. Tobias for reading the early chapters, to Donald McCormick for information on Harvey, to Dr A. E. J. Hollaender, to Mr J. L. Howgego, Keeper of Prints and Pictures at the Guildhall Library, and to C. W. Shepherd ('Shep') for watching over it from the beginning.

To Gerald Howson for the illustrations to Chapter 3 and for generously letting me read and quote from his biography of Jonathan Wild, *Thief-taker General*, while it was still in manuscript. To James Wright who saw that a book was possible and showed me how to make one from my inky pages. In both instances, the friendship that has resulted has been one of the more valuable rewards for writing this book.

Finally to my wife who has had to put up with the high as well as the low.

DONALD RUMBELOW

Foreword

BY

SIR ARTHUR YOUNG, C.M.G., C.V.O., K.P.M.
Commissioner of Police for the City of London

IT is a pleasure to write this foreword to Mr Rumbelow's book; indeed, it is with a feeling of pride that I do so.

The Force has received many requests for information of its early history, and though we were aware that much material was available no authentic coverage has previously been attempted.

Mr Rumbelow has done an enormous amount of research into the early history of policing in the City of London from the time of Elizabeth I to Queen Victoria, and this is the first full account of the difficulties of the first Commissioner and the formation of the Force following the City of London Police Act, 1839.

Much painstaking work has uncovered unpublished material from which the author has built up not only a vivid portrait of the changing face of the City of London through several centuries but also intimate portraits of the men themselves.

In this book a balance has been struck which lifts it above a catalogue of crimes and produces a rich social history illustrating in depth the often brutal conditions in which the City Marshals and early City policemen lived and worked.

26 Old Jewry,   ARTHUR YOUNG
London, E.C.2.
April 1971

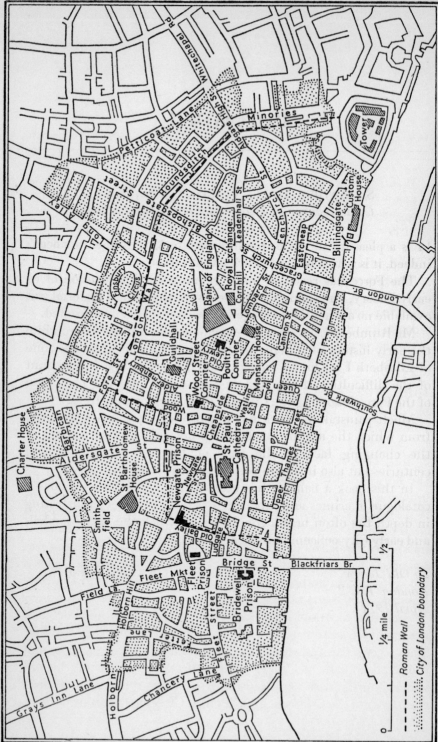

The City of London at the beginning of the Nineteenth Century

Introduction

Wanted, a hundred thousand men for London watchmen. None need apply for this lucrative situation without being the age of sixty, seventy, eighty, or ninety years; blind with one eye and seeing very little with the other; crippled in one or both legs; deaf as a post; with an asthmatical cough that tears them to pieces; whose speed will keep pace with a snail, and the strength of whose arm would not be able to arrest an old washerwoman of fourscore returned from a hard day's fag at the washtub; whose constitution is worn-out in hard service, either in the army or navy, some unhealthy business, or from the effects of a gay and profligate life; and that such will neither see or hear what belongs to their duty, or what does not, unless well-palmed, or garnished for the same.

JOHN PEARSON'S mock advertisement is the conventional picture of the London watchmen of the past, of gouty old men, wheezing with asthma, hobbling through the streets with mountains of capes on their bent backs, lighting lords to brothels, or fingering bribes, or tippling with prostitutes, or huddling in the snug warmth of their watchboxes bawling the hour and ignoring the dark and unprotected beats they had left to thieves to plunder. Nineteenth-century England fully shared his amused contempt for these feeble guardians of the night. Perversely, it insisted on their retention. And when this antiquated system was swept away, against its wishes, it rounded fiercely on 'Peel's bloody gang' and others of the New Police. 'Down with the Raw Lobsters, Blue Devils!' it screamed.

Such hatred would have been understandable if the police had inherited a tradition of violence and repression. But they had not. They were steady, efficient and reliable. The corruption and indiscipline that had been such a notable feature of the old watch had likewise been purged from their ranks. (In the first eight years the Metropolitan Police Commissioners reputedly

dismissed, from a force of over 3000 men, 5000 men, and a
further 5000 resigned.) This meant little. In the early part of
the nineteenth century there was widespread belief that a police
force was no more than an instrument of repression. In confirma-
tion of this men looked to the Continent, to France, where the
absolutism of the Bourbons had been replaced by the absolutism
of Napoleon. In the hands of Joseph Fouché, Napoleon's Minister
of Police, the police state had been brought one step nearer to
perfection. 'Police' had long been synonymous with spies and
agents provocateurs. The word, and its associations with France,
aroused the same kind of feelings in nineteenth-century England
that the S.S. or the K.G.B. have aroused in the twentieth. No
other police system could be envisaged. In 1818 a Police Committee concluded:

> Though your committee could imagine a system of police that might
> arrive at the object sought for; yet, in a free country, or even in one
> where any unrestrained intercourse of society is admitted, such a
> system would of necessity be odious and repulsive, and one which
> no country could carry into execution. In despotic countries it has
> never yet succeeded to the extent aimed at by those theorists; and
> among a free people the very proposal would be rejected with
> abhorrence; it would be a plan which would make every servant of
> every house a spy on the actions of his master, and all classes of
> society spies on each other.

This feeling lingered on well into the century. It was behind the
public jubilation at the killing of Constable Culley in a riot in
1833, and the reason why banquets and medals were given to the
inquest jury that brought in the iniquitous verdict of 'Justifiable
homicide'. Yet this feeling has so often been misunderstood or
ignored that the desperate struggle of wards and parishes to
retain the old watch system has frequently been wholly inter-
preted as resistance to change, which is only partly true, or
worse, the cynical protests of men intent only on retaining and
exploiting the watch system for their own criminal ends. Always
the worst fulminations of this kind have been hurled at the most
powerful and vociferous of all these alleged opponents of change,
the City of London.

The term City of London as it is used in this book applies to the kernel of the metropolis, the one square mile, and not to London as a whole. Throughout the centuries, from its Roman beginnings as a military supply-base on the north bank of the Thames to later times, the City's shape and size was determined by the surrounding wall and ditch. Strategically the military importance of the City lasted to the seventeenth century and ended only with the Civil War. By the thirteenth century, when detailed records for the City begin, the defence system that had evolved rested on a standing and marching watch of constables. Their function was to defend the City from external attack. At night half manned the walls and half patrolled Thames Street along the undefended shoreline. As the strategic importance of the City gradually declined the role of this standing and marching watch changed also. By Stow's time it was only a ceremony.

The constables were reorganised on a ward basis. Since 1550 the City has had twenty-six wards. Each has as its head an Alderman, who is also a magistrate, and who is elected to office. Subject only to his resignation or his removal for misconduct, his office is tenable for life. Every year one of the twenty-six is elected Lord Mayor by the others. Together they form the Court of Aldermen. They have precedence over the Court of Common Council which nowadays is the more powerful of the two courts. This consists of the Common Councilmen of each ward. The number sent from each ward varies according to its size. For the period covered in this book the total number varies from roughly 200 in the seventeenth century to a maximum of 240 in the nineteenth. They assist the Alderman of their ward. But until the late seventeenth century the office of Common Councilman was so resented and considered so burdensome that meetings of the Court of Common Council were rare. Correspondingly the powers the Court of Aldermen wielded were immense. With growing political and civic consciousness this later changed and an intense struggle lasting nearly 150 years developed between the two courts for control of funds and policy.

Neither side could always maintain a united front. The Alderman's office was not a hereditary one. And the Common Councilmen had to seek re-election each year. As late as 1820 there were less than forty democratically controlled boroughs in the country. Of these the City was the most powerful. Because they were dependent for re-election on a popular vote the Common Councilmen jealously guarded the privileges and powers of their own ward. Rather than centralise for improved efficiency in some things and submit, however limited in form, to the partial domination of the Aldermen, they preferred to have a massive duplication of offices. Besides having its own beadle, scavenger and constable, each ward had its own nightly watch. This was based on the old seasonal watches that had been formed in the past at Christmas and Easter and on other special occasions to quell disturbances and to maintain order. Gradually they had been established on a nightly basis and consisted of unpaid conscripts, the householders of each ward taking turns by rotation. The constables were their overseers.

To both the duties were irksome. For refusing office fines or imprisonment or both could be, and were, imposed. And still they could be compelled to take office. This was necessary since no other form of policing existed. To ease the burden on them the hiring of substitutes was permitted. Generally these were the oldest men of the ward. Service in the watch was an acceptable way of keeping them off the rates. In spite of the Aldermen's frequent orders to the contrary, they would rarely pursue a criminal beyond the boundary of their own ward. To co-ordinate the ward watches and impose on them some semblance of unity, the Court of Aldermen appointed its own law officers – a City Marshal, Under Marshal and six marshalmen. From the sixteenth century until 1789 when the place of execution was moved to the front of Newgate gaol, it was part of their duties to escort the condemned carts up Holborn Hill to the gallows at Tyburn. In the beginning they were elected officers of the Corporation. But in 1691 the City of London was declared bankrupt by Act of Parliament. Offices had to be sold to pay off debts. The highest bidders bought them for investments and mined them ruthlessly. The legacy of this policy was even wider corruption. From this emerged a piece of gallows bait, at first only the unsworn marshalman to a corrupt and homosexual Under Marshal but later the self-styled Thief-taker General of Great Britain and Ireland, Jonathan Wild. Uniquely combining the roles of thieftaker and thief he reorganised the eighteenth-century underworld. From his gang-breaking skills, his smuggling, his warehouses of stolen goods and his thieves it has been estimated that he earned in modern values half a million pounds; his nineteen sword and pistol wounds, his cut throat and his morticed skull-fractures testified to the brute animal courage and cunning that made this possible. After his death his methods were imitated by the heirs to his criminal empire. By working together in gangs, as he had taught them to do, the underworld challenged the old watch system with impunity. Passers-by were ambushed and openly attacked in the streets. In the alleys and lanes of the metropolis, said the novelist Henry Fielding, a 'thief could harbour with as great a security as wild beasts do in the deserts of Africa and Arabia'.

Partly as a result of his experiences as a magistrate at Bow Street, Fielding and his blind brother John founded the Bow Street Runners. At first there were only six of them. Like the marshalmen they assumed the role of co-ordinating some of the watchmen scattered throughout the hamlets and villages that outside the Cities of London and Westminster comprised the rest of the metropolis. In actual numbers this meant about 1000 men, or about half the police of the metropolis. The other half was in the City of London. In 1780 not even this concentration of power could quell the disturbances provoked by the Protestant Association and its patron Lord George Gordon. Rioting broke out in Westminster and quickly spread to the City. 'No Popery' was the shout. But, in Defoe's words, few knew if this was a man or a horse. For over a week the rioting continued. Bridewell, Newgate and the Fleet were among the prisons burned. By night pillars of flame were visible more than forty miles away. Bow Street was also burned, the Bank of England was attacked and the homes of Catholics, especially those of the Irish weavers in Moorgate, looted and gutted. The Lord Mayor, who was a former brothel-owner, would do nothing. Eventually the guards were called out by George III who threatened to read the Riot Act himself if his magistrates were afraid to do so. London, said one eyewitness, 'offered on every side the picture of a city sacked and abandoned to a ferocious enemy'.

More than 300 rioters had been killed. Twenty-five more were subsequently hanged. In the aftermath the old watch system came in for some rough handling and was widely blamed for letting the riots spread. Fresh calls were made for reform, and five years later Pitt's Solicitor-General introduced the London and Westminster Police Bill into Parliament. Immediately it came under heavy fire. Some of the powers demanded for the bill were so arbitrary that as one of the Aldermen pointed out 'a constable might break open any man's house, and enter his wife's bedchamber, and so far was he from being liable to an action for trespass, if the master of the house molested him, or endeavoured to prevent such an outrage, he was liable to the severe punishment of imprisonment for several years or of being sentenced to transportation'. Because the City was so prominent among the opponents of the Bill it has always been blamed for the Bill's withdrawal. In this instance, as in so many others, 'the City' has been a convenient label with which to tag the opposition. On the contrary, although the City objected to some of the powers demanded for the Bill, they agreed with it in principle and indicated that they were willing to support it. The fact that the Bill was subsequently withdrawn is perhaps not unconnected with the reasons which prompted the Government to withdraw Colquhoun's four police bills in 1799, and for which likewise no explanation was ever given.

From this has stemmed the legend that the City was opposed to any reform of the watch system. Nothing is further from the truth. The Aldermen and their supporters were constantly urging reform on the more stiff-necked of their opponents in the wards. But because of their greatly reduced powers they were unable to force reform on them as they had done in 1737 when Parliament had approving the forming of the country's first professionally paid watch-force. However, they had been able to form a Day Police and equip it with the policeman's familiar blue coat and trousers; this was only two years after one of the parliamentary select committees considering police reform rejected yet again the forming of a professionally paid police-force. The country still had to rely on the gallows, the stocks, the whip and the transportation ship to maintain a stable society. In 1828 Peel, who was Home Secretary, packed a select committee with known reformers and the following year brought in his bill for a police force for the metropolis including the City. There was little support for the Bill even among members of Parliament. The City was sharply divided against itself. Some were for the Bill and some were against. The wards counted on their political allies, the Whig opposition, to force Peel either to withdraw the bill or to exclude the City. This he agreed to do, as he had probably intended from the beginning, in return for Whig support and token opposition only to the rest of his plan for a metropolitan police-force. Several months later the first metropolitan policemen marched out from Scotland Yard to the shouts and jeers of hostile Londoners.

Suggestions that the police and watch of the City should be remodelled on similar lines only roused the fury of the wards who were more determined than ever that control of the police should be in their hands alone. But they were fighting a rearguard action. Support for the reformers grew, and over the next ten years this was steadily reflected in the annual wardmote elections. Reform seemed certain but progress was proving too slow. In 1839 Parliament intervened, wrested control from the wards and placed it in the hands of a Commissioner, Daniel Whittle Harvey. They made it impossible for the Court of Common Council to dismiss him. This could be done only by the Court of Aldermen or one of the Secretaries of State. The wards' powers were limited to finance, clothing and equipment. With these as their weapons the diehards fought the Commissioner for the next twenty-three years.

From the records in the possession of the Corporation of the City of London it has been possible to piece together this complex story. It is long overdue. For centuries, until the beginning of the nineteenth, London was the one square mile, and it is strange that apart from one small article written in 1927 almost nothing has been written on the important part it played in the forming of the country's police forces. Almost certainly, without the City it would have been impossible for Peel to have passed his Metropolitan Police Bill through Parliament in 1829. The purpose of this book has therefore been parochial and I have not set the City against a larger framework. For most of the period covered by it the City acted as a self-contained unit, and as such I have treated it. Although my main interest has been the police and its growth from the old watch-system, I have also tried to show how it grew side by side with the underworld beginning with the old monastic sanctuaries of Tudor times to the thieves' kitchens of the Dickensian City. These I have set against the changing face of the City itself.

I. The City Marshals

1. *Watchman*

1

Watch and Ward

For it was then (saith mine author) a common practice in the city, that a hundred or more in a company, young and old, would make nightly invasions upon houses of the wealthy, to the intent to rob them; and if they found any man stirring in the city within the night that were not of their crew, they would presently murder him, insomuch that when night was come no man durst adventure to walk in the streets.

John Stow, *Survey of London*[1]

THE medieval City of London was a fortified town on the north bank of the Thames protected on three sides by a wall 'in form of a bow, except denting in betwixt Cripplegate and Aldersgate'[2] with a line of battlements and towers stretching along the river between its eastern limit, the Tower of London, and its most westerly limit Blackfriars. The wall was surrounded by a ditch, in places 200 feet wide, and entry into the City was through one of its seven gates – Aldersgate, Moorgate, Cripplegate, Bishopsgate, Aldgate, Ludgate and Newgate. Every evening the gates were shut as curfew was rung at St Martin's Le Grand. The portcullises were lowered, the gates were chained from both within and without and locked, and the City kept in a state of siege until morning when a bell was rung at St Thomas of Acon in Cheapside.[3] The ringing of curfew was the signal for the taverns to shut and the nightly watch to muster at the gates, each man wearing a quilted leather jacket or light cuirass and armed with either a sword, halberd or longbow.[4] The watch was then divided into two parts, half to patrol Thames Street while the other half mounted guard on the wall and gates.

The gloom that hung over the City was broken only by the flickering torches of the watch, or that of 'some great lord or other substantial person of good reputation, or a person of their household, who from them shall have warranty, and who is going from one to another with a light to guide them'.[5] Yet in spite of strict orders that 'no person shall be so daring as to be found walking through the streets after curfew rung at St Martin's Le Grand', there were frequent clashes between the watch and the armed gangs that nightly roamed the dark streets and alleys openly robbing, murdering or plundering houses. Maintaining law and order was secondary to the watch's main task of defending the City from external attack, and resistance to these gangs was left to the citizens themselves. Occasionally they were able to do this, as when

> a crew of young and wealthy citizens, assembling together in the night, assaulted a stone house of a certain rich man, and breaking through the wall, the good man of that house, having prepared himself with others in a corner, when he perceived one of the thieves named Andrew Bucquint to lead the way, with a burning brand in the one hand, and a pot of coals in the other, which he essayed to kindle with the brand, he flew upon him, and smote off his right hand, and then with a loud voice cried 'Thieves!' at the hearing whereof the thieves took their flight, all save he that had lost his hand, whom the good man in the next morning delivered to Richard de Lucie, the king's justice.[6]

Otherwise the citizens had to rely on the watch to protect them but even that was looked on by some as an excuse for licensed plunder. The Chronicles tell how in 1262

> the citizens kept watch and ward, riding by night throughout the city with horse and arms; though among them a countless multitude of persons on foot obtruded themselves; some evil-minded among whom, under pretext of searching for aliens, broke open many houses belonging to other persons, and carried such goods as were there to be found. To restrain the evil designs of these persons, the watches on horseback were therefore put an end to, and watch was kept by the respective Wards, each person keeping himself well armed within his own ward.[7]

These however, were only seasonal watches and the large, medium and small-sized wards continued to send twelve, eight and six men (these numbers were later dropped to eight, six and four) to man the walls at night.[8] A proclamation of Edward I in 1283 stresses 'that the watch shall be set at night within the City in due manner, and when need shall be. That is to say, in each Ward certain persons shall be chosen, up to a certain number, according to the size of such Ward, and at times when there is great resort of people unto the City.'[9] The frequency with which the ward watches were used increased during the Wars of the Roses, and the times between them grew less. By 1509 they were organised on a nightly basis and, the practice of manning the walls having by this time been discontinued, the City was left with one nightly watch-system organised on a ward basis. It is on this basis that the policing of the City depended for the next 400 years, and it is because of the inherent defects in this system that it was to prove so ineffective.

The City was divided into twenty-five wards (twenty-six since 1550), each ward being a self-contained unit, under the control and direction of an Alderman and small group of common councilmen. The right to elect these officers was confined to the freemen of the ward – anyone practising a trade or business in the City had to be a freeman – but the minor officers such as the beadle, constable and scavenger were elected by both freemen and non-freemen alike. Each Alderman represented his ward in the Court of Aldermen. Up until the end of the seventeenth century the Lord Mayor and Court of Aldermen framed policy for the City as a whole although it was left to the Aldermen as individuals to see those policies carried out within their wards. However, many of the wards had acquired, by virtue of the churches or monasteries within their precincts, certain grants or privileges; Whitefriars, for instance, was exempt 'from all taxes, fifteenths and other burdens of scot, and of watch and ward' as well as 'the office of constable, scavenger, and such officers of charge . . .'.[10] They therefore resented any common policy likely to increase taxation or curtail their privileges, and this attitude lasted until the nineteenth century. There is no doubt that some centralisation and common policy would have benefited both them and the City as a whole, as in 1654 when an attempt was made to organise street-cleaning on a central basis. Unfortunately the hostility of the citizens was such that it

could only be made to work on a ward basis and this remained
so until almost the nineteenth century.[11] Obviously there could
only be a common policy for the City as a whole if the citizens,
through their wards, desired it. To put it in its crudest form there
were in the City twenty-six separate authorities under the
general direction of a Lord Mayor and Court of Aldermen
incapable of enforcing a common policy unless the wards allowed
them to do so.

The Alderman maintained order in his ward through the
beadle and ward constables, the number varying according to
the number of precincts, there being 240 precincts in the City
with a constable for each one. Each constable made a list of the
people living in his precinct giving their names, surnames, trades,
professions and precinct where they lived 'wherein the place is
to be specially noted by the Street, Lane, Alley or Sign'. On the
basis of these lists every householder was liable for election to one
of the minor ward-offices such as beadle, scavenger or constable.
In theory they were elected to office but in practice they were
nominated, the office usually going to the oldest non-serving
inhabitant. A householder was defined as anyone rated for a
house, 'paying scot' or 'bearing lot' and this definition was a
major cause for the corruption and inefficiency of the watch.

The term 'bearing lot' referred to certain duties the ward
required every householder to perform such as sweeping the
ground in front of his house, hanging out a lantern in the winter
months, placing a bucket of water before his door in case of fire
and taking his turn as ward beadle, constable or scavenger.
'Paying scot' was the payment of rates for tasks that should have
been performed by paid employee but were often undertaken by
the citizens themselves.[12] This system of ward service was the
same, except for minor changes, in the nineteenth as it was
in the thirteenth century, and although most of the City
records relating to this earlier period have been destroyed it
is possible by quoting later examples to show how the system
worked.

As early as 1341, when twenty-eight citizens living in
Cordwainer, Bishopsgate and Broad Street Wards were fined for
refusing office, there was a marked reluctance on the part of the
citizens to serve as constable, beadle or scavenger.[13] Their period

2. *Bellman and Billman*

of office lasted one year, and not only was it unpaid but they were expected to earn their living during the day, be on duty at night and cope with any other emergency that might arise. Long before Tudor times the practice grew up of allowing constables to hire substitutes but many householders avoided this unnecessary expense by having their servants or apprentices deputise for them. Under these circumstances it is hardly surprising that the constables were lethargic or indifferent in the performance of their duties and one can readily understand the attitude of the constable who answered every complaint with 'God restore your loss. I have other business at this time.'[14] The worst abuses, however, were created by the definition of a householder as anyone rated for a house, 'paying scot' or 'bearing lot'. This considerably increased the number of persons liable for service as it could be applied not only to residents but non-residents as well. Although the following cases are considerably later than the period we are at present speaking of, the principle was the same as it was in medieval times. John Kirkman was in partnership with his brother who managed their London business from his house in the Ward of Farringdon Without. John transacted his part of the business from Coventry where he lived and worked, but because he paid half the expenses and taxes of their London house he was classed as a householder although he was clearly a non-resident. He was ordered like his brother to become a constable for the Ward. He asked to be exempted from office but his petition was refused. Samuel Bruckfield was likewise elected constable for Bread Street Ward seventeen years later on the grounds that he paid half the taxes on his partner's warehouse; similarly he was not discharged from office although he too lived in Coventry. Under such circumstances a man had no alternative but to take office or to hire a substitute for one year. If he challenged the system in the Courts they always firmly upheld such elections as without them there was no force to maintain law and order except for the trained bands or militia. One who did challenge his election in the courts in 1664 was Richard Clarke. For refusing to serve Clarke was charged with contempt of the King's Majesty, but he withdrew his action and took office as constable when the court clearly indicated that they intended to uphold the validity of his election, and the Ward

Alderman further indicated that even if Clarke was discharged from serving he would make sure that he was elected to office again the following year.[15]

Other aggravations were that service in one ward did not exempt a man from service in another. A man might live in one ward and have his business in another, thus making him liable for office in both. Similarly foreign traders found that having to be freemen to trade in the City also meant that they could be elected constables. Anthony Bomyri, Peter de Bulleyn and other strangers were threatened with imprisonment if they did not take office, while John Box, a Dutchman, was actually committed.[16] Surgeons were exempt from office as were others, like the verger and bellringers of St Paul's and the clerks of the compters and Mayor's Court.[17] Occasionally men were discharged through advanced age or sickness, but the greatest burden of all fell on those who were too sick to serve but not discharged and yet, because they could not pay the fine or hire a substitute, were forced to take office themself although its acceptance meant their ruin. Possibly the author of the following extract, William Brown, citizen and barber, exaggerated his ills although there is no reason to think so; it was to cases like this that Defoe was referring in 1714 when he spoke of 'the imposition of the office' of constable as 'an unsupportable hardship; it takes up so much of a man's time that his own affairs are frequently totally neglected, too often to his ruin'.[18]

Brown was appointed a constable for the Ward of Vintry

Wherein Your Petitioner, neither pays any Tax whatever nor even [h]as his Name on the Parish Books. Likewise Your Petitioner States that through the decay of Trade, He does not realise on an average more than five shillings a Day; for the Maintenance of Himself and Family. Also Your Petitioner, is troubled with shortness of Breath, and is likewise grievously troubled with two Ruptures, for which, he wears a Double Truss, and which Complaint; subjects Your Petitioner to a faintness, & weakness, so much so that he is frequently obligated to lay down, for two or three Hours at a time. And Lastly, Your Petitioner is warned out by his Landlord; the beginning of March next, by reason of the New Bridge taking place; & which unfortunate circumstance alone, will infallibly be His ruin, as he Your Petitioner, knows not where to go, to carry on his

Business; having only had the Four Years and one Quarter, though
He is turned of 50 Years of Age. Hoping these foregoing Reasons
which Your Petitioner will if required; Substantiate upon Oath, will
have their due weight, with Your Worship, Your Petitioner will
always be in Gratitude as well, as Duty bound to Pray.[19]

Inevitably such men avoided the performance of their duties and
the office was soon brought into the greatest contempt.

The earliest mention of the watch occurs in the City records
at the beginning of the thirteenth century. Its origins are
uncertain but the custom of manning the walls went back to a
time 'whereof the memory of man is not to the contrary'.
Clearly the City being the capital had always had some such
defensive system and this practice continued until the beginning
of the sixteenth century when life grew more settled. There is an
implied distinction in the City records between the nightly
watch and seasonal ward-watches. The former's task clearly was
to defend the City from external attack, and that of the latter to
maintain law and order. The walls were manned by the men
from the nearest wards while the remainder patrolled the shoreline along Thames Street. This was probably where the terms
'standing watch' and 'marching watch' originated. The shift
away from defence seems to have happened in Stow's lifetime.
According to the old chronicler there were more than 240
constables in London, one half of whom went each night in the
marching watch while the other half 'kept their standing watch
in every street and lane'.[20] Possibly this was the final variant,
with the marching watch patrolling the City as a whole before
the final breakdown and reorganisation on a ward basis. In the
thirteenth century the large, medium and small-sized wards sent
twelve, eight and six men respectively to the nightly watch.
This number was later reduced to eight, six and four, and in the
City Journals for 1448–54 there is an order that 200 persons with
two aldermen were to keep the nightly watches, to wit 100
persons with one alderman for Thames Street and the like for the
City walls as particularised.[21]

Originally the seasonal or ward watches were under the control
of the two City Sheriffs but their duties were taken over by the
ward Aldermen. These watches patrolled within the limits of

their own wards. The Alderman rode ahead of the watch on horseback and in the year 1297 householders were ordered to remove pigsties from the streets and 'that pentices which are too low shall be forthwith pulled down, that so persons may ride on great horses beneath'.[22] The most important seasonal watch was that lasting from 24 December to 6 January. The watch had to make sure that street lanterns were hung outside every house, arrest all those who passed through the streets wearing a 'visor or false face' while the Alderman's task was to ensure that there was no overcharging for bread and ale.[23] Frequently the beadle was left in charge of the watch and in the event of any trouble he was ordered to raise hue and cry by horn and voice. Several incidents are recorded in the Court Rolls of fights 'without a light and with edged weapons'[24] between the watch and armed men prowling the streets. On one occasion the beadle was run through the arm with a sword. Other references are more light-hearted, as when the watch arrested some apprentices who 'had filled an empty cask with stones on Monday midnight, and set it rolling through Graschurchestrate to London Bridge to the great terror of the neighbours'.[25] The main task of the watch as they conceived it was to act as guardians of public morality. It appears that after complaint to the wardmote and a warning to the owner of a suspected disorderly house the beadle and watch could break in and render the house uninhabitable by removing all the doors and windows! In 1305 'Thomas, late Vicar of the Church of St Sepulchre without Newgate, and John Le Copersmyth charged with entering the house of William Cok, butcher, in Cockes Lane and tearing away eleven doors and five windows with hammers and chisels'.[26] Frequently the watch dispensed with formalities as in the year 1366 when they broke into the house of Joan Upholdestere to see 'if she was harbouring any men of ill-fame and conversation' and left with the doors and windows doing 100 shillings' worth of damage.[27] On yet another occasion they were charged with breaking into a house 'on a rumour that Reginald [the Chaplain] was with Isabella as her paramour' beating them up and demanding money as the price of their silence.[28]

Each householder took his turn in the ward watch serving in rotation according to the list held by the Alderman. Unlike the

B

constable he only watched one night, the frequency with which he did so varying according to the number living in his ward. Even this was felt to be too much and those that could afford it clubbed together and paid the beadle a small sum to hire substitutes in their place, it being part of the beadle's duties to warn those whose turn it was to watch. By the middle of the sixteenth century the Aldermen had stopped supervising the watch and the beadles were able to exploit their position to the full. Not only did they hire the cheapest labour, generally the oldest and most decrepit in need of work, but judging by later evidence they rarely hired their full quota of watchmen and pocketed the difference.[29]

The final collapse came when the Aldermen stopped riding through the watches and left the supervision of them to the beadles and constables who were appointed joint heads of the watch. The Aldermen had been able to check the worst abuses of the system but these were now exploited to the full, as it was against their own interests for the beadles, constables and watchmen to make the watch an effective force. The watch rapidly developed into a farce, and the literature of the period mirrors the contempt that was felt for it. Shakespeare's Dogberry and Middleton's 'Blurt Master Constable' are just two examples.

Individually the watchmen were nicknamed 'Brown Bill' from the rusty halberds they carried, broad-bladed instruments on the ends of staves,[30] and everyone agreed that they were notorious for 'abusing the time, coming very late to the watch, sitting down in some common place of watching, wherein some falleth on sleep by reason of labour or much drinking before, or else nature requireth a rest in the night. These fellows think every hour a thousand until they go home, home, home, every man to bed. Good night, good night! God save the Queen! sayeth the constables, farewell neighbours.'[31] Frequently the watchmen were in league with thieves, and their corruption was such that in 1591 the Lord Mayor had to come to terms with them. Watchmen were set at the gates to confiscate all meat brought into the City during Lent. The meat was to be sold and the proceeds go to the hospitals and prisons within the City. The conduct of the watchmen was such that the Lord Mayor was forced to recommend to the Lords of the Council, the scheme having proved ineffective, that the watchmen be allowed half the meat confiscated and only half go towards the benefit of the hospitals and prisons.[32]

There were some, however, who realised that if 'this watch be not better looked unto' then 'no man shall be able to keep a penny, no, scant his own life in a while. For they that dare attempt such matters in the city of London, what will they do in houses smally guarded, or by the highway?'[33]

2

The City Marshals

*Yet alas, what shall I doe poore knave? I could go to London
and lurcke in some baudie Lane; And in the Nighte when the
watch is either a slepe or gone awaie (For when the most nede
is then are the watch soonest gone,) I could then with my
companions, with hookes, picklockes, or ladders, or Gon-
pouder, to open lockes, or a Crowe of yron, make shifte For
a bootie of plate, clothes &c. But I doe feare the Galows.*
William Bullein, *A Dialogue against the Pestilence*[1]

IN spite of rigorous controls to limit building the City of London
in the sixteenth century was already beginning to expand and
push beyond its medieval wall. The surrounding ditch was
choked with weeds and rubbish and in parts built over. Houndsditch, so called because the Common Hunt flung into it the
carcases of slaughtered dogs, was paved over in 1503, and the
area rapidly became a quarter for dealers and sellers of second-
hand clothes. Every available piece of land in the City was built
upon. Temporary sheds giving way to more permanent structures
were erected in gardens and churchyards. Extra storeys were
added to houses, each new storey jutting over the one below,
creating the impression from the street that the houses on either
side were toppling towards each other. Cheapside was a broad
open thoroughfare but the majority of streets were narrow and
unpaved, in wet weather morasses of mud and in summer
stinking pools and stagnant kennels of dirty water. Garishly
painted shop and tavern signs whirled and clattered above the
rumble of carts carrying hides and meat to Leadenhall, or fish
from the boats moored off Billingsgate. Cattle, sheep, oxen and
horses stumbled through the streets to market in Smithfield.
The salt air stank with the smell of stale beer and excrement,

and vibrated with the raucous cries and shouts of itinerant
street-traders bawling down one another's wares. Above this
hubbub and confusion rose the towering spire of St Paul's
Cathedral. The lesser spires of 114 churches clustered about it
like a phalanx of spears. The destruction of many of these in the
Henrician dissolution released yet more building-land. Twenty-
three monasteries were among those either pulled down or converted to other uses. The Lady Chapel of St Bartholomew the
Great became a private house. A large wine-tavern was erected
on the site of St Martin's Le Grand. This wholesale destruction
in part explains the reason why for the next 150 years the City
was to become the centre of London's underworld.[2]

Many religious houses before their destruction offered immunity of arrest or sanctuary to debtors and other fugitives from
the law. The Reformation Parliaments swept this and other
ecclesiastical privileges away but sanctuaries of a sort remained.
The practice of compelling sanctuary men to flee to either Ireland
or the Continent was abolished on the partial grounds that the
Army and Navy were losing possible recruits. An Act of 1540
created instead a number of 'bastard sanctuaries' throughout the
country. London had three. Westminster and St Martin's Le
Grand, 'the one at the elbow of the City, the other in the very
bowels', and Whitefriars adjacent to the Temple on the south
side of Fleet Street.[3]

The latter was the most notorious quarter in London. The area
was rebuilt when the monastery was pulled down and for a time
was fashionable with the more wealthy citizens until the excesses
of the sanctuary men drove them out. Whitefriars then de-
generated into a slum. The former mansion of Sir John Parker
was divided into 'twentie severall tenements' and that of Francis
Pike into thirty-nine. Brothels, taverns and fencing schools
flourished. In 1609 there were eleven taverns where six were
considered sufficient. Cellar shops and taverns in Fleet Street
concealed masked entrances into the sanctuary through which
the sanctuary men could pass to commit fresh crimes and return
again with safety. The absence of any ward officers such as
constable, beadle or scavenger accelerated the rate of decay.
Water Lane was 'soe stopped with dunge and dirte that the
passengers can hardlie pass and the pavement soe broken and

ruyned that if speedilie redresse be not had neither horse can drawe his load nor passengers goe that waie'.[4]

Equally troublesome were lesser places of refuge scattered throughout the City on the sites of former churches or monastic houses. The privileges that remained to them were swept away in 1623 but they continued to flourish in spite of the law. They were still being claimed in 1754. A typical example was Dukes Place, a miniature stronghold surrounded by a wall and gates, forever asserting its independence of the City and constantly challenging the authority of the Lord Mayor. It maintained its independence until one night in 1674 when a constable from Aldgate Ward chased a man into Dukes Place and was violently assaulted, not by the wanted man, but by Richard Tyler, the constable for that place, for having invaded the sanctuary of Dukes Place. Tyler was ordered to appear before the Court of Aldermen to explain his offence but he answered their summons with 'very rude and contemptuous expressions' and aggravated his offence still further by saying of one of the Aldermen, 'A ffart and a turd for him. A pox confound him for a son of a whore.' The inhabitants of Dukes Place approved of Tyler's conduct, which so incensed the Lord Mayor and Aldermen that they invaded the place and carried off the gates.[5]

It was not always so easy for the City to impose its will on the 'bastard sanctuaries'. In 1608 the Lord Mayor had been given a limited jurisdiction over Whitefriars, or Alsatia as it was renamed, but in spite of the warrants his officers had carried they had been refused admittance and thrown out.[6] Law officers, especially if trying to make an arrest, were greeted there until 1691 with shouts of 'Clubs' and 'Rescue'. They would be given a sound drubbing and the pulp tossed back into Fleet Street.

Murderers, robbers and other felons were theoretically denied sanctuary, but in practice there was no civil power strong enough to winkle them out of these rookeries of crime. Although the following figures must be treated with caution it has been estimated that in 1517 the number of beggars in London was about a thousand. The immediate effect of the dissolution of the monasteries, land enclosures and a growing population was to push this figure up to alarming proportions, so that by 1594 the

number had risen to over 12,000.[7] Harsh penal laws were passed
to check this rise and the corresponding increase in crime with
the law making little or no distinction between those who could

3. *The Pillory*

and those that would not work. Vagabonds over fourteen could in
1572 be 'grievously whipped and burned through the gristle of
the right ear with a hot iron of the compass of an inch' unless
taken into service for a year.[8] Beggars were taken to Leadenhall
before being thrown out of the City, a 'V' (for Vagabond) of yellow
cloth was fastened to their breasts and they were then driven
along Cheapside to the ringing of bells.[9] Women were ducked in

the ducking-stool at Queenhithe or in the pond at Smithfield.
Privy Bribers and Pykers were forced to wear paper hats marked
'For Privy Pykers' in the pillory in Cheapside; one ear was nailed
to the boards and they were threatened with the loss of the other
if they returned to the City.[10] Many offences were punished with
carting. Men and women were stripped naked, tied to a cart's tail
and whipped through the streets by either the executioner or
constables before being released with a collar of iron, stamped
with the City arms, riveted about their necks.[11] In spite of these
measures it was impossible to check the flow of beggars to
London. A shanty town grew up on the site of the Haymarket,
and the fringes of the City – Houndsditch, Barbican and Smithfield – rapidly acquired unsavoury reputations. Many vagrants
genuinely wanted work but as this was denied to them they were
forced either to live by crime or starve to death. Children were
particularly vulnerable as Fleetwood, the City Recorder,
discovered when the watch raided Wotton's Alehouse at Smart's
Key near Billingsgate. The alehouse was also a school

> set upp to learne younge boyes to cutt purses. There were hung up
> two devises, the one was a pockett, the other was a purse. The pocket
> had in yt certen cownters and was hunge aboute with hawkes bells
> and over the topp did hannge, a little sacring bell; and he that could
> take owt a cownter without any noyse, was allowed to be a publique
> Foyster: and he that could take a peece of sylver owt of the purse
> without the noyse of any of the bells, he was adjudged a judiciall
> Nypper. Nota that a Foister is a pick-pockett, and a Nypper is termed
> a Pickepurse, or a Cutpurse.[12]

Children were prostituted at an early age, and unwanted
babies left in the streets or flung on dungheaps to die. Many
beggars were either too old or too weak to work and starved to
death in the streets. At night it was a common sight for the
watchmen to see these wretched creatures lying under stalls, in
porches and doorways, or huddling for warmth in the sheep pens
of Smithfield.[13]

The City was ahead of informed opinion when it acknowledged
the fact that this was a problem that would not be solved with
whipping. A survey showed that there were three categories of

beggars – 'the succourless poor child, the sick and impotent, the sturdy vagabond or idle person'. In 1547 they pioneered a bold experiment by rating the citizens for poor relief and assuming responsibility for the beggars by feeding, sheltering and disciplining them in the institutions they provided for the purpose. The crumbling Greyfriars Church in Newgate Street was converted into an orphanage and rechristened Christ's Hospital. St Thomas's and St Bartholomew's Hospitals became shelters for the sick and aged. The third category, 'the sturdy vagabond or idle person', by far the greater number, created more of a problem as the City had to provide them with a building large enough to be both a prison and workhouse, where men could be whipped into virtue and the unemployed find work. In 1552 they successfully petitioned Edward VI for his Palace of Bridewell (the mother of all bridewells), 'a wide large empty house' overlooking the Fleet river.[14] The palace was a warren of alleys and outbuildings and the atmosphere was poisoned with the smell from the river. The smell had steadily been getting worse ever since the early thirteenth century when the Carmelite Friars had begged of the King 'Help, lest we perish of the stench', to 1652 when the Fleet was described as impassable 'by reason of many encroachments thereupon made by keeping of hogs and swine therein and elsewhere near it, the throwing in of offals and other garbage by butchers, soucemen, and others, and by reason of the many houses of office standing over and upon it'.[15]

Work was begun on converting it and a young labourer caught breaking open a chest was strung up on hastily erected gallows in the courtyard. Workshops and apprenticeship schemes were in operation by 1557. Two corn-mills turned by treadmills were manned by eighteen vagabonds; Bridewell also boasted a glove-making factory, bakehouse and clothworkers' shop for women.[16] For some years the distinction between the prison and the workhouse was strictly maintained; the unemployed were paid for their work but prisoners were manacled or whipped, frequently both, and on one occasion at least are known to have been tortured.[17] However the distinction between the two sides could not be maintained for ever, and after the turn of the century disappeared altogether, leaving Bridewell to be remembered only for its harshness and cruelty.

B2

Sixteen beadles of beggars were appointed to patrol the wards and gates and daily carry off the beggars to these institutions.[18] Oak cages were erected for their prisoners at Billingsgate, Cornhill, Aldersgate and London Bridge – yet another City street in itself, the road running between two rows of houses, many six storeys high, and complete with its own shops and chapel. The beggars avoided capture by hiring watermen to ferry them across the river from Southwark.[19] The number of beadles was too small to cope with the problem, and they were helpless against the discharged soldiers and sailors, many of whom had been allowed to keep their arms and uniforms to sell to make up deficiencies in pay, and who travelled to London in disciplined bands. In 1569 500 threatened to loot Bartholomew Fair in Smithfield and had to be dispersed by force.[20] Other bands were led by the upright men and their doxies.[21] The symbol of the upright man's authority was the staff, five or six feet in length, which he carried. Similar staves were carried by the anglers or hookers with a hole drilled through about one inch from the end. This was concealed with the hand when carried but by fitting it with a hook the angler could insert the stave through a small opening and empty a chest of drawers or strip a bed of its linen by drawing out the articles.

Then, as now, the underworld had its own slang or thieves' cant.[22]

MAN. *Yonder dwelleth a queer cuffin. It were beneship to mill him.*
Yonder dwelleth a hoggish and churlish man. It were very well done to rob him.

ROGUE. *Now bing we a waste to the high-pad; the ruffmans is by.*
Nay, let us go hence to the highway; the woods is at hand.

MAN. *So may we happen on the harmans, and cly the jerk, or to the queer-ken and scour queer cramp-rings, and so to trining on the chats.*
So we may chance to be set in the stocks, either be whipped, or had to prisonhouse, and there be shackled with bolts and fetters, and then to hang on the gallows.

ROGUE. *Gerry gan!! the Ruffian cly thee!*
A turd in thy mouth! the Devil take thee!

MAN. *What! Stow your bene, cove, and cut benat whids! And bing we to Rome-vill, to nip a bung. So shall we have lour for*

> *the bousing ken. And when we bing back to the dewse-a-vill,*
> *we will filch some duds off the ruffmans, or mill the ken*
> *for a lag of duds.*
>
> What! Hold your peace, good fellow, and speak better
> words! And go we to London, to cut a purse. Then shall
> we have money for the ale-house. And when we come
> back again into the country, we will steal some linen
> clothes off some hedges, or rob some house for a buck of
> clothes.

'Priggers of prancers' were horsestealers; 'Abraham men'
counterfeited insanity; 'demanders for glimmer' and 'freshwater
mariners' claimed to have been ruined by fire and shipwreck;
the 'dummerers' feigned loss of hearing. In dealing with these
types constables frequently resorted to methods which, although
normal to them, would certainly not be condoned by any court
of law today. Thomas Harman in his *Caveat for Common
Cursitors* tells how he tied a halter about a 'dummerer's' wrists
'and hoisted him up over a beam, and there did let him hang a
good while. At the length, for very pain he required for God's
sake to let him down. So he that was both deaf and dumb could
in short time both hear and speak.'[23]

The Justices of the Peace failed to maintain an adequate supervision and were frequently lax in enforcing the law. Gradually
a system of central governmental control was developed and
their work came to be supervised by the Privy Council who issued
the necessary directives and demanded reports in return. From
time to time they ordered the appointment of Provost Marshals
to strengthen the local watch or constabulary. Frequently it was
necessary for the City to make this appointment itself. In 1570
there was an outbreak of plague and, as was customary, the
watch was disbanded to limit the spread of infection, and
constables confined to noting the infectious houses in their
precinct marked with a blue cross. Beggars flocked into the
City, and John Read and William Sympson were appointed
Provost Marshals. Each man was paid 6s 8d a day, and
the money advanced them, £35 9s 4d for twenty-eight days'
work, included the hire of twelve marshalmen at twelve
shillings a day.[24]

Similar appointments continued to be made for the next thirty years. Each appointment was of limited duration, generally twenty-eight days, and only once is there any indication that it was for a longer period. In 1595 beggars attacked an escort of prisoners and rioted through the City.[25] The Privy Council appointed Sir Thomas Wilford Provost Marshal, and the Common Council furnished him with ten men mounted on horseback from 26 July until the 14 October 'if the Queens pleasure should be so long to continue it . . .'. Wilford's authority, like that of his predecessors, was not limited to the City but extended to the counties of Kent, Middlesex, Essex and Surrey. His orders were to hunt down and punish 'such notable rebellyous and incorrigible offenders worthilie to be speedilie executed by Marshalle Lawe to attach and take such personnes and in presence of the said Justices accordinge to Justice of Marshall Lawe to execute them uponn Galows or Gibbett . . .'.[26] Executions were commonly carried out at Tyburn but just as frequently performed near to or on the spot where the offence was committed. The City provided him with portable gallows and Wilford used them when he hanged five men on Tower Hill.[27] The purpose behind these wheeled gallows was to illustrate the awful horrors of hanging to a large number of spectators. In 1517 thirteen boys, some not in their teens, were hanged at Leadenhall, Newgate and Aldgate. The formalities were observed if the condemned man was a gentleman of rank. In the reign of James I a fencing master, John Turner, was murdered in a Whitefriars tavern by two assassins hired by Lord Sanquhar in revenge for Turner having blinded him in one eye with an accidental swordthrust. Sanquhar was hanged outside Westminster Hall and the two murderers opposite the Whitefriars sanctuary. One of the men, Carlisle, a former page of Sanquhar's, was hanged six feet above the head of his accomplice as he was born a gentleman, while his fellow was not.[28]

From 1570 to 1596 the City police-system was controlled and directed by a very able and energetic Recorder, William Fleetwood. The Privy Council co-ordinated mass searches throughout the City and the surrounding counties to prevent criminals fleeing over the borders into neighbouring counties to escape arrest. They were timed to begin at ten o'clock in the evening

and frequently lasted all night. Fleetwood needed little prompt-
ing to organise these man-hunts and would frequently do so
without being ordered. His letters make grim reading:

Upon Thursday at even her Majesty in her coach near Islington
taking of the air, her Highness was environed with a number of
rogues. One Mr. Stone, a footman, came in all haste to my Lord
Mayor and after to me and told us of the same. I did the same night
send warrants out into the said quarters and into Westminster and
the Duchy; and in the morning I went abroad myself, and I took
that day seventy-four rogues, whereof some were blind and yet
great usurers and very rich; and the same day towards night I sent
for Mr. Harris and Mr. Smith and the governors of Bridewell and
took all the names of the rogues and sent them from the Sessions
House unto Bridewell, where they remained that night. Upon
twelfth day in the forenoon the Master of the Rolls, myself and
others received a charge before my Lords of the Council as touching
rogues and masterless men and to have a privy search. The same
day . . . I met the governors of Bridewell and so that afternoon we
examined all the said rogues and gave them substantial payment.
And the strongest we bestowed in the mill and the lighters. The rest
we dismissed with a promise of double pay if we met with them
again. Upon Sunday . . . I conferred with [the Dean of Westminster]
touching Westminster and the Duchy, and then I took order for
Southwark, Lambeth and Newington, from whence I received a
shoal of forty rogues, men and women, and above. I bestowed them
in Bridewell. I did the same afternoon peruse Paul's, where I took
about twenty cloaked rogues that there use to keep standing. I
placed them also in Bridewell. . . . Upon Friday morning at the
Justice Hall there were brought in above a hundred lewd people
taken in the privy search. The Masters of Bridewell received them
and immediately gave them punishment. . . . Upon Friday last we
sat at the Justice Hall at Newgate from 7 in the morning until
7 at night, where were condemned certain horse-stealers, cutpurses
and such like to the number of ten, whereof nine were executed,
and the tenth stayed by a means from the Court. These were
executed upon Saturday in the morning. . . .[29]

There was a regular traffic in pardons between the Royal
Court and the more affluent criminals who often escaped the
gallows by this means. Fleetwood commented on this practice,

'That when the court is furthest from London then there is the best justice in all England.'[30]

These man-hunts continued until the time of the Civil War, and the evidence shows that the constables had little liking for their task. Frequently they had to whip the beggars 'till their backes be bloodye', and while they were expected to carry it out with a brutal thoroughness there were doubtless some among them who mitigated the punishment by reddening the lash of their whips so that it left only red stripes on their victim's back. They were expected to relieve the Provost Marshal of his prisoners but this they frequently refused to do. The Marshal then incurred their dislike still further by reporting them to the Aldermen who either fined or committed them as they did when Roger Clarke called the Marshal and his men 'Rascall, Knaves &c'.[31] From the frequency with which it is entered in the journals it seems fairly certain that the constables avoided the Marshal's attentions by making recognition impossible, as they did not wear uniforms, by removing their white staff of office with the Royal coat of arms hanging by their street doors and marking their dwelling-place. Clearly the time had come for stricter supervision, and in 1603 the office of Provost Marshal was made a permanent one.

The Court of Aldermen appointed Roger Walronde Provost Marshal and clearly defined his task. It was to carry off rogues and vagrants to Bridewell or inflict punishment according to the law. His more general duties consisted of supervising the constables, reporting them for neglect of duty, to 'sometimes ride or goe abroad in the night to see the Watches duely kept and performed as they ought', clearing the markets and streets of itinerant 'ffruiterers Hucksters and others', maintain supervision over the beadles and scavengers, to see that the regulations appertaining to the plague were strictly observed and to 'take up those yonge huswyves that wander upp and down the streets selling of fishe oisters and such like unless they be licensed . . .'.[32] He was also made responsible for Royal processions through the City. Walronde was given two assistants, or marshalsmen, and in 1617 this number was increased to four. Walronde was as much disliked as his predecessors but he appears to have carried out his duties in a conscientious manner. Possibly he earned the dislike of the public as well for he became in time the City's press-gang officer and escorted prisoners to their ships. This was one aspect of Bridewell that was only gradually developed, and it became a temporary holding-house for pressed men. Vagrants too were transported from there, the Irish to Ireland and the remainder cheerfully banished by James I to 'The Newfoundland, the East and West Indies, France, Germany, Spain and the Low Countries or any of them' anywhere in fact except England.[33] With increasing trade between these countries, particularly the American colonies, prisoners simply marched off one ship and boarded another and re-entered the country by a different port.

In 1619 Bridewell appointed its own Provost Marshal, William Davis.[34] To avoid confusion this needs some explanation. Until 1626 Davis's services were exclusive to, and paid for, by the Governors of Bridewell and completely separate from the City Marshal's duties, although the purpose of both was basically the same. In that year his office was placed under the control of the Court of Aldermen and he became assistant or Under Marshal to the City Provost Marshal. The word 'Provost' fell into disuse and the latter was simply known as the City Marshal. The City Marshal was paid £80 and the Under Marshal £66 13s 4d per annum; each was paid a further sum of £10 per annum for a horse 'to ride up and down this Citye upon these services'.[35] Their six marshalmen were each paid twelve pence a day from a quarterly sum allowed to the City Marshal and provided with a uniform hose and jacket or other suitable apparel. Each man carried a halberd.

This small band of men was frequently expected to cope with tasks hopelessly beyond their resources. In 1625 they were attacked and beaten by a mob of 300 apprentices for escorting an apprentice who was being carted from Aldgate to Fleet Street.[36] Three years later there was yet another outbreak of mob violence when Dr Lambe was murdered in Cheapside. Lambe was a quack necromancer with an engaging method for dealing with those who doubted his powers. A lady of the court once consulted him in the presence of her friends with the obvious intention of amusing herself at his expense. The lady left abruptly and covered in confusion when Lambe opened his séance by observing that she was the mother of two bastards. He had, however, a less pleasant side. Twice he was sentenced to death, the first time for poisoning and the second time for raping a young girl in prison, on each occasion only being pardoned through the intervention of his patron the Duke of Buckingham.[37] The London mob hated Buckingham and loathed Lambe, and when he unwisely walked down Cheapside late one night he was attacked by the mob, dragged back and forth along the street and systematically beaten up. The mauling went on long enough for news of what was happening to reach Charles I in Whitehall and for him to ride to Cheapside to rescue his favourite's necromancer. The mob at first refused to hand Lambe over and when they did his injuries were such that he died soon after. The King demanded that the ringleaders be punished, but the only victims were two marshalmen, Edward Grubb and William Towlson, who had witnessed the mob fury but made no attempt either to rescue Lambe or send word to the Lord Mayor or Aldermen who might have done so.[38]

The Lord Mayor shifted the blame for this and similar outrages onto the constables whom he justly accused of neglect of duty and lack of action. A portion of blame was reserved for the citizens whom he accused of refusing to assist in the apprehension of offenders 'much less to apprehend the offenders themselves and bring them to some officer or minister of justice'. The frequency with which successive Lord Mayors issued proclamations on this point shows just how helpless the authorities were in trying to impose 'watch and ward' on an indifferent citizenry that stubbornly refused to accept it. A random sample shows that in 1628 the Lord Mayor protested once again that the constables were abusing their office to such an extent that he strictly forbade the hiring of deputies.[39] He imposed a fine of twenty shillings for every default or neglect of duty and insisted that the constables' staffs be placed by the doors of their houses 'to the end that every man that hath occasion to use the ayde or assistance of a Constable, may know where to finde him.'[40] A proclamation issued two years later shows that matters had deteriorated still further and once again the hiring of deputies was forbidden.[41] This was repeated again in 1661.[42] A proclamation of 1673 notes the outrages and disorders in the street, the most notorious being a murder, and orders the constables to search the taverns every night beginning at ten o'clock.[43] This practice is amusingly described in Ned Ward's *The London Spy Revived* and is worth quoting:

. . . and as we were contending with the drowsy master for the other quart, who should come in and put an end to our controversy but a tall, meagre carrionly Cony-fumble, and with him his crazy crew of corniferous halberdiers, who looked together like Judas and his accomplices, or a parcel of Tom T . . . d-men with their long poles coming to gauge a vault: when he had given us a fair sight of his painted authority, which he stamped down upon the boards before him, with as much threatening violence, as a Jack-Adams in a music house, at the end of every strain, when dancing with a quarter staff; then with as much pride as a loobily Mayor of a Country Corporation, he opened his mouth, like Balaams ass, and thus spake, 'Look ye, do ye see me gentlemen? 'Tis an unseasonable time of night for people to be tippling; every honest man ought to have been in bed an hour or two ago.' 'That is true,' said I, 'for nobody ought to be up so late, but constables and their watches'; at which some of the company tittered, which gave great offence to the choleric conservator of Her Majesty's peace, who commanded us instantly to be gone, or he would commit us to the Compter. A Wine Cooper in the Company, being well acquainted with this shred of authority, used importunate solicitations for the liberty of drinking another quart, saying 'Pray, Mr. Constable, do not be thus severe with us, it was but last night you and I were drinking at a later hour together, I therefore hope you will not deny us the privilege yourself has so lately taken.' This bitter reflection, tossed into the very mouth of a magistrate, had such an unsavoury relish, that he could not swallow it, but commanded his blackguard to take us to the Poultry Compter, who presently fell on like so many foot pads, first secured our weapons, and then led us along by the elbows. . . .[44]

It has frequently been alleged that the Lord Mayor and Aldermen tolerated a weak police-system as to have reformed it would have meant some curtailment of their own privileges. This simply is not true. The written record disproves it. Undoubtedly there were Aldermen hostile to reform but, nonetheless, genuine attempts were made over a considerable period of time to strengthen and improve the City police system. That they failed was due to the indifference, corruption and hostility of a stubborn citizenry. The power of the Court of Aldermen was weakened still further by the rise of the Court of Common Council at the end of the seventeenth century. This gave to the citizenry a bigger representation and more say in the affairs of the City; by this means they were able to block many reforms that would have benefited the City as a whole but which they deemed to be against their own interests. The logical answer to this problem was a paid police force but even supposing that it had been thought of, which it was not until the 1750s, there is no doubt that it would have been conceived as an attack upon the liberty of the individual and regarded with even more horror in the seventeenth century than it was in the nineteenth when it was forced on an unwilling public. Under these circumstances what other system than watch and ward was there for maintaining law and order? The militia could only be used in exceptional circumstances and then with difficulty, and a paid police-force was not thought of. We have come full circle. The watch system based on personal service was the only answer to this problem, and that it was not allowed to work was the fault of the times and not of the system.

The corruption was so great that it quickly infected the Marshals. In 1627 Charles I appointed Davis Provost Marshal to the Earl of Holland's relief expedition to the Isle of Rhe.[45] The City allowed him temporary leave of absence and with their approval Davis nominated Nicholas Bestney as his deputy. When Davis returned two years later he was so broken in health that he was given a further leave of absence to go to Bath.[46] The Aldermen wished to replace him with a more fit and able man, but Davis thwarted their efforts to do so by using his influence with Charles I and the Earl of Holland who, remembering his service at the Isle of Rhe, successfully intervened on his behalf.[47] The impetus to oust Davis from office and again in 1631 probably came from his deputy, Nicholas Bestney, who, while performing all the duties of the Provost Marshal, received only a percentage of the wage that was paid to Davis as office-holder. He was utterly dependent on Davis for how much he received and, judging from the evidence of other cases, he could not have received more than half the Provost Marshal's wage and, since he was Davis's nominee, the figure was probably much less. For

five years he held the office in Davis's absence and then in
January 1632 the Aldermen caused an inquiry to be made into
his conduct and that of Henry Fitch, the Under Marshal, 'con-
cerning their letting out of Bridewell one Walter Lawrence a
known common thief and letting him go at liberty whereby he
hath lately committed a felony' and one other charge, the details
of which are not given, against Bestney. Bestney reacted to these
charges in the worst possible manner by abusing the Governors
of Bridewell; and for this and for his misdemeanours he was
promptly dismissed from office and flung into prison. In April
1632 being then a 'prisoner in Newgate for debt' Bestney
petitioned the Court of Aldermen for relief and was given forty
shillings.[48]

The Aldermen wished Davis to resume his office but he, firmly
in favour with his patrons and sure of their protection, declined
to do so. When summoned to appear before the Aldermen he
refused and caused them to appoint yet another deputy, Richard
Parker, in his stead. The Aldermen halved Davis's salary to £40
per annum, giving the other half to Parker, and this treatment
so incensed Davis that he complained yet again to Charles I and
the Earl of Holland who forced the Court of Aldermen to increase
Davis's salary to £60 per annum and to make up the difference
to £80 with two freedoms a year to sell. Eventually the Aldermen
brought him to heel by withholding payment for five years. In
1637, after ten years' non-performance of office, Davis asked to
be reinstated and the Aldermen agreed on condition that he
never again asked either the King or the Earl of Holland to
intervene on his behalf. Parker was dismissed with £20 and two
freedoms a year for life and Davis was paid the money that was
owing to him, £325. The concession they had wrung from him
stood the Aldermen in good stead; Davis and Fitch, the Under
Marshal, were so incompetent and abusive of their powers that
the Aldermen considered the City to be put to an unnecessary
charge in maintaining them and in 1642 sacked them both.[49]

The outbreak of the Civil War and the uncertainty of the
times probably account for the stability of their successors, for a
time at any rate, although, then as before, they neglected to
supervise the watch. The latter was badly in need of reorganisation, and in 1663 an act of Common Council was passed 'for the

better ordering of the Night Watches within ye City of London and liberties thereof'.[50] The watches were described as 'weak and wanting' by virtue of the fact that many citizens either claimed exemption from watching or that they should not watch with any constable other than the constable of their precinct. This point was taken up, and the act affirmed once more as had been done for the past hundred years that a constable's authority was not limited to his own precinct but extended to every part of the City.

One of the major defects in the old system was that watching was done by precincts and meant, in fact, that about 250 constables had to be on duty every night to supervise the watchmen in their precincts. It was humanly impossible for the constables to work all day and at night as well, and so the watch was reorganised into twenty-six ward-watches with only one constable on duty in each ward at night. This allayed a major grievance as the constable's tour of duty now averaged one night in ten. The number of watchmen each night was fixed in proportion to the number of persons living in the ward, and so that none should escape their turn, either by serving personally or by hiring a deputy, they took their turn from a rota, drawn up from the ward registers, and published 'every several nights'. These rotas were fixed on posts in the streets and market places so that everyone could see when they were to watch, the constable and beadle in charge, the date, place and time of meeting. To make doubly sure that everyone was warned the beadles and constables were given similar lists and told to warn their watchmen either by word of mouth, or by leaving a copy of the list at their house. Those that failed to turn up or neglected their duty were marked down on lists and sent before the Lord Mayor and Aldermen who fined the watchmen twenty shillings and the constables, because of their rank, five pounds. The fine was automatically trebled if the offender refused to go before the Lord Mayor or pay the original fine, and the money recovered with an action for debt. The case would be tried before the Lord Mayor and Aldermen and the prosecutor, the beadle, received one half of the fine, the other half going to the poor of the ward, after the Chamberlain had recovered his costs.

The most startling innovation was that, if they fell within the definition 'by reason of their habitation, occupation or dwelling', then the watchmen could be women! The 1663 Act, like the consolidating Act of 1705, is quite explicit on this point. If women did serve in the watch then it must have been on extremely rare occasions for one cannot imagine the satirists of the time ignoring such a subject. It would therefore be fair to assume that most if not all women hired deputy watchmen.

This Act was a solid and imaginative piece of reconstruction and should have provided the City with a good, efficient and workable watch-system. Unfortunately the reformers on the council had to combat not only the prejudices of the citizens but also overcome the hostility of fellow aldermen and common councilmen who regarded reforms such as this as yet a further attempt to weaken the power of the wards and strengthen the central administrative machine. When discussing this subject one tends to forget the reformers and remember persons such as the Alderman, who, in 1667 as Lord Mayor, reputedly rejected a number of would-be watchmen in the following terms:

If the whole City came to be entirely bereft of all its watchmen (which in God's name I pray may not happen) I would be loath to give employment to the likes of you.

The watch must be left for the aged, the infirm and the not over robust.

Some of you are still under 70 years of age and fit in mind and limb, and still have the audacity to seek employment in the watch.

I tell you that you are able-bodied, lazy, idle, shiftless knaves. The Watch hath no place for you.[51]

Men such as this condoned malpractices in the watch system hoping thereby to win favour with the citizens and to strengthen their own following in the wards. A little-known document in the Guildhall Records Office written in 1678 by a City constable, Robert Wilkins, a former High Constable of a Hundred in the county of Kent, and appropriately entitled 'Miscariages of Watching', shows how little the 1663 Act was allowed to achieve.[52]

The main point stressed throughout this document is 'the want of a horss man or two well mounted and armed in nature of a Scout or petrowle to ride the rounds of the City' to supervise the watch. The words 'Scout or petrowle' cannot disguise his true meaning that this is an attack upon the City Marshals, and by attributing the inefficiency and corruption in the watch to their neglect, still more so by his offer efficiently to undertake similar duties himself, Wilkins's motive in writing this document is transparent. Fortunately the points he makes are confirmed from other sources.

The constables, he alleged, frequently absented themselves from their duties a month or two at a time and left the beadles to supervise the watch. Even when on duty they never watched more than three or four hours except when they knew the Lord Mayor or Aldermen to be about. A more serious allegation was that constables have seldom or never 'theire full nomber of men but put the over plus of theire non appearance in to theire own pockets'. Now this was a point that had been specifically dealt with by the 1663 Act. The beadles had been forbidden 'any allowance of watchmen called dead pay for or in respect of their nightly watching' and the wards apparently agreed to pay them instead a salary rather than have the Court of Common Council intervening into what was after all a ward matter. The inhabitants, however, preferred not to pay the extra money and continued to condone 'dead pay', the beadles never hiring their full quota of watchmen and pocketing the difference between the number of men they were paid to hire and the number the Act required of them. John Strype confirms this in his 1755 edition of Stow's *Survey of London*.

There is a late settlement made of the Watch, yet not founded upon any law, wherein the watchmen have little or no dependence upon the constables; but the Beadle provides them, and he makes a Roll of the Yearly rate upon the inhabitants, in effect, at his own discretion. By which settlement, there attend thirty at Bishopsgate, and their pay is said to be sixpence a night; whereas, by the aforesaid act, there were appointed eighty; which being put in strict execution . . . the said duty came round the said ward but once in one and twenty nights, at eighty men per night. But the number of watchmen is since reduced from eighty to thirty; so that, were the Inhabitants now obliged to watch in their turns, or send fit persons so to do, the whole charge would be but sixpence once in about fifty six nights, for any one Housekeeper in the said ward, according to the present number of watchmen, and the pay they receive; which is not one half of what is now paid.[53]

The 1663 act fixed the number of watchmen in twenty-one of the City's twenty-six wards at 747; in practice less than half, 353, were hired.[54] In 1705 the wards pressurised the Court of Common Council to accept these lower figures, roughly half the numbers fixed by the 1663 Act, and caused them to pass an act to legalise the position.* In doing so the wards successfully paralysed, for a time at any rate, any further moves towards reform.

Wilkins has little new to add to what we already know about the watchmen, whom he describes as 'Antient and Infirme men, and not fitt for soe lively and Active a duty' armed with weak and rusty halberds 'not fit for offence or defence'. They neglected to patrol the alleys and lanes where crimes were most frequently committed preferring, no doubt, to shelter in the watchhouses and boxes that were slowly being erected throughout the City.[55] The impetus for these began when the watch for Aldgate was provided with a converted lodge, and other constables and watchmen in 1648 with a wooden shed erected by the City carpenter near Moorgate. The most interesting point in Wilkins's petition is that the watches, having neither uniforms nor a password, could not differentiate between the watch from another ward and the small bands of criminals that moved about the City at night armed with halberds and lanthorns similar to the watchmen's and when challenged claimed to be a watch from another part of the City. The watch was forced to let them pass, and so they went their way crying 'Good-night brother.'

Clearly the watchmen were no match for the sanctuary men and bullies of Alsatia who strutted through the streets with their flapping hats pinned up on one side and iron swords at their sides. Supremely confident when 'in defence perhaps of a Paultry Whore, or a Punctilio of mistaken Honour; they think it no Crime to pass through the Bowells of their neighbours, or wade in his Bloud to accomplish their Barbarous and Wicked Passions'. That this was no exaggeration can best be illustrated with the follow-case. On 3 December 1684, between eight and nine o'clock in

* An Act of Common Council, 16 June 1705. See Appendix 1

the evening, John Sparks 'having by the Darkness of the Night, and Tarrying to make water' was running down Fleet Street when by chance he brushed by a bully of Alsatia, John Hutchins, who was picking up a whore in Fleet Street. Hutchins cursed and drawing out his sword drove it through Sparks's body. The fact that Hutchins was later captured and tried for murder was a matter of pure chance.[56]

4. *Bullies of Alsatia*

By the end of the seventeenth century the City had managed to bring in various ways nearly all the sanctuaries under their control with the exception of Whitefriars. The signal for its end came in 1691 when the Templars, tiring of their villainous neighbours, tried to brick up the entrance in King's Bench Walk into Whitefriars. As fast as the workmen laid bricks the Alsatians tore them down. A furious fight between the two sides developed with swords and pistols being used. Several persons were wounded

and one killed. The City authorities raided the sanctuary in force
and arrested seventy Alsatians. The leader of the mob was
hanged in Fleet Street. In 1697 Parliament finally stripped
Whitefriars of its privileges and so swept away the last remaining
sanctuary in the City.[57]

The underworld had long foreseen that the usefulness of the
sanctuaries must one day come to an end. The bands of discharged military men and the beggars, led by the upright men,
had gradually been replaced by gangs of well-trained and well-
organised criminals. The oldest, cunningest and most experienced thief was usually their Captain or Superior. He commanded their instant obedience and worked each man according
to his own peculiar skill. Novices, before they could be accepted
into the gang, were first tested and then trained according to
their inclination and ability. Each man carried 'his private badge
whereby the Society may know what he is when they meet him;
the Robbers bear always a glove hanging and made fast by one
finger, the Cheats button their doublets by intercession one
buttoned and the next unbuttoned, the *Stafadours* always stroke
their moustaches every three or four steps, the cutpurses have a
little white mark in their hatbands etc.'[58] Certain laws had to
be observed by all (see Appendix 2). They were never to quarrel
with one another unless it was done so as to avoid suspicion. They
had never to be seen in the same company more than once in
ten days. Neither could they travel about the City in pairs nor
should they when in strange company show that they knew each
other. There were only certain places where they could meet as
a gang – one of these places in 1657 was 'the house of the
common hangman of the City of London' – and they met every
Saturday night 'to give an account of each employ[t], the manner
and purchase of it, and that they divide among themselves
according to their several shares. . . .'[59]

Opposing them were the watchmen – old, weak, indifferent to
their duties, trailing their rusty halberds through the streets,
drinking in taverns or lighting some noble lord to a brothel for a
piece of change but best of all snuggling down in their watch-
house or box where John Pearson found them in the early nineteenth century – 'for the thieves are out in all weathers, and the
more it rains, the more it blows, the more it hails, and the more

it snows, the more charley will stick hard and fast to his box, and bawl the hour, first putting his head this way and then that way, and no fool either; it is them and only them, who are the fools, who erect these retreats for poor old cripples, worn down with age and infirmities, to go to sleep in them, called in ridicule, guardians of the night. . . .'[60]

3

The Marshal and the Bucklemaker

And by this means all the numerous officers belonging to and depending on the Law, who were at first no doubt designed for the service of the public, in the administration of justice, and the defence of the rights and liberties of the people, are now by this lewd toleration of the buying and selling of places, become so desperately wicked, that they seem to be joyn'd in unanimous and direct conspiracy to rob and defraud the rest of mankind, and violate all the rules of justice and good policy.
James Whiston, *England's Calamities Discover'd*[1]

IN 1694 the Orphans Act was passed at the City's request and Parliament confirmed, what many had long suspected, that the City of London was bankrupt and could not repay the £700,000 it held in trust for the orphans of freemen. It was the practice in the City on a freeman's demise for a third of his estate to be set aside for his children's future use and administered by the City Chamberlain on their behalf until they either married or came of age. Instead of this money being administered in a separate fund, however, it was treated instead as income and by 1680 the City's debt to the orphans fund was a staggering £558,920. The Corporation tried for years to stave off the threatened bankruptcy by numerous short-term measures to increase revenue, including the sale of offices, a common enough practice at the time, but one that necessarily meant a certain loss of corporate control over the conduct of purchasers who were none too scrupulous in the methods they employed to recoup the money on their investments. The markets in Honey Lane, Leadenhall and Newgate, for instance, were farmed out in 1676 for £2000 a year; the bidding for them, however, rose sharply over the next fourteen

years when it became known that the purchasers were successfully extorting more than £13,000 a year from the tenants![2]
The Corporation was forced to turn a blind eye to many practices
it should have condemned and resignedly accepted the common
view 'That the Officers buy their places, and therefore 'tis
Reasonable in them they should make the best of them.'[3] Certain
other offices were sold by the Lord Mayor and Sheriffs to defray
their expenses while in office, since the Corporation's lean purse
could not provide them with yearly allowances as the Court of
Common Council wished; and at some unspecified date between
1652 and 1696 the posts of City Marshal and Under Marshal
were placed at the Lord Mayor's disposal, the former selling in
1696 for £800 and the latter for £300.[4]

In January 1712 the Under Marshal's office was sold for nearly
£700 to Charles Hitchen, a cabinet-maker, living in St Paul's
Churchyard, the money being raised by his wife Elizabeth who
sold her moiety in some family property in King's Waldon, Herts,
to buy the office for him.[5] Hitchen frankly admitted that he
wanted the office for what he could make from it and soon
became a familiar figure in the Three Tuns and Black Horse
Taverns in Moorfields, the Goat in Smithfield, the Blue Boar in
Barbican, the King's Head in Ivy Lane and other thieves' taverns
on the fringes of the City, openly touting for and buying stolen
goods. These, he suggested, in the anonymous letters he wrote
to the thieves' victims, could be returned to them if they contacted Mr Charles Hitchen in St Paul's Churchyard, 'the greatest
Proficcient in the Business of Thief-taking in England', sternly
warning them, however, to come 'to him with your Pocketts
well-lin'd, or he'll have nothing to say to you'.[6] Hitchen's chief
interest was in pocket books, private papers and bills of exchange,
generally things of little or no value to the average thief but of
some intrinsic value to their owner who was usually prepared
to pay handsomely for their return. The prices he paid for these
stolen items were arbitrary, since the laws against receivers had
been further strengthened by two new acts – Statute 3 William
and Mary *c*. 91 (1691) and the Tyburn Ticket Act (1706) – which
had added branding, transportation and hanging to the usual
punishments of fining or whipping, their combined effect
frightening off all but the most hardy receivers. Those few

that remained, like Hitchen, ran minimal risks, and since they now had a monopoly paid only nominal sums for stolen goods. 'Unconscionable devil!' said one woman of Hitchen when threatened by him with Bridewell if she did not comply with his terms, 'when he gets five or ten guineas not to bestow above five or ten shillings upon us unfortunate wretches'. Hitchen could afford to incur their enmity since on one occasion he boasted that he was receiver to over 2000 thieves, among them a gang of young pickpockets he daily met in Moorfields and whom he styled 'his Mathematicians'.[7] Hitchen's interest in these boys was not entirely professional, for he was a noted homosexual and well known at Mother Clap's in Holborn and the male brothel in the Old Bailey where it was customary for the men to address each other by the title of 'Madam' or 'Ladyship'. Complaints of these and other matters were made by irate citizens to the Court of Aldermen within the first eight months of Hitchen's appointment as Under Marshal and a Special Committee was appointed to inquire into his conduct – perjury, blackmail and the receipt of stolen goods being just three of the matters alleged against him. Hitchen delayed answering these charges for several months and then counter-attacked by calling his accusers 'thieves' and 'persons of little or no credit'. The Court of Aldermen suspended him from duty on 24 June 1713 for his accusers 'to prosecute him (if they think fit) for the crimes aforesaid',[8] but this they failed to do and he was consequently restored to office on 6 April 1714. It was in the intervening period that he struck up his infamous partnership with Jonathan Wild.

Wild was a strong, stocky man, five feet six inches tall, lame or deformed in some way (a contemporary pamphlet says that he was able to dislocate his hip joint at will but such a trick is physically impossible) with a dry wit and strong animal magnetism attractive to women – at least five among his many mistresses having the dubious pleasure of calling themselves his wife. Not surprisingly in those days when children not twelve years old roamed the streets 'half eaten up with the foul distemper'[9] of venereal disease, Wild later suffered from syphilis and more serious still from a bungled attempt to cure it. His hazardous career brought him many enemies and when he died he was still suffering from the effects of a cut throat in a body

5. *The Thief-Taker General*

scarred with seventeen different wounds and two fractures in a skull mortised with silver plates.

The exact date of Wild's birth is uncertain, but it was probably about 1683, in Wolverhampton. He was apprenticed to a bucklemaker before coming to London in about 1709. Almost immediately he was arrested for debt and committed to the Wood Street Compter where he spent the next four years, serving one year in 'the Hole', an underground cellar forty-two feet long by fifteen feet wide and twelve feet high, without heat or light, the prisoners only telling if it was night or day by the light or lack of it shining down the chimney flue. There was little ventilation and no sanitation for the seventy men, women and children that existed there on scraps of food flung through the grating and so vile were the conditions that apothecaries refused to descend into 'the Hole' for even a few minutes. Wild suffered terribly from his time underground, but by running errands for his gaolers and the more wealthy prisoners he was taken out and made a 'trusty'. He soon struck up acquaintance with a 'buttock and file' (pickpocket/whore) Mary Milliner, whom Wild, it is said, later marked for a bitch by cutting off an ear with his sword, and when he was released under a general pardon in December 1712 he moved with her into lodgings in Lewkenor's Lane.[10] For a time they worked the 'buttock and twang', Wild's mistress luring anxious customers into dark alleys and 'whilst the decoy'd Fool is groping her with his Breeches down, she picks his Fob or Pocket of his Watch or Money. And giving a sort of Hem as a Signal she has succeeded in her Design'. Wild would then attack the unsuspecting man from behind and knock him down.[11]

The money from these robberies financed Wild's more ambitious scheme to act in direct competition to Hitchen as a receiver of stolen goods. The last four months of his imprisonment in the Wood Street Compter had coincided with the investigation into the Under Marshal's conduct, and from the other prisoners Wild had pieced together Hitchen's importance as a receiver and the reason for his monopoly of stolen goods in the City. Hitchen's office was all that protected him from the worst effects of his indiscretions, but Wild could run no such risks, and it is a tribute to his evil genius that he spotted the loophole in the law that would not only protect him but through which

he could work. For the successful prosecution and conviction of
a receiver it had to be proved that at some point the stolen goods
had been in the accused's possession; this point vitiated the laws
against receivers for Wild saw – and this was the simplicity of his
scheme – that if he never took possession then he never could be
convicted of receiving and on this technicality built the foundations of his criminal empire.

The first thing he did was to strengthen his links with the
underworld by moving to Cock Alley in Cripplegate into the
heart of the area most under Hitchen's control. Here, among the
jerry-built houses, taverns and brandy shops beneath the
crumbling battlements of the City's north wall, Wild successfully
competed with him for stolen goods and by paying higher prices
broke his monopoly and rapidly expanded his business at the
Under Marshal's expense. The stolen goods, although purchased
by Wild, were retained by the thief while Wild went to the
victim, hat in hand, to inform him that he knew where his
goods might be found or that he knew who had possession of
them, and offer to treat with the thief on the owner's behalf for
their return, advising that the matter be left in his hands lest
the thief take fright and put the goods beyond all possible chance
of recovery. If, as sometimes happened, this offer aroused the
deepest suspicions and Wild was questioned as to how he knew
so much he would answer 'That it was meerly Providential;
being, by meer Accident, at a Tavern, or at a Friend's House in
the Neighbourhood, they heard that such a Gentleman had his
House broken open, and such and such Goods Stolen, and the
like!' If this answer failed to allay the person's suspicions then
Wild would put on some show of righteous anger and indignation :

> Sir, (says Jonathan) I only come to serve you, and, if you think
> otherwise, I must let you know, that you are mistaken; I have told
> you, that some goods being offered to pawn by a suspected person,
> the broker had the honesty to stop them; and therefore, Sir, if you
> question me about thieves, I have nothing to say to you, but that
> I can give a good account of myself; my name is Wild, and I live in
> Cock Alley by Cripplegate, where you may find me any day in the
> week; and so, Sir, your humble servant.[12]

His resentful words seldom failed to convince the loser of his
honesty, and when a bargain had seemingly been concluded

with the thief Wild would take the loser to his house in Cock Alley and show him an open panel in the wainscotting through which a hand would appear clutching the stolen pocket-book, letters or papers which Wild, at this time, dealt in; these the owner would take and place in the upturned palm the sum agreed on for their return, neither party to the transaction witnessing at any time the other's face. In this way Wild avoided the extreme penalty of the law for he could safely claim that he neither touched the stolen goods nor received the money for their return but simply acted as the intermediary between an honest citizen and a thief.

Wild's methods crippled Hitchen's business to such an extent that shortly after the Under Marshal's suspension from office he approached Wild with the offer of an alliance to make the underworld submit to their terms:

> I am very sensible that you are let into the knowledge of the intrigues of the Compter, particularly with relation to the securing of pocket books: but your experience is far inferior to mine; I can put you in a far better method than you are acquainted with, and which may be done with safety; for, though I am suspended, I still retain the power of acting as constable, and, notwithstanding I cannot be heard before my Lord Mayor as formerly, I have interest among the Aldermen upon any complaint. But I must first tell you, that you will spoil the trade of Thief-taking, in advancing greater rewards than are necessary; I give but half-a-crown a book, and, when the thieves and pickpockets see you and I confederate, they'll submit to our terms, and likewise continue their thefts for fear of coming to the gallows by our means.[13]

Wild agreed to this offer and so their short-lived partnership began with Wild becoming an unsworn marshalman.

The importance of Hitchen to Wild's career should not be underestimated, for when their partnership began both men were ostensibly on opposite sides of the law and theoretically enemies, Wild as a receiver of stolen goods and Hitchen as an officer of the law. Their partnership, however, showed Wild that the gulf between them was not so wide, that the two sides could be bridged, and Wild's subsequent career as a thief-taker must be regarded as the logical development of his friendship with Hitchen.

c

The expression 'thieftaker' was just coming into common usage at the beginning of the eighteenth century but their prototypes are easily discernible in Elizabethan 'rogue' pamphlets where they are called 'Black Dogs' and 'Cony Catchers'.[14] Their methods were the same then as in Wild's time when, armed with warrants, some genuine, others false or out of date and primed with the whispers of numerous underworld informers, they blackmailed thieves into further committing crime. The average citizen gratefully thought they did their unpleasant work from a keen sense of public duty and this opinion the thieftakers bolstered still further by sacrificing to the law the petty thieves and first offenders they arrested; their methods encouraged thieving since they preferred the professional criminal to be at large, for the longer he continued his thieving the greater was the share of the thieftakers' profits. Not surprisingly the crime rate rose alarmingly and the authorities tried to check the rise in the only way they knew how by increasing the number of hanging offences. Between 1690 and about 1760 the number of capital indictments rose from just under 80 to over 350, and many were the legal arguments as to what a man could or could not be hanged for. Other acts intended to reinforce these unwittingly strengthened the power of the thieftakers still further. The intention behind these acts was to encourage thieves to inform on one another, and in doing so to break up the organised gangs. In 1692, the Highwayman Act (4 and 5 William and Mary *c.* 8) offered a reward of £40 to anyone who arrested and prosecuted to conviction a highwayman; section seven of the Act offered a free pardon to anyone, not in prison, who turned informer. The 'Tyburn Ticket' Acts of 1699 and 1706 exempted from parish duties those who had successfully convicted a felon and received the £40 reward; possession of the ticket freed a man from the irksome office of constable or from the charge of hiring a substitute and they changed hands at high prices, 'Tyburn Tickets' frequently being advertised for sale by public auction. The 1706 Act also offered a £40 reward to informers and similar rewards were offered by banks, private individuals, town councils and the Post Office. What the legislators had not foreseen was that these acts would create an army of professional informers, men ready to commit perjury for the sake of the offered rewards. The thieftakers could now more easily black-mail thieves into a life of crime, for if they proved recalcitrant they could be framed with old evidence and dance aloft while the thieftaker and his accomplice shared the £40 reward. The extent of the thieftaker's power was now unlimited, as one thief explained:

For, said he, the Thief-Catchers are our absolute Masters; and they have Intelligence from Tapsters, Ostlers, and Porters etc., at Inns, and from People, that only for a Disguise, cry things about the Streets; and others, who draw in Servants to be accessory in robbing their Masters; and they send us into several Wards and Stations, (as a Corporal sends Soldiers to stand Centinel); and if we refuse to go, they'll immediately have us committed for some former Crime . . . he told me that there was at that Time, six Thief-Catchers that he knew, and where they kept their nightly Clubs, to which if their Gangs did not repair, they were in Danger; and from thence they must go wherever they sent them. He said the Thief-Catchers went every morning to all the Prisons, to seek for new Offenders; where they ask'd them their Case, and taught them how to plead; and if they had Money, would find some Contrivance, as in our Case, to bring them off; and whichever Thief-Catcher came first to such new Offender, he must be his Slave for ever after, and rob when he bid him, or be hang'd for refusing.[15]

The partnership between the Under Marshal and the Buckle-maker, as Hitchen called Wild in allusion to his former trade, lasted just over a year, from the latter half of 1713 to the winter of 1714–15. According to the *Tyburn Chronicle* they then 'fell to loggerheads about one another's honesty, and so they parted' but in the pamphlet war that finally terminated their friendship they left an unflattering account of some of their more scandalous experiences together.

According to Wild,[16] they made their first evening patrol together on the same day as he agreed to act as Hitchen's assistant. The relative importance of their positions as they walked down Fleet Street was readily discernible from the tall, strutting figure of Under Marshal Hitchen, with a sword by his side, resplendent in a silver-buttoned coat and knotted peruke, in striking contrast to the small, stocky man that limped beside him in his shadow.

They called in at various brandy shops and were offered punch, brandy and fine ale by the owners but Hitchen wanted information about pocket books and other stolen items only as 'pay back' for his protection. The prostitutes they met with were soundly berated and threatened by Hitchen with Bridewell if they continued to give the things they stole to the bullies and rogues they lived with. 'What do you think I bought my place for,' he asked them,

> but to make the most of it? and you are to understand this is my man (pointing to the Bucklemaker) to assist me. And if you at any time for the future refuse to yield up the watches and books you take, either to me, or my servant, you may be assured of being all sent to Bridewell, and not one of you shall be permitted to walk the street. For, notwithstanding I am under a suspension, (the chief reason of which, is, for not suppressing the practices of such vermin as you) I have still a power of punishing, and you shall dearly pay for the least disobedience to what I have commanded.

Some nights later the two thieftakers went to a brandy shop near St Paul's Cathedral and seized a 'buttock and file' whom Hitchen knew to be in possession of a stolen pocket book and watch. Hitchen bullied and threatened her with the Compter until Wild took her quietly to one side and told her that the Under Marshal would certainly carry out his threat to commit her to the Compter unless she handed them over. Hitchen offered a guinea for both items and with some reluctance increased his offer when the woman told him that the watch had been pawned. From the fifty shillings he gave her the woman paid forty to redeem the watch, and Hitchen was left in possession not only of the pocket book but a watch worth £7–8. This he kept but the pocket book presumably earned him a reward.

The Under Marshal treated both guilty and innocent alike. A 'file' successfully relieved a gentleman of his watch in the Blue Boar and with the aid of another woman pawned it to a watchmaker for fifty shillings. Wild arrested her, and Hitchen, on hearing her story, promptly seized the innocent watchmaker and threatened him with Newgate if he did not give up the watch. The bewildered watchmaker pointed out that the real thief could be traced through the woman who had pawned the watch to him, not realising that her accomplice, the 'file', was standing by him and listening to his tale. Hitchen irritably answered that he was not interested in who stole it but only in the person who had possession and once more threatened the watchmaker with Newgate if he did not hand over the watch, slily adding that the watchmaker should 'return him thanks for his civility which deserved five or ten pieces'. This broad hint was lost on the unfortunate man, who, as Wild cynically pointed out, was unaccustomed 'to unfair dealings', and who, in spite of his protestations, was finally made to yield the watch up to Hitchen who was rewarded by the owner with three guineas for his trouble. On yet another occasion a reward of thirty pounds was offered for the return of a pocket book stolen near Charing Cross by a pickpocket with a 'lame' hand. From the description, Hitchen knew the thief to be one that had done him some favours and whose 'pilfering employment' (pickpocketing) at the Royal Exchange he condoned. The thief, in spite of past favours, was blackmailed into handing over the pocket book, for if he did not, Hitchen had threatened, he could 'never expect to come within the City gates; for if you do, Bridewell at least, if not Newgate, shall be your residence'.

His treatment was equally outrageous when dealing with the ordinary citizen:

One night the Marshal and the Buckle-maker being abroad in their walks, not far from the Temple, they discovered a clergyman pissing against the Wall, in an Alley to which he had retired, as persons frequently do on account of modesty and decency. Immediately a woman of the town lying in wait for prey, brushed by, the clergy-man saying aloud, 'What does the woman want?' The Marshal instantly rushed in upon them, and seized the clergyman, bidding his man secure the woman. The clergyman resisted, protesting his innocence, (which his language to the woman confirmed) but finding it to no purpose, he at last desired that he might be permitted to go into an Ironmongers house near by; but the Marshal refused, and dragged the clergyman to the end of Salisbury Court in Fleet Street, where he raised a mob about him; and two or three gentle-men that knew the parson, happening to come by, asked the mob what they were doing with him, telling them he was chaplain to a noble lord. The rough gentry answered, 'Damn him, we believe he's chaplain to the devil, for we caught him with a whore.'

The Marshal further threatened to commit him to the Compter 'unless he gave very good security for his appearance the next morning, when he would swear, that he caught him with the whore, and his hands under her petticoats. The clergyman seeing him so bent on perjury, which would very much expose him, sent for other persons to vindicate his reputation, who, putting a glittering security into the Marshal's hand "which they found was the only way to deal with such a monster in iniquity, the clergyman was permitted to depart".'

The partnership soon broke up, for Hitchen's crude tactics unnecessarily alienated the support of those people on whose goodwill Wild was utterly dependent for the continuing success of his prospering Lost Property Office. He moved to bigger premises, to the Blue Boar tavern in Old Bailey, opposite Newgate Gaol.* The two main wings of the prison, covering what is now Post Office Yard and the Central Criminal Court, were separated by a central tower sixty foot high built over the main gate. Like other City offices, the post of Keeper was for sale, the present Keeper having paid £5000, at least £4000 of which it is said he recouped in one year, in 1715, from Jacobite prisoners. Prisoners were expected to pay for their comforts. Furniture could be rented for ten shillings a week and habitable rooms reserved for the more wealthy for non-returnable deposits ranging from £21 to £500, exclusive of rent. If a prisoner refused to pay the fees but looked as if he could do so, he could be loaded with chains, the most painful being the shears, 3-foot bars weighing 50 lb fastened to the ankles and the groin, limiting movement to 3 to 4 inches at a time. As their funds diminished so did the prisoners move down to the lower levels in the gaol, but while the money lasted they could drink beer in the 'Cellar', play cards and dice in the 'Buggering Hold' or watch the hangman in Jack Ketch's Kitchen boil the heads of traitors in Bay salt and cummin seed for spiking on the City gates. Those who had no money were placed in the Stone Hold beneath the gate and left without light or water, and forced at night to sleep on the stone floor on the cockroaches and lice that crackled beneath their bodies. The stench polluted some of the houses opposite

* I should like, once again, to express my indebtedness to Mr Gerald Howson for allowing me to use this material, some of it still unpublished.

and in consequence Wild had some very poor neighbours indeed.

Wild's methods changed with the opening of the Lost Property Office and he no longer waited on the public, hat in hand, but was consulted by them for a fee of five shillings as the first step towards recovering their property. Each item was entered into a register and later checked for discrepancies against the actual property that had been brought to him by the thief. His book-keeping made it possible for Wild not only to maintain discipline over his men but enabled him to tell which thieves or gangs were outside his control. Apart from a small bodyguard, Wild was independent of gangs but used the law to discipline those that failed to obey him, getting one thief to impeach two more, and then a fourth to impeach the first and so on until gangs, twenty to fifty strong, were either wiped out or brought under his control. The registers gave rise to a curious piece of folk-lore that when a thief brought his stolen goods to Wild, the par-ticulars were entered in a register and a cross marked beside his name if there was sufficient evidence to hang him; if this evidence was subsequently used and thief hanged, a second cross was added to the first to show that this had been done, this being termed a 'double cross'. Wild organised those that remained into groups, each specialising in a particular form of robbery; some robbed only at churches during Divine Service, others at the Court, fairs or the Houses of Parliament. His 'Spruce Prigs' went to Court 'on Birth-nights, to Balls, Operas, Plays and Assemblies for which Purpose they were furnished with lac'd Coats, brocade Waistcoats, fine Perriwigs, and sometimes equipp'd with hand-some Equipages, such as Chariots, with Footmen in Liveries, and also Valets-de-Chambres, the Servants all being Thieves like the Master.' Wild sometimes paid for a dancing-master to teach them to dance. By 1724 he had over 7000 thieves trained as servants to rob exclusively in private houses. Vast quantities of stolen goods were stored in several warehouses, one in Smithfield, another in Southwark, and a team of artists permanently em-ployed in altering watches, jewellery and snuff boxes and other valuable items prior to their being smuggled out of the country in Wild's own vessel to Holland where they were disposed of by a 'superannuated Thief'. All of this was carefully concealed from

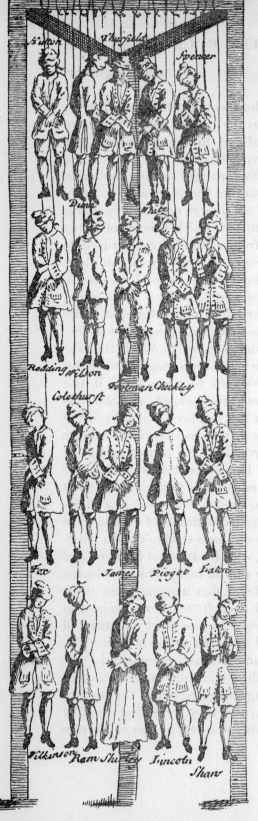

the public who, from 1716 onwards, were dazzled by the exploits of Jonathan Wild, self-styled 'Thief-taker General of Great Britain and Ireland'. In a series of well-publicised and sensational arrests Wild quickly caught and held the public's favour and while it is true to say that the motives behind some of the arrests were calculated to uphold 'his authority among his People', it is equally true to say that he was efficiently performing tasks which the law officers, such as Hitchen, lamentably failed to carry out. Wild himself listed seventy-six men and women he had 'discovered, convicted and apprehended', sixty-seven of whom were hanged; but this figure does not include the names of those 'too tedious' to insert and the true figure is probably in excess of 120.

Among Wild's numerous enemies was the City Recorder, Sir William Thomson, a corrupt lawyer and politician, notable only for his determination to hold as many offices and draw as many salaries as possible. In 1725 Wild was arrested and charged with helping the captain of his smuggling vessel, Richard Johnson, escape from custody by attacking the arresting constable and his officers. The charges against him were

6. *Jonathan Wild's Victims*

extremely flimsy but Thomson created a sensation by cataloguing Wild's crimes as sufficient reason to hold him in gaol, although there is little to suggest that Sir William had any hard evidence to sustain his allegations. Wild might still have escaped the gallows had he not blundered badly by confusing the charge against him for another matter, a hanging one, of which the prosecution knew nothing. Such a terrible blunder can only be excused on the grounds that Wild's throat had been cut three months previously and he was still suffering from the effects of that dreadful wound. He was sentenced to death and although contemporary opinion had it 'There's Nothing to being hang'd, but a wry Neck and a wet pair of Breeches' he tried to commit suicide on the morning of his execution. A too-massive dose of laudanum caused him to vomit much of it up and he was only partially conscious as the execution cart pulled him up Holborn Hill through the jeering, stone-flinging crowd to the triple tree at Tyburn. On former execution-days Wild had ridden ahead of the condemned cart to tell the spectators 'with the greatest joys and exaltation imaginable' that some of his 'children' were coming; his

C2

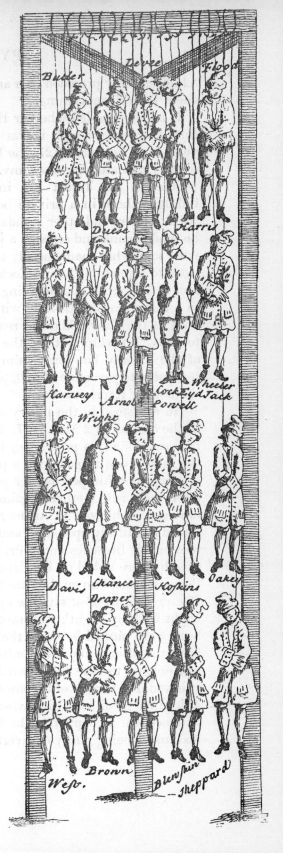

'children' now preceded him and mockingly told the crowd that their 'father' was coming.

It is not recorded whether Hitchen accompanied Wild on his final journey although it was part of his duties to do so. Two years later, in April 1727, the Under Marshal was charged with sodomy and attempted sodomy. Hitchen was well known to the waiters in the Talbot Inn in the Strand for he frequently indulged there in a private bedroom in 'sodomitical practices' with 'soldiers and other scandalous fellows'. On 29 March 1727 he made drunk and seduced a young man, Richard Williamson, who, somewhat shamefacedly the next morning, told the whole story to a relation, Joseph Cockcroft. On 9 April a message was sent to Cockcroft, and hurrying to the Talbot he caught Hitchen in a compromising position with another man. 'Sir,' said Cockcroft as the Under Marshal reached for his sword,' if you offer to draw, I'll whip ye thro' the gills.' A Jury acquitted Hitchen of the sodomy but found him guilty of the attempt. He was sentenced to pay a fine of £20, to stand in the pillory and to suffer six months' imprisonment.[17]

He was stood in the pillory at the end of St Catherine Street in the Strand on 2 May 1727. The mob had good reason to hate him and for extra protection, besides the Under-Sheriff's men, the pillory was ringed with a protective barricade of carts. The howling mob jumped over or pushed these aside 'and used him after their ruff method, against which he was well provided, having clad himself in Armour to stand their Batteries, which flow'd plentifully upon him, and finding him Armour proof, they tore off his Breeches and Shirt from his Back . . .'. Part 'of his Cloaths were pull'd off his Back, his Breeches down and several Persons struck him on the bare Skin with the end of their Canes'. *Parker's Penny Post* says 'he appear'd as a tatter'd scarecrow to fright Owls by Night'. Resistance was impossible. His wrists and head were pinned between the wooden boards. He nearly died from the attacks and after only half an hour the Under-Sheriff was obliged to take him down. His six months' imprisonment followed. His neglect of his office made it possible for the Court of Aldermen to dismiss him when he had nearly completed his sentence. On 31 September he was dismissed 'from his Office on Account of being guilty of several notorious practices and having for upwards of six Months past totally neglected the Duty of his Office'. He died soon afterwards in extreme poverty. His wife applied to the Court of Common Council for relief.[18]

Unfortunately the problems Wild and Hitchen had set could not be solved by their deaths.

7. *The End of Jonathan Wild*
Woodcut at the head of *A True Discovery of Receivers, Thief-Takers*, etc.,
by Charles Hitchen, the City Marshal

Riot and Reform

*But when a Mob of Chairmen or Servants, or a Gang of
Thieves and Sharpers, are almost too big for the Civil
Authority to suppress, what must be the Case in a seditious
Tumult, or general Riot of the People?*
Henry Fielding, *An Enquiry into the Causes of
the late Increase of Robbers*[1]

MUCH public anxiety was caused in the next two years by the
small number of persons convicted at the Sessions and the even
smaller number hanged. So few were hanged, in fact, that com-
parisons must inevitably have been made with 1706 when the
shortage of hangings forced the hangman, Richard Pearse, to
beg the Court of Aldermen for something to keep himself from
starving, he being 'ffitt for no other imployment . . .'.[2] Some
attributed this to a reform among the rogues themselves and
others more accurately to the want of a proper person to detect
them. The paucity of convictions was compared unfavourably
with Wild's heyday, his ruthless thieftaking efficiency and the
spectacular successes that had caused pragmatists like Cesar de
Saussure to question the wisdom of hanging him by arguing that
though they might rid themselves of a rogue he was still 'only
one and by his help several were hanged every year'. Public
opinion turned so much in Wild's favour that the *Daily Post*
jeeringly commented, 'Since the Death of Jonathan Wild has
been so much lamented for Want of his useful Intelligence, this
is to inform the Publick, that his Ghost gives constant Attendance
every Night at a certain House in Bury Street; where he resolves
all Sorts of Questions. N.B. As his former Business was to discover
Robberies committed, he has now the Gift of revealing Rogueries
intended.'[3]

His criminal empire was broken up but his methods lingered on in the numerous gangs that modelled themselves on his organisation. Thirty years later, one such gang, numbering nearly a hundred men, was not only adept in 'every Art of Cheating, Thieving, and Robbing' but had also 'Officers and a Treasury' and if caught 'rotten Members of the Law to forge a Defence for them, and a great Number of false Witnesses ready to support it'. By working together in gangs twenty to thirty strong, criminals were guaranteed near immunity from arrest. Passers by were openly attacked and robbed in the centre of London and those that resisted risked being either cut down or brutally maimed. Constables unashamedly admitted that in certain parts of the metropolis they kept their warrants in their pockets and slunk past the very men they were expected to arrest for fear of reprisals.[4]

The authorities responded to this challenge in the only way they knew how, by increasing the number of hanging offences. Crime, they believed, could be checked by terror, by more frequent use of the gallows. Within a few years, travellers could not approach the capital without passing by some gallows or gibbet or the corpse of some highwayman or footpad rotting in chains by the roadside.

Free pardons continued to be given to criminal informers and the number of rewards were further increased; but they became so divided up that frequently they were not worth collecting. On 3 February 1775, a gang numbering thirty to forty persons armed with 'Cutlasses, Blunderbusses, Pistols, and other offensive Weapons' surrounded the watch-house in Moorfields about ten o'clock in the evening and demanded the release of one of their number held prisoner by the constables and watchmen. They 'being refused, broke the Windows of, and fired into the said Watch-house, forced open the Door with an Iron Crow, cut, wounded and maimed the Officers and Watchmen there in a most cruel and terrible manner' and escaped with the prisoner. In Halfmoon Alley in Bishopsgate they met with the watchman, Philip Moss, and mutilated him so badly that he died of his wounds. The Court of Aldermen offered £50 for the arrest and conviction of one or more of the offenders. Two of the gang were arrested two nights later and thirteen others soon after. Twenty-six persons petitioned for the reward. Each was given a guinea.[5]

Forty pounds was the statutory reward for the more serious offences, and thieftakers acting as *agents provocateurs* would incite petty criminals to commit more serious offences and then arrest them when they 'weighed the forty'. Others trapped and framed their victims, often innocent of any charge, with a criminal offence and convicted them with perjured evidence. Ten 'Blood Money Conspiracies' are known to have been committed by one group of thieftakers alone; seven of their eighteen victims were hanged (three of them earning the conspirators, in this instance, believed to be fifteen, £540), two others were transported and one young boy died in gaol before he could be released. The profession of thieftaking was held in such loathing and contempt that John Fielding was forced to conceal the names of his four Bow Street Runners from the public for fear of reprisals. 'Blood Money Conspiracies', however, were one of the penalties that had to be paid for a weak police system and in the year 1772, according to a Member of Parliament, at least twenty persons were known to have fallen victims to similar conspiracies.[6]

Little was done to curb the thieftakers since they were considered necessary adjuncts to the existing police system. Judging from subsequent statistics, it seems unlikely that London's constables and watchmen ever numbered more than 2000 men and almost half this tiny force was concentrated in the City of London (see Chapter 5, page 97).

Though well policed in comparison with the rest of the metropolis, certain parts of the City were hazardous to pass through even in daytime. Moorfields was known as 'Sodomites Walk' because of the numerous young men that pounced on male passers-by and threatened to charge them before a magistrate with unnatural acts unless they bought their silence.[7] The crumbling tenements in Golden Lane, Smithfield and the adjoining Liberty of Saffron Hill were openly let to thieves who adapted them to sudden escapes; wanted men could escape through an upstairs window of the Red Lion Inn on a sliding plank that would roll them over the Fleet Ditch to a house on the far side where the plank could be drawn in behind them.[8] Jack Ketch's Warren, as the area was called, was equally famous for its pickpocket schools and pickpockets, many of them poor boys originally found drifting in Smithfield where the marshal-

men waited on Sundays to fine and punish drovers who, to
secure the best places, brought their herds and flocks in before
market day. The drovers evaded these penalties by hiring poor
boys to bring their animals in for them; flocks of sheep, fourteen
to fifteen hundred at a time, belonging to thirty or forty persons,
were brought in by these boys, 'who are not able to pay the
Penalty, And who Instead of minding the Shame of sitting two
Hours in the Stocks, Will sit a whole day with Pleasure for a
Small matter of Money.'[9]

One Smithfield publican had a 'club of boys, whom he
instructed in picking pockets, and other iniquitous practices;
beginning first with teaching them to pick a handkerchief out
of his own pocket, and next his watch; so that, at last, the
evidence was so great an adept, that he got the publican's watch
four times in one evening, when he swore he was as perfect as
one of twenty years' practice. The pilfering out of shops was his
next art; his instructions to his pupils were, that as many
chandlers, or other shops, as had hatches, one boy was to knock
for admittance for some trifle, whilst another was lying on his
belly, close to the hatch, who when the boy came out, the hatch
on jar, and the owner withdrawn, was to crawl in, on all fours,
and take the tills or anything else he could meet with, and to
retire in the same manner. Breaking into shops by night was
another article which was to be effected thus: as walls of brick
under shop windows are very thin, two of them were to lie
under a window as destitute beggars, asleep to passers by, but,
when alone, were provided with pickers to pick the mortar out
of the bricks, and so on till they had opened a hole big enough to
go in, when one was to lie, as if asleep, before the breach, till
the other accomplished his purpose.'[10]

Building restrictions to limit the City's growth had caused
many houses in Jack Ketch's Warren and other parts of the City
to be neglected and ultimately abandoned to the poorer and
criminal classes. Thieves and prostitutes lived in wooden shacks
'under the City Wall from Aldgate to the Postern on Tower Hill'.
In the Blackfriars district were numerous 'laystalls and bawdy
houses, obscure pawnbrokers, gin-shops and alehouses; the
haunts of strolling prostitutes, thieves and beggars', which, it
was argued in 1756, would be worth the cost of building Black-

friars Bridge to remove them.[11] Rebuilding, in fact, broke up
some of the City slums, but the jerry-built houses that replaced
them staggered skywards on walls one brick deep and that made
of partly warmed earth dug from the foundations or human filth
quarried from the scavengers' muck heaps, one of which was not
cleared from the streets until the following century when it was
sold to Russia for the rebuilding of Moscow. Thomas Copping,
however, was not so enterprising and not only obstructed naviga-
tion on the river but created a hazard to shipping by emptying
over 2000 cart-loads into the Thames.[12]

The older properties on the fringes of the City, the great houses
and gardens that had survived the Fire, were built over and
turned into streets, alleys and squares. Though buildings were
compelled by law to be of brick, fires were frequent, Londoners,
according to Defoe, being 'the most careless people in the world
about fire'; however, even the inhabitants in and about Shoe
Lane were provoked into complaining of Mr Lemon's chemical
experiments and 'excessive feirce fires' which, twice within
seven weeks, had set fire to his laboratory, a converted stable in
Shoe Lane. Future experiments had threatened to incinerate the
neighbourhood.[13]

The increasing complexity of the City's streets, lanes, alleys
and courtyards were perfect for concealment and, in Fielding's
view, had they been intended for that purpose 'they could scarce
have been better contrived'. Even its traffic facilitated street
robberies though the streets had been widened and the gates
demolished,* except for Temple Bar, to ease the ever-increasing
flow of coaches and sedans into the City and the heavy carriers
that rumbled down from Glasgow, Doncaster and Northampton
to coaching inns like the Belle Sauvage on Ludgate Hill, which
Parson Woodforde found 'a very good house' and where he slept
very soundly though 'bit terribly by the Buggs'. Brewers' drays
and scavengers,' carts, locked wheel to wheel in Fleet Street
and Ludgate Hill, frequently trapped fashionable ladies in their
carriages for more than an hour at a time and by preventing
them from getting out nearly ruined the mercer's trade.[14] The
coachmen would ply their whips on their horses and each other

* Bishopsgate, Cripplegate and Ludgate were pulled down in 1760, Aldgate
and Aldersgate in 1761, Moorgate in 1762 and Newgate in 1777.

to free themselves. When the marshalmen, William Payne and Thomas Linton, arrested a hackney coachman, they were prevented from taking him off his box into the Compter by a carman 'passing along the Poultry with his Horse and Cart' who stopped them by whipping up the coach horses and causing them to stampede, flinging Payne to one side of the street and almost trampling Linton to death. The carman was arrested, but as the marshalmen took him into the Compter a mob gathered, and the horse and cart 'went away'. The Court of Aldermen reluctantly settled out of court.[15]

Conditions on the pavement, the space between the wooden pavement-posts and the building-line, were equally ruinous to trade; and traders complained of the whining beggars by their doors and, in Fleet Street and Ludgate Hill, of the great number of prostitutes that walked up and down between St Paul's and Temple Bar.[16] The prostitutes worked with bullies and pickpockets and created diversions for them.

> They create a bustle and, try over the pockets of unsuspecting persons; till at length having marked out one, the accomplice shoves him hard up against other persons (usually some of the gang) who naturally repress the intrusion. Thus wedged in they hit him over the head with a stick, when he, to save his hat, or to resent the insult, lifts up his arms. A third or fourth still further behind gives one more shove, rams his flat hand hard against the belly of the person marked out to be done, and pulls out his watch.[17]

Far more troublesome to the traders on and about Tower Hill were the pickpockets, gamblers, thieves and itinerant traders of the weekly Rag Fair 'a Sort of Fair with Raggs and Old Cloths which are conceived for the most part are the ill got Effects of Thieves and Robbers and no little Encouragement to such bad Practices'. Fish, fruit, roots and herbs were offered from baskets set down in the middle of the highway; stolen goods were sold side by side with the butcher's and baker's stale meat and bread. By 1787 Rag Fair stretched northwards from the Tower through the Minories and Houndsditch though numerous attempts were made to suppress it.[18]

The citizens formed associations to protect themselves and to stamp out particular evils. The merchants formed a river-watch

force named 'Merchant's Constables' to stop the river pirates
from plundering their vessels; it was estimated that in eighteen
months the river pirates had robbed the merchants of over
£100,000 worth of goods.[19] Parishes hired their own watchmen,
traders had themselves sworn in as extra constables and the
Marshals hired men to act as constables.[20] Inevitably there were
demands for a stronger watch.

The power in the City still lay with the Court of Aldermen;
in 1726 their already delicate relationship with the Court of
Common Council had become even worse when they used their
influence with the Crown to cause a statute to be passed in their
favour giving them the right to veto resolutions of the Court of
Common Council which did not meet with their approval.[21] This
bitterly antagonised the Court of Common Council who spent the

8. *Watchmen*

next twenty years in fighting back through the wardmotes by electing only Aldermen pledged to repeal the hated veto; but in the intervening period they were helpless to oppose any changes and it was against their will that for the second time in thirty-two years far-reaching changes were made in the City watch-system.

The 1705 Watch Act had broken new ground by permitting the hiring of substitutes; the new Act followed this through to its logical conclusion by abolishing the old system of personal service and substituting instead a force of professional watchmen maintained from a rate levied, not on just the few, but on everyone living in the City.[22] This did not affect the obligation imposed on every householder to serve as constable, but the bill did remove two major sources of grievance. Parliament's approval was sought for such far-reaching changes. Possibly the Court of Aldermen considered that should their veto be abrogated, as it was nine years later, the Court of Common Council would have great difficulty in reverting to the old system. In 1737 Parliament passed 'An Act for the better regulating the Nightly Watch and Bedels within the City of London, and Liberties thereof; and for making more effectual the Laws now in being, for Paving and Cleansing the Streets and Sewers in and about the said City.'*

The Lord Mayor, Aldermen and Common Councilmen 'in Commons assembled' were empowered between 1 October and 20 November each year to make a Watch Act for the next year, beginning and ending on 25 December; to fix the number of watchmen to be hired, how they were to be armed, their wages and hours of duty, matters formerly settled by the wards themselves. The wards, however, did not lose all control over their

---

* One point should be cleared up. In discussing this, Leon Radzinowicz (*A History of Criminal Law and its Administration from 1750*, vol. 2, p. 180) says that bellmen were appointed after 1756. In fact, the date is much earlier. The City's first bellmen, Clement Foreman and Robert Egam, were hired on 22 January 1569. Each was paid five marks a year for nightly walking through the City and crying 'with a lowde voyce in every strete and lane wherein they shall watch these words "remember the Clocke Loke well to your Locke fyer and your light and god geve you good night for nowe the bell ringeth" '. Each ward was made to have a bellman by 'An Act for Preventing and Suppressing of Fires within the City of London and Liberties thereof'. (1667).[23] The bellman's task was to give warning of fire, that of the watchman to maintain law and order. Both called the hours but this is all they had in common.

own watch and could not only collect and administer their own watch rate but, provided they did not conflict with the general orders of the Watch Act, could also make additional orders and regulations for their own ward watch.

When the Court of Aldermen's powers began to wane, the wards began to vary the number of watchmen they hired and some concealed the discrepancies by not registering the changes in the Watch Acts. This was not to conceal any malpractices by them but was done through their natural antipathy to the Court of Aldermen and the wish to manage their own affairs. A Committee reported that, for many years after the passing of the 1737 Watch Act, the wards kept as strictly as possible to the Watch Acts.

> They caused half the number of Watch Boxes to be placed in their Wards, as they were allowed of Watchmen; so that one half of the Watchmen did Duty at those Stands, and were relieved every hour by the other half, who, when off from that Duty waited in the Public Watchhouse. But of late years, it being found that able and fit Men could not be procured at such low Wages as £13 per Annum, several of the Aldermen, with their Deputies, and Common Council, have, without any alteration in the Watch Acts, altered the method of watching their Wards, and the wages of the Watchmen; some by employing only half the number of Watchmen; but those Able Men, to whom they have given double Wages, and Compelled them to keep their stands all night, without being relieved – others have lessened the number of Watchmen, and appointed Patroles, with greater Wages than £13 per annum; but have all, in General, taken care not to expend more Money than by the Watch Acts they have been empowered to raise and levy for that Service.[24]

How great this discrepancy was can be seen by comparing the Watch Acts for 1774 and 1775, the year of the report (see Appendix 1).[25] In 1774 the number of watchmen supposedly hired is 922 but the figures for 1775, including possible increases, show that not more than 736 watchmen could have been hired, a staggering twenty per cent difference. The wards were forced to register the changes from 1775 onwards by the Recorder and Common Serjeant, who pointed out that unless the facts agreed with the Watch Acts then distress warrants for non-payment of the watch rate would be considered illegal in a court of law.

This was the last major piece of legislation on the City watch for the next hundred years. By 1746 the Court of Common Council had elected a sufficient number of Aldermen of their persuasion to repeal the Aldermanic veto and the struggle between the two bodies became centred instead on the Marshals and marshalmen.

The Marshals' offices were sold, and continued to be sold, by the City Lands Committee until 1779 by public auction, the highest bidder being declared the purchaser. He immediately paid down ten per cent of the purchase money as a deposit to be forfeited in case the remainder was not paid within fourteen days.[26] Only once, in 1771, had the Court of Aldermen refused to ratify a sale, when a notorious extortioner and gallows cheat, James Bollond, had tried to invest part of his infamously earned money by offering them £2400, £500 more than his nearest rival, to be the next City Marshal; his deposit money was returned, and six months later Bollond's rival, now the City Marshal, hanged him at Tyburn.[27]

Other bidders, though not so blatant in their conduct, were no less unscrupulous and, once in office, exacted 'money from a great number of Inhabitants within the said City and Liberties particularly of Brewers, Distillers, Vintners, Keepers of Coffee Houses, Victuallers, Bakers and others dealing in a public way under pretence of excusing or conniving at illegal practises and Misdemeanours'.[28] Thomas Hurnall, for eleven years the City Marshal, was a dealer in rum and bought office to force his competitors 'to deal with him on his own extravagant and oppressive terms' or be ruined by him; this he did on one occasion by terrorising guests and closing down the premises on the pretext that it was a disorderly house.[29]

In 1746 Edward Richardson, his Under Marshal, bought his office for £900 and fully exposed the Corporation to the hazards of their policy. Like his predecessors he was completely unsuited to his task and twice within the next three years he was suspended from duty, once being sharply reprimanded for kidnapping a runaway slave, William 'Beau Billy' Stanford, from his pregnant wife and two children, by pretending that he was taking him to the Lord Mayor's court, but instead shipping him, handcuffed and bound, on board a slaver.[30]

Richardson had contracted numerous debts in the victualling trade. His creditors harried him so much that he could not perform his duties, and on 22 April 1749 he was made bankrupt; his estate and office were assigned to the creditors who asked the Court of Aldermen to transfer the office to them formally to resell. The Court of Aldermen could only do this with Richardson's consent, but this was withheld and the office could not be alienated without exposing the Court of Aldermen to legal proceedings and risk of heavy damages. Richardson's stubbornness meant that the creditors had to find other ways to oust him from office or to leave him in possession, and to accept more than £200 of debts offset only by a meagre £150 from the estate.

The creditors petitioned the Lord High Chancellor who, on 4 August 1749, ordered Richardson to surrender his place and the creditors to find a buyer. The creditors immediately accepted Henry Buck's offer of £850 for Richardson's place, but Richardson stopped him from being sworn in by twice ignoring the Court of Aldermen's summons to make his surrender; he answered their third summons on 17 October 1749, but contemptuously refused to comply with the Lord High Chancellor's order. Ten days later the Lord High Chancellor issued a warrant for his arrest and to the creditors' dismay Richardson absconded and went into hiding. He was still in hiding four months later, on 27 February 1750, when the Lord Mayor and Court of Aldermen seized the initiative, as they had done with Hitchen, and dismissed him for nonattendance and neglect of duties. His dismissal solved nothing, for they were still without an Under Marshal, and they still could not swear in Buck in his place.

Richardson was in hiding another six months before he was arrested and committed to the Fleet Prison. The Lord High Chancellor told him that he would stay there unless he surrendered his place on or before the first day of the Michaelmas term. Though he was guaranteed his release and the creditors offered to waive their claims over more than £100 worth of household goods and offered him a similar sum in cash besides, Richardson still would not let them dispose of the office 'let the Consequence be what it would'.

The impasse was only broken on 21 December 1750 by the Lord High Chancellor guaranteeing to indemnify the City against any claims made by either Richardson or his nominees if, without Richardson's consent, they swore in Buck as Under Marshal and let the creditors have their money. Even so, Richardson still proved capable of making difficulties, and it was not until seven months later, on 9 July 1751, that Henry Buck was sworn in in his place, twenty-three months after he 'bought' the office.[31]

Though they had been held to ransom and risked being done so again, the Corporation continued to sell the Marshals' offices. The speculators' interest waned, however, when the City Lands Committee publicly proscribed the taking of illicit fees and gratuities. This bit deep and Hurnall's successor, Osmond Cooke, complained that after paying interest and £51 insurance* on his purchase money, his income amounted to less than £50 per annum.† The Marshals began to look about for other sources of income and unwittingly sparked off a whole series of major reforms.[32]

For nearly 150 years prior to 1723, it was the accepted practice for the Marshals to appoint their own men and later, when the offices came to be sold, for them to keep the marshalmen's purchase money. But in 1723 the then Lord Mayor claimed that the right of appointment was his, and in spite of the Marshals' protests both he and successive Lord Mayors used the money to subsidise themselves in office. The Lord Mayor's claim was not seriously challenged again until in 1771, nearly fifty years later, when the Under Marshal, Thomas Gates, claimed the right of appointment in a petition to the Court of Aldermen; he further angered them by telling them that he had appointed his brother, Joseph Gates, a marshalman and wished him to be sworn in as a constable as was customary.‡ His petition was unanimously rejected by the Court of Aldermen who swore in instead the Lord Mayor's nominee, John Bradley, who had purchased his place of the Lord Mayor for £500. Gates angrily protested that

---

* The purchase money was insured with the Corporation and repaid on death or resignation on payment of an annual premium of £3 for every £100: Cooke bought his place for £1700.

† This figure seemingly excludes the fees worth £95 and is apparently based on just the yearly wage of £135 (see Appendix 3).

‡ The Marshals and marshalmen had no special oath of office and from 1643 or earlier were sworn in as constables.

this was an infringement of the Marshals' rights and asked the Court of Common Council to intervene as the Lord Mayor's action was a clear contravention of the Act of Common Council of 29 August 1643, a report to the Court of Aldermen of 4 April 1626 and the Orders of the Court of Aldermen of 26 August 1625 which were given to them when they took office.[33]

The investigating committee that was appointed was the City Lands Committee. They were also asked to consider the Marshals' allegations that the marshalmen not only refused to obey or assist them but held themselves to be 'Marshalls Men to the Lord Mayor and not subservient to the Marshalls'. On 28 October 1773 the City Lands Committee reported to the Court of Common Council that there had been 'no Act Ordinance or Bye Law' to abridge the Marshals' right of appointment and that the Lord Mayor's claim was founded on an opinion only of the Court of Aldermen of 30 April 1723, which not only contradicted the Act but the 'terms of admission on which the present as well as all former Marshals had purchased' office.[34] The Committee's decision also meant that marshalmen could no longer refuse to obey the Marshal's orders or withhold their services which they had formerly considered exclusive to the Lord Mayor.

The Committee's decision irritated the Lord Mayor who promptly whittled down the marshalmen's perquisites and withdrew from four of the six the privilege of dining at the Mansion House, the principal inducement for them buying their places and worth to each of them an estimated £20 to £30 per annum. Including £2 5s 0d for clothes and an annual bonus of £8 6s 8d, their yearly wage was a meagre £28 16s 8d, and without such extras they could not support themselves. With some justification they blamed Gates for their troubles and sought compensation from the Court of Common Council, though each of them had bought his place from the Lord Mayor. William Martindale, for instance, had bought his place for £467, including the Swordbearer's fee of six guineas and five guineas to Gates who had 'told him that there were considerable perquisites at the Old Bailey and that he would have the right to wait at the Sword Bearers table and to Board at the Lord Mayors House and that Gates told him that he would employ him to attend upon Publick Processions and other occasions and should pay him for his

attendance that Gates did accordingly employ him for two or
three years afterwards and paid him 3s 9d a time (Gates charging
five shillings as he understood). . . .'

The City Lands Committee suggested that the Act of Common
Council of 26 August 1643 should be repealed and that for the
future the Marshals and marshalmen should be elected to office
by the Court of Common Council and have fixed salaries; the
present marshalmen could then be compensated with the return
of their purchase money. This provoked an immediate reaction
from the Court of Aldermen's supporters in the Court of Common
Council as not only did the proposals mean that control of the
Marshals and marshalmen would pass to the Court of Common
Council, but that the independence of the Court of Aldermen
would be progressively weakened by the subsequent loss of
income. The Committee was asked to reconsider its recommendations but they reported back in even stronger terms on 23 June
1774. In the original proposals the Court of Aldermen's powers
had been limited to suspending or dismissing the marshalmen
for misbehaviour; these were abrogated still further and it was
now recommended that they should only be able to suspend them
for misbehaviour until the next Court of Common Council. The
Court of Common Council could not agree on the proposals and,
Tinsdale having died, the City Lands Committee was ordered to
sell the City Marshals' office 'subject to such restrictions as they
should think proper'.[35]

This meant drawing up new orders and regulations for the
Marshals' office and the Comptroller was ordered to search the
City's books and make abstracts of entries on the nature and
duties of the Marshals' office. In the opinion of the City Solicitor
and the City Recorder who examined them, not only was the
original patent for the office of Provost Marshal founded upon a
mistake and therefore invalid, but that subsequent orders were
either illegal or obsolete like the Act of Common Council of 26
August 1643 which was never meant to bind the City in its
dealings with the Marshals.[36]

This ruling left the board free of all corporate and legal
tangles, and on 26 May 1775 a motion was agreed to that for the
future the appointment of the marshalmen should be in the
Court of Common Council and that they should be elected annu-

ally at the first Court after 12 February. The City Lands Committee had likewise recommended that the Marshals should be elected to office as it 'would then be more easy for the Corporation to cheque or control them in the execution of their office, for tho' every abuse of an office implys a forfeiture, there are many practices which the Corporation might wish to restrain that in strictness in Courts of Law might not be deemed so and the difficulty of proof of them, when they actually exist makes that a precarious security for the good of an officer. . . .' The first elections took place on 10 April 1778. Gates polled 107 votes and was made City Marshal with an increased wage of £250 per annum; his purchase money was returned to his father-in-law. William Miller, with eighteen votes less, became the new Under Marshal and was given a yearly wage of £200.[37]

Gates quickly organised the marshalmen into an effective crime-fighting force, and the following year successfully broke up 'a Gang of very daring and Desperate Persons at the Ship Alehouse in Gravel Lane', though Miller and several of the marshalmen were badly wounded in the fighting.[38] Far more worrying to them was the increase in popular disturbances, though rioting was expected when the flying horses and show-men's booths were erected in Smithfield for Bartholomew Fair, and on Lord Mayor's Day when the Marshals' finery was customarily bespattered with filth, their silk sashes ruined and maces broken.[39] The social and economic consequences of the Industrial Revolution were beginning to be felt, and behind the shouts of 'No Gin. No King' and 'Wilkes and Liberty' and 'Wilkes for Ever' there was 'a groping desire to settle accounts with the rich, if only for a day, and to achieve some rough kind of social justice'.[40] From 1760 onwards the Marshals found it more and more difficult to control the riots and with increasing frequency the Lord Mayor was forced to ask for military assistance from the Tower of London 'the Civil power not being found sufficient to quell the said riot'.[41] Without military assistance it was inevitable that the City watch, the strongest in London, should eventually be overwhelmed as it was in the Gordon Riots of 1780.

Rioting began on Friday 2 June 1780 when Parliament rejected a petition from the Protestant Association, led by the eccentric Lord George Gordon, demanding the repeal of the Catholic Relief Act of 1778. That night, 'to get the Papishes on the hop', a mob shouting 'No Popery' burned to the ground the chapel of the Sardinian Ambassador in Lincoln's Inn Fields and ransacked the chapel of the Bavarian Embassy in St James's. The following day they gathered in Moorfields where there was a large colony of Irish weavers, and encouraged by the supineness of the Lord Mayor and the tacit support of the ward constables, many of whom flaunted the blue cockade of the Protestant Association, they attacked, shortly after eight o'clock on the Sunday evening, the mass house in Ropemaker Alley, shattering first its windows with a volley of stones and brickbats before setting it alight.

For the next two days, chapels, mass houses and the homes of respectable Catholics were ransacked and in some cases gutted with fire. Doors and panelling were torn from houses and burnt with prized household possessions on numerous street bonfires; canary birds, screaming in their cages, were hurled into the flames because they were 'Popish birds'. Catholics were attacked in their homes and in the streets. John Geary strutted from a burning house, naked except for the bodices of the two servant-girls he had raped and left behind in the flames to die. Gates, the City Marshal, found that too many of the constables sympathised with the aims of the rioters and would not help him; one marshalman, John Bradley, told him that he would not protect 'such Popish rascals'. The Lord Mayor, Brackley Kennett, a former brothel-owner, was equally indifferent to their plight. His attitude amazed even his contemporaries. 'The whole mischief seems to be,' he said, 'that the mob have got hold of some people and some furniture they do not like and are burning them and what is the harm in that?'

Other City magistrates were equally reluctant to interfere, not only through 'lack of conviction' but, it was suggested, because some of them, those most adversely affected by the cessation of trade with the American colonists, were staunch supporters of the Protestant Association and hoped that the riots would topple Lord North's administration and bring about the termination of the war with America. Similar riots broke out in Westminster, Wapping and Spitalfields.

Parliament reassembled on Tuesday 6 June, and the rioters gathered in Westminster to overawe and intimidate the members. Justice Hyde courageously read the Riot Act and had ordered the Horse and Foot Guards to disperse the mob, when, in a voice that 'boomed like the crack of doom', James Jackson, one of the 'captains', riding a cart horse and waving a red and black flag, bellowed 'Hyde's house a-hoy' and led them away; by early evening the contents of Hyde's house were burning in half a dozen bonfires in St Martin's Street, Leicester Fields. Some rioters carried the flames to the Bow Street offices of the 'Blind Beak' himself, Sir John Fielding, while others followed Jackson, still riding his horse and waving his flag, towards the City, and shouting 'A-hoy for Newgate'.

The two great wings of London's strongest gaol were centred on the Keeper's house which immediately became the focal point of attack when the Keeper refused to surrender his prisoners. One hundred constables went to his aid but were quickly surrounded and beaten up and their broken staves used as firebrands to spread the flames about. The flames quickly spread from the Keeper's house to the chapel behind, and from there to other parts of the prison. Some of the rioters attacked the prison gates with sledge hammers and pick axes, while others tore out the rafters in the roof to get at the shrieking prisoners inside; as they dragged them out by their hair, legs and arms, red hot bars and great pieces of masonry thundered to the ground about them.

That night the flames of six fires could be seen from the Clerkenwell Bridewell, with the great flames from Newgate towering over the others and turning the night sky blood red.

The next day was 'Black Wednesday'. It began with sporadic attacks on Catholic property and the destruction of public houses in Golden Lane and Whitechapel. In the evening the riots began again in earnest and centred on Langdale's distillery at the corner of Holborn and Fetter Lane. By nine o'clock the building was in flames. Delirious men, women and children flung themselves on the ground and greedily lapped at the raw gin that spewed from the broken stills into the street. As the flames took hold the vats ignited and 120,000 gallons of raw spirit roared into the air in a great column of flame visible for thirty miles around.

Two fire-engines tried to douse the blaze, but the rioters substituted gin for water and the flames spread to the adjoining houses, burning twenty-one of them. A watchman passed by 'calling the hour as if in a time of profound tranquillity'.

Nearby was the Fleet Prison, and that too was fired. The King's Bench Prison, the New Gaol, Southwark and the Surrey House of Correction on the south bank of the river were likewise left in flames, and the prisoners in the Marshalsea released. From Blackfriars Bridge thirty-six fires were visible. Thick flakes of soot blotted out St Bride's steeple. The toll houses on Blackfriars Bridge were set ablaze, but the rioters refused to disperse until the military fired a volley into the crowd and then broke it up with the bayonet, forcing many into the Thames, killing about a hundred.

Other rioters, meanwhile, were massing in Cheapside with the firm intention of attacking the Mansion House and the Bank of England. The Lord Mayor had been given prior warning of the attack, and troops and civilian volunteers stood ready in front of the Royal Exchange. As the sun began to set, the mob made its first attack, shouting, screaming, waving flags, cutlasses and iron bars, urged on by a brewer's drayman on a horse ornamented with chains from Newgate. Cables had been fixed between the pavement posts in Cheapside and Cornhill to break the charges up, and as the mob reached the lines the order was given to fire. At least twenty people were killed with the first volley and many more wounded. The mob pulled back to regroup and reform, and ten minutes later hurled themselves a second time at the scarlet lines. Again they were beaten off.

The third and final attack came between three and four o'clock in the morning. It was the climax of the riots. Through sheer numbers the mob was able to beat off the Horse Guards and forced the Foot Guards to come to their rescue. Some of the rioters were armed with muskets, and the Foot Guards opened fire. The mob recoiled on itself and broke.

'Such a time of terror,' wrote Dr Johnson to Mrs Thrale, 'you have been fortunate in not seeing.'[42]

The New Police

*Your Committee have not failed to observe, that the City of
London, from the nature of its Magistracy, the description of
its various public Officers, the gradation and subordination of
their various classes, the division and subdivision of its local
limits, affords an example of that unity, and of that dependence of parts on each other, without which no well constructed
and efficient system of Police can ever be expected. If such a
system could be successfully imitated in Westminster and its
Liberties, and within the other adjacent Parishes which have
hitherto formed an unconnected mass of scattered and un-
controlled local Authorities, considerable benefit might be
expected to ensue. . . .*

Report on the Nightly Watch and Police of
the Metropolis, 1812[1]

MOST of the escaped prisoners, nearly 2000 of them, were re-
captured within a few days and temporarily caged in wooden
sheds in the King's Bench Prison and St Paul's Churchyard until
the charred shells of Newgate and the other prisons could be
rebuilt. Among those sentenced to death was the hangman,
Edward Dennis, who from the condemned cell begged the Court
of Aldermen to appoint his son executioner in his stead – a request,
which, had it been granted, might have necessitated the son
hanging the father.[2] The 'Yeoman of the Halter' was needed,
however, to hang his fellow rioters; sixty-two had been sentenced
to death and twenty-five were eventually hanged – one, at least,
on perjured evidence, his accuser being a thief-taker named
Connor who 'for some years lived by the price of Blood'.[3]

Order continued to be maintained throughout the capital at
the point of a bayonet. Civilian volunteers shouldered muskets

Down with the Bank!

No POPERY

NO POPERY or NEWGATE REFORMER

9. *This is believed to be the hangman, Edward Dennis*

with the regulars, and for some time afterwards armed detachments of the London Military Foot Association assisted with arrests and searches. No immediate steps were taken to strengthen the existing police-systems and there was a total reliance on the military to suppress the '*guerre des pots de chambre*' as a Member of Parliament contemptuously called it.[4] In 1781, the following year, Sheridan called for a committee of enquiry into the state of the police and magistracy of Westminster where the riots began. In debate the Commons unanimously con-

An Exact Representation of the Burning, Plundering and Destruction of NEWGATE by the Rioters

1. Gordon Riots – the burning of Newgate Gaol

demned the Westminster police as 'wretched and miserable' and branded the Middlesex justices as men of 'tried inability and convicted depravity'; but these were held to be insufficient reasons for changing the system, and the Solicitor-General complacently summed up in favour of the police 'in its present form' which had 'been found, throughout the course of ages, adequate to every common purpose'; the riots he dismissed as a 'single instance of a defect in the civil power which, in all probability, would never again occur'. The motion was rejected.[5]

In spite of the fact that crowds of victims were harvested every two or three months on the gallows, crime continued to increase. On 23 June 1785 leave was given to Pitt's Solicitor-General, Sir Archibald Macdonald, to bring in a 'Bill for the further Prevention of Crimes and for the more speedy Detection and Punishment of Offenders against the Peace in the Cities of London and Westminster, the Borough of Southwark and certain parts adjacent to them'.[6] The bill proposed to merge these areas into one 'District of Police' which could then be divided, irrespective of boundaries, into nine police divisions, the first division being the City of London. In 1812 the City, with twelve per cent of London's population, had forty per cent of its police.[7] In 1785 it had had at least half. Since the old watch system was to be retained unchanged this automatically meant that half the watch and police forces of the metropolis would still be concentrated in one division. On to the old watch system the bill[8] proposed to graft a central police force of 'Ministerial Officers of the Peace' called Petty Constables of the Division, some to patrol on foot and others on horseback; each of the nine divisions was to be commanded by a Chief Constable answerable to a High Constable of the Peace who was to have the overall supervision. The force was to be commanded by three Commissioners of Police (also Justices of the Peace) in whose hands would 'be concentrated the whole power of the police'.[9]

The Solicitor-General proposed to form his 'Ministerial Officers of the Peace' into 'a number of patroles divided into parties of twenty-five to each division, twelve of whom, with a leader, were to be on duty every night', 108 by day and 117 by night. Not only were these numbers hopelessly unrealistic, but they weakened still more a plan already vitiated by the decision to

D

leave in the hands of innumerable parochial and ward authorities the existing watch systems, without either changing their traditional structure or method of rating which would have made this possible – in the City of London, for instance, the nightly watch-rate could not be used to pay for other forms of police, such as the Marshals and marshalmen, who were paid for from the City's cash. From the bill it is clear that the main task of the petty constables would have been to co-ordinate and supervise the local systems; for this reason and because of their small numbers, the Bill armed them with extremely wide powers, and persons who neglected or refused to obey them could be fined or imprisoned. As the bill stood 'a constable might break open any man's house, and enter his wife's bedchamber, and so far was he from being liable to an action for a trespass, if the master of the house molested him, or endeavoured to prevent such an outrage, he was liable to the severe punishment of imprisonment for several years, or of being sentenced to transportation'.[10]

In spite of the obvious impracticalities of trying to work so unwieldy a system with so few men, the Solicitor-General wanted his plan tried for an experimental period of one year at least. Quite clearly the purpose of the bill was to improve the efficiency of the nightly watch of the metropolis and not to create a police force, in the modern sense of the term, as some writers have tried to suggest. Unless at the end of the experimental period there had been a vast increase in establishment, the only protection the Bill would have offered the metropolis by day was a scattered force, twelve men to each division, of 108 men, roughly the size of the later-established Bow Street Patrol, which it clearly foreshadows.

Leave was given for the Bill to be brought in on 23 June. On 27 June it was read for the first time, but the following day notice was given that the Bill had not been properly prepared; leave was given for it to be withdrawn and a new one presented.

Less than forty members had been present when the Bill was brought in. Through 'an accident' a copy of the Bill had not been sent to the Lord Mayor until the Sunday evening of 26 June, three days later. The Court of Aldermen was convened and met two days later, on 28 June, *as the Bill was being withdrawn in*

Parliament.[11] The contents of the Bill it was said, 'created great alarm and uneasiness in the city of London; so much so, that if a torch had been applied to the buildings there, it could not have created greater alarm'.[12]

Parliament, it must be remembered, was still at this time a 'marketable thing'. Less than 6000 voters could elect 254 members, and the corruption in Parliament itself was still increasing; by 1820 '144 peers nominated 300 MPs, and the government and 123 persons together nominated 187 more, thus making an actual majority however high the division figures might be'.[13] In the country there were less than forty democratically controlled boroughs, and of these the City of London was the spokesman and the most powerful.*

The Bill as it stood would not only have overridden the chartered rights of the City of London but placed in the hands of the Government 'a strong professional force under its undivided control and independent of the civil power as exercised by the Justices of the Peace. Its jurisdiction would have extended over the whole metropolitan area, and its powers would have encroached upon those of the justices, overriding many ancient municipal rights and possibly impinging upon the liberty of the subject.'[14] This was the crux of the City's argument, and the same point is stressed again and again. The Bill was a threat to the 'Liberties of the Kingdom' and the 'Constitutional Rights of the Nation'; it was 'utterly subversive not only of the Chartered Rights of the City of London but to the constitutional liberties of all his Majesty's subjects . . .'. The teeth in the Bill were the 'extraordinary and dangerous powers' to be given to the central police force. The City was not alone in fearing that with such powers the police might be used by the King or his Ministers,

---

* 'In 1769 Common Hall issued a list of instructions to its parliamentary representatives. Among other things they were to keep a jealous watch over the Habeas Corpus Act, parliamentary privilege, and the rights of electors which they judged were in danger of attack. They were to veto any use of public money in elections, the bribery of Members of Parliament or any increase in the power of the army. They were to advocate shorter parliaments and do everything possible to uphold the independence of the magistrates and to preserve the public faith. Much of what they advocated were the tenets of nineteenth-century reformers, and they were the political convictions of the City throughout the greater part of the eighteenth century.' (Rosamond Bayne-Powell, *Eighteenth-Century London Life.*)

working through a bought House of Commons, to act in a yet more arbitrary manner. Nor were these fears exaggerated or unnecessarily alarmist.

Only five years previously the Commons had passed their famous resolution 'that the influence of the Crown has increased, is increasing and ought to be diminished'. Nor was it so many years before that Wilkes had been expelled from the Commons because he was anathema to the Crown, and a Lord Mayor and an Alderman been committed to the Tower because they had shielded with the City's privileges a printer who had offended by printing and publishing the Commons debates.

On 29 June the Sheriffs came to the bar of the House of Commons and presented a petition against the Bill from the Lord Mayor and Court of Aldermen. None of the Aldermen (the City's MPs) who took part in the subsequent debate were aware, until told by the Speaker, that the Bill had been withdrawn and that a new one was to be brought in. One of the Aldermen moved that the new Bill should be discharged unseen, but neither of his colleagues would support him; Alderman Townshend said

> it was not to be disputed, that they were got into a lamentable state of police, and as thieves and rogues of all denominations had increased to an almost incredible number, he would not second a motion for discharging an order to bring in a bill for the prevention of robberies and burglaries. He thought the title of such a bill was sufficient to induce gentlemen to wait till the bill was before the House, in order to see when it came, whether it was a bill fit to be received or not.[15]

The motion was withdrawn and the way was clear for the Solicitor-General to bring in the new bill which 'he hoped, with the joint assistance of the abilities of the whole House, to make a beneficial bill to the public'.[16]

However, opposition was now mounting from other quarters. Though it had been withdrawn, the Bill had been so badly drafted that it had antagonised as well the Justices of the Peace, the publicans, the pawnbrokers and certain other trades it had intended to license; the Press had been equally critical of the Bill — one newspaper had thought it 'radically bad'.[17] The Solicitor-General's inept handling of the whole affair completely prejudiced the chances of the new bill and compelled Pitt to shelve it until a more favourable moment. This never came. Possibly it suffered the same fate as Colquhoun's four police bills in 1799 and which likewise were never heard of again. War soon followed, and for the next twenty years this island was locked in mortal combat with the eagles of France.

No comparable measure was introduced into the House of Commons for another forty years. To compensate for a weak police-system the nation's penal laws were ruthlessly enforced intead. Eight persons could swing side by side on each of the beams of the 'Three-Legged Mare' at Tyburn. It was a capital offence not to remain in quarantine, to cut down trees or river banks, to make a false entry in a book of the Bank of England, to impersonate a Greenwich pensioner, to cut down hop vines, to damage Westminster Bridge and to steal in a dwelling-house to the value of forty shillings, though judges and juries in collusion often mitigated the severity of sentence, and goods whose actual value was forty to fifty pounds were often deliberately undervalued at thirty-nine shillings; between 1781 and 1787, there was not, in the opinion of an old Bow Street runner, 'an execution wherein we did not grace that unfortunate gibbet with ten, twelve, to thirteen, sixteen, and twenty [persons]; and forty I once saw at twice . . .'.[18]

In 1783 the shambles of 'Tyburn Holiday' were brought to an end, and the place of execution moved to an open space in front of Newgate gaol. Unlike the 'Three-Legged Mare' the new scaffold was not a permanent one, and had to be erected the night before by twenty men working through the night from ten o'clock in the evening until seven o'clock the next morning for a pint of porter and 6s 8d each. The contractor, Mr Banner, soon became accustomed to workmen resigning rather than help to erect it.[19]

The 'gallows groaned', and eighteen out of every twenty persons hanged in the metropolis were under the age of twenty-one. The criminal careers of most of them began when they were urchins, six to ten years old, sent by their parents, or the thieves who worked them, to pick pockets, to take things 'on their hands and knees, from shops such as haberdashers and linen-drapers' or from windows by 'starring the glass' with a knife. Occasionally they were encouraged with small sums of money but at other times could be seen sleeping in cellars, markets and cattle pens, too afraid to go back without the sixpence they had been sent to either beg or steal. If caught they were committed to the 'nurseries of vice', Newgate and the hulks, and corrupted completely by the old thieves, transports and condemned men sharing with them; sometimes the magistrates found it possible to commit the boys to Bridewell or correct them with thirty-five lashes, but in the opinion of two of the Marshals this not only marked them for life but hardened them as well, half of those so punished being invariably convicted a second time at the next sessions where they were tried, whatever their age, before a judge and jury.[20] One eye-witness saw 'a baby of seven years of age turned back into the Newgate from the Old Bailey Court, convicted of felony' and the Ordinary of Newgate told a Select Committee on Police in 1816 of four boys, aged nine, eleven, twelve and thirteen, who between them had been in custody more than seventy times. The youngest had been abandoned by his parents when he was six, and since that time he had existed on the streets, keeping himself and his girl, by begging and pilfering; now aged nine, he was under sentence of death.[21]

The lives of these boys, and the girls they lived with, centred on 'flash houses' like the Barley Mow in Field Lane, the Red Lion in Fleet Market, the Magpie and Stump in Skinner Street, and the Cock in Bishopsgate where there was a 'most desperate set of Boys, Girls and Men . . .'. The 'flash houses' were useful sources of information to officers of the law and thief-takers who were on 'familiar terms with the landlords and landladies; hailing them in a friendly manner, winking at them, whispering and drinking drams with them'. 'It was very difficult to distinguish the thief from the policeman: they spoke the same slang language, they frequented the same flash public-houses, and their habits and manners and conversation were so much alike, that it was difficult to tell one from another.'[22] They were equally useful for keeping an eye on known thieves until they were 'worth the forty'; a thief generally knowing when he was ready for 'consumption' by the 'weight of his Cly'.[23] This was explained in the following manner to the victim of a robbery who wrongly identified one of his attackers:

'You were certainly very much deceived, sir, respecting this man; though, to be sure, he is a thief, and has not left the ballast-lighter above a month; but he does not yet do anything so considerable as your affair was; he is only in a low way yet, such as picking of pockets and robbing of carts; and, at the very time you were robbed, he was robbing waggons in another part.' I interrupted them here, by asking them, 'as they knew this, why they did not prosecute him?' They smiled at me, in a seemingly contemptuous manner, and made use of these particular words: 'Oh! God bless you, sir, it is our interest to let little fish go, that we may get great ones!'[24]

Successive Marshals tried to stamp out the City 'flash houses' but new ones were constantly being found – the Dolphin, the Crown and Sugar Loaf, the Horse Shoe and Star, and Gurney's Tap which kept open for thieves until four o'clock in the morning.[25] Other useful sources of information were the lodging-houses in Spitalfields, Shoreditch and Whitechapel, such places being kept by 'men of the lowest and vilest description, who live by the plunder those boys and girls collect'. In some houses lived '18 and 20 men and women, boys and girls, in bed together, all in two rooms. The fellow who keeps the house has a sort of table for them; some pay 6d for their bed, some 4d, and they all go out thieving. If they steal a handkerchief, the man says, "You had your dinner yesterday, that was 4d; I will take this handkerchief for it;" and if they steal a watch, which is worth perhaps 20l. or 25l., it will fetch 20s or 25s in the market, and he says, "This will go on for next week".' In the daytime they hunted 'about Whitechapel, on both sides of the way until eight o'clock, when the City Day Police go off; then they go across Whitechapel into Aldgate, and prowl along up to the Mansion-House, and round that neighbourhood, and commit all manner of depredations'.[26]

The City Day Police they took such pains to avoid had been formed by the Lord Mayor in 1784 and in its early years was known as the City Patrol. It was formed on the orders of the Court of Common Council who had expected it to operate for a short time only, at the City's expense, for a sum not exceeding £300, from 1 December 1784 to 1 April 1785;[27] the fact that it was continued might owe something to Pitt's Solicitor-General

and the favourable reference he seems to have made to it when
he brought in the London and Westminster Police Bill. 'He had,'
he said,

> in his researches for information, conversed with every man whose
> situation had led him to a knowledge of the subject, and among the
> rest, with a very respectable judge (baron Eyre), who was once
> Recorder of London; from whom he had learnt that a patrole was
> established in a certain part of town, where robberies and other
> enormities had been much practised, and that the consequence was,
> that for two sessions, he could not pretend to say, that not any,
> but very few capital convictions took place at the Old Bailey. He
> should therefore propose a similar plan, but to extend generally to
> every part of the town, and its environs; for if it were to be confined
> to the heart of the city, it would drive the robbers to the out-skirts,
> and if it were only to be applied in the out-skirts, it would bring
> them all to the centre. And he had been informed, that in conse-
> quence of the vigorous exertions of this patrole, a mode of robbing
> was adopted by those who were confined by it to the interior parts,
> vulgarly called the 'rush'; which signified a number of persons
> assembling at a door, and as soon as it should be opened, rushing in,
> binding the family and servants, and then plundering the house.[28]

It was on this patrol that he had hoped to model his central
police patrols.

In 1791 the City Patrol was issued with uniform – boots,
round hats and Kersey greatcoats. Subsequent issues were so
infrequent, however, that for some years following the men were
compelled to buy their own. Eventually they could no longer
afford to do so, and in 1801 the Corporation agreed to issue them
with boots every two years and a blue-cloth greatcoat every four.[29]
The colour might have been suggested by Jonas Hanway, who
thought that constables on duty at executions might wear 'a
uniform of dark blue or other garb of distinction'. However,
until 1824 the wearing of uniform was not compulsory. It seems
to have been worn so infrequently that it was possible for the
City Marshal, in 1822, to tell the Select Committee on Police
that the Patrol never wore uniform. This was two years after
they had petitioned for an early issue of clothing as the 'weather
was very sharp' and on 'cold nights and muddy streets' greatly

needed.[30] A possible explanation is that the men were often
working for, and had their wages paid by, the victims of crime.
In 1838 it was explained that their wages were stopped when
they were investigating robberies as it was thought proper 'that
when city officers were sent after robberies, those who had
been robbed ought to pay them. That . . . was not disputed by
an individual in the court [of Aldermen], and therefore it may
be inferred it was their opinion, that persons who have paid to
the police rates for 20 years, ought to pay the officers out of their
own pockets for the recovery of property of which they have
been robbed.'[31]

The wages were frequently inadequate, and often the men
were compelled to seek extra work. A common complaint against
the watchmen was that they were often employed in running
errands and shutting up shops. In 1802 the wages for the City
Patrol were 4s 6d a day.[32] In 1812 this was increased to 5s 3d a
day for the Day Patrol who had complained that being on duty
from morning till night stopped them from taking on any other
trade or occupation'; though according to the City Marshal,
Philip Holdsworth, they had 'an opportunity of getting money,
because where they are employed, whether it is where burglaries
are committed, or where they are put on a particular duty, the
gentlemen employing them give them something for their
trouble, but of that they must tell the Lord Mayor; they run a
risk of losing their situation if they accept a present without
informing him'.[33] The plight of the Night Patrol was far more
invidious. They were obviously expected to find other work. They
were not given the same increase as the Day Patrol, and when
the City Patrol, now the Day and Night Police, was reorganised
in 1824 their wages were actually *reduced*, after 22 years, from
4s 6d a day to 4s.

In 1824 the wearing of uniforms was made compulsory for
both the police and the Marshals and marshalmen. There had
been frequent complaints that the Marshals never wore uniform,
understandably so, as it was hopelessly impractical for police
work and reflected more the ceremonial duties with which they
were becoming increasingly involved. Each Marshal carried a
silver gilt mace and wore a scarlet tunic with gold epaulettes and
a military cocked hat with plumes; on execution day and on

D2

" Forward, I say, are you all Beetles—Constables, clear the way, and
let the cavalcade advance with all becoming grace ; and, Bill, do
you make the best of your way to ' the Goose and Gridiron,' in St.
Paul's Church-yard, and get ready a pint of gin for the gemmen in
armour. The fog is as thick as mustard, and the air is heavier than
their brass doublets—stop as you go by at White's, the hatter, in
Cheapside—tell my old lady I'm a coming. Tell her too to have no
fears for me, for, with the fate of Wontner before my eyes, I've secured a horse that can't fall down, if he would, for I have appointed
two of the City police to watch each leg, and to take him into custody if he dare to make a false step. The procession will, as usual,
' take water' at Blackfriars, but if I take a drop of water this
blessed day I'll de d——d."

Long may's thou mount thy generous steed,
    The glory of all London town ;
Alike prepared to fight or feed—
    May vile Reform ne'er cut thee down.
Long may the bottle paint that snout,
    And viands choice thy system nourish ;
Still bid defiance to the gout,
    And long thy wand of office flourish !
" First fiddle in my Lord Mayor's Show,
    Folks shan't suppose that I'm a sammy ;
Il'll let each base plebeian know
    That I'm the City Marshal—damme !"

10. *Neville Browne, the City Marshal*

The allusion to Wontmer makes it almost certain that this figure is
meant to be his successor Neville Browne. Wontner was City Marshal
from 1816 to 1822. He was badly injured when he was thrown from
his horse and was forced to retire. He became Keeper of Newgate.

other important occasions he rode a horse with a richly ornamented saddle and hand-painted leopard-skin saddle-cloth. The
marshalmen wore military cocked hats with double gold stays
and rich spangled loops and buttons.[34] The uniform for the Day
Police was more sober – blue coat, blue trousers and a drab waist-
coat with the City button; the Night Police wore dark grey coats.
In 1828 a round button of the City arms on a plain shield was
appended to the coat and the Smithfield men were issued with
hats marked 'CITY POLICE'.[35]

Between 1791 and 1801 the City Patrol was increased from
twelve to seventeen men, and by 1822 consisted of twenty-three
Day Patrol and sixteen Night Patrol. In 1824 this was reorganised into twelve Day Patrol and twelve Night Patrol; each
patrol was broken down into pairs, and each pair was based on a
main watchhouse or police station.[36] Primarily these were
assembly points in case of riots. In 1824 they were the Mansion
House, London Bridge, Portsoken (Aldgate), Bishopsgate, Fleet
Market and St Andrew, Holborn. These were open every day
from nine o'clock in the morning until the Watch was set and
persons wanting assistance could leave their names with the
Station Officer – a senior constable not 'capable of much active
duty' – who would then inform the Patrol who came back every
hour to sign their names in the station register. Eight other
constables patrolled Smithfield market and looked for stolen
horses. The overall supervision was left to the Marshals and
marshalmen and the immediate supervision to two newly
appointed 'Inspectors of Police' or Superintendents (both terms
are used); the Superintendent of the Day Police was the senior
and this was reflected in his wages, 7s 6d a day; the wages of his
assistant, the Superintendent of the Night Police, was 5s 6d a
night.[37] In 1824, excluding the Watch and including the Marshals
and marshalmen, the number of police in the City was forty-
eight.

In 1828 this number was nearly doubled when the City's
thirty-two street-keepers were ordered into police uniform;
besides dealing with street nuisances they helped to overlap the
awkward changeover period when the City Patrol and the Nightly
Watch were not on duty. According to the time of year, this
could be as much as eight hours and was never less than four.

In this time, the Lord Mayor complained, warehouses were robbed 'after the watchmen have left their stations, by persons who either secrete themselves in the night within the houses, or enter early in the morning by means of false keys; a town cart is called by a well dressed person; he stands at the door with a book, pretending to enter the goods, while two or three persons are loading into the cart'.[38] Some wards began to hire patrols just for the changeover period, and by 1828 they were compulsory for every ward. The Nightly Watch Committee fixed the numbers in each ward at not more than one-fourth or less than one-eighth of the number of watchmen for that ward. In practice this meant that in fifteen wards the number of men patrolling was three or less. A total of sixty-three men was hired at 15s a week. Some wards began to use them to supervise the Watch, but this was stopped and left to the ward constables, nineteen out of every twenty of whom now served by deputy by paying substitutes £8 to £15 per annum.

The substitutes were mostly small shopkeepers, and the money supplemented in nearly all cases an existing income. Unlike the watchmen they did not have to exist on the meagre wage of, on average, thirteen shillings a week, and consequently were not so susceptible to bribes. In 1816, the Lord Mayor, Alderman Matthew Wood complained,

> The beats or rounds of many watchmen are so short that they take only five minutes to walk them; which, being twice within the hour, he is either fifty minutes in his box, or what is more frequent, they meet two or three together, and are in conversation a considerable time; frequently they are employed in shutting up shops, and going of errands for the inhabitants, going into public houses with prostitutes; and although the streets are crowded with disorderly women, they will not interfere, or take the least notice of their conduct; also from the practice of their being fixed in stations or boxes for many years, there is no doubt but some of them receive bribes from persons who commit robberies in the streets as well as in houses; for it is a well known fact, that notorious characters attend Fleet Street and other public streets every night, and are in constant conversation with prostitutes, and must be well known to the watchmen.

The watchmen's wages were so small that they freely admitted that they ignored offences rather than take them to court and miss a day's work.[39]

Wood called himself a Radical Reformer. He supported the Whigs and championed vote by ballot and unlimited free trade. He was born in 1768. At the age of fourteen he was apprenticed to his cousin, a chemist and druggist, and within a few years became a traveller for druggists. He established himself in the City as a wholesale druggist in Devonshire Square, and widened his field of operations by becoming a hop merchant in Southwark and by interesting himself in the working of copper mines in Cornwall. In 1804 he was elected to the Common Council of Cripplegate where his counting-house was; in 1807 he was elected Alderman, and in 1815 he became Lord Mayor. From 1817 to his death in 1843 he was one of the City's four members of Parliament. His championship of George IV's queen, Caroline of Brunswick, earned him great popular support though some accused him of cynically exploiting the situation. *The Times* wrote, 'Looking, however, at the disfavour with which the King and the Ministers were regarded in the city, as well as the partiality entertained towards the Queen, he must have perceived that the occasion was one which he might turn to good account in augmenting his own influence and in advancing the interests of the political party to which he had attached himself.'[40] Ministers, however, did not like his politics and would not dine with him as was customary in the Guildhall when he was re-elected Lord Mayor in 1816. His re-election to the mayoralty broke several hundred years of tradition.

For the next twenty-five years, in committee and behind the scenes, he fought to reform the City's police and watch. When Lord Mayor he visited every watch-house and examined 'every man as to his health and his age, and he had all those discharged that were unfit, notwithstanding any length of service; if they were to be remunerated, he said, the wards must do it, and he would have more efficient men'.[41] The watchmen, he thought, were too static, and he proposed instead that the City should hire 400 patrols and forty superintendents and give them wages of twenty-one and thirty shillings respectively each week. The patrols, he suggested, could go on duty at nine o'clock in the

evening, wear dark-brown or drab coats with the initials of the
ward and a number on the arm, and be armed with short staves;
they would have neither lanterns nor watchboxes, and would
patrol for two hours and then go to the watchhouse for one hour.
Beats would be changed every night and there would be one
superintendent to a small ward and two to a large one; they
would be issued with dark-blue cloth greatcoats and come on
half by night and half by day to assist the Day Police.

Wood tactfully outlined his plan to the ward authorities before
submitting it to the Court of Common Council who referred it to
a Committee. The plan was thought far too radical and was
butchered completely. The Committee rejected its own Sub-
committee's recommendations and made only one suggested
change to the Court of Common Council, that they should hire
sixteen superintending watchmen; even this they made certain of
rejection by putting the men under the Lord Mayor's control and
by recommending that their wages should be paid by the wards.

Yet another plan submitted by Wood suffered a similar fate
the following February. This time it was for a Horse Police of
one hundred men. The plan 'was calculated to strengthen the
civil power and to obviate the necessity of introducing the
Military in case of tumult', an obvious reference to the riots of
2 December 1816, two months before, when a mob of several
thousand had marched on the City from Spa Fields and seized
a store of firearms by breaking into a gunsmith's shop in Skinner
Street on Snow Hill and killing the owner. They had then
marched down Newgate Street and Cheapside firing the guns
into the air. Wood, with two friends, four policemen and the
City Marshal, had attacked the head of the column on the north
side of the Royal Exchange and seized four prisoners. 'Fire away,
you rascals,' he told two rioters who levelled their muskets at
him. One did so and missed. The prisoners were dragged into the
Royal Exchange, and with great difficulty the police officers
closed the gates on the mob who fired beneath them at their
feet and legs. Wood quickly swore in several thousand extra
constables and with the aid of the military the riot was crushed
the same day.[42]

He promptly urged that some watchhouses should be turned
into stations where the ward and special constables could assemble

in times of 'Riot, Tumult or public disturbance' and where the inhabitants could go for help by day or by night.[43] They were most of them in a 'most wretchedly degraded state'. When they were inspected in 1836 it was found 'that 14 of the watchhouses had cells, and 16 were without; many of their cells were nothing but cupboards; they had no urinals, no place of easement for the prisoners . . .'. One of the watchhouses, in the parish of St Bride's, the one in Blackhorse Court, was surrounded entirely by brothels; 'there is a complete avenue of brothels, and the watchhouse is in the centre of them'.[44] Cheap watchhouse became the Central Station and in their divisional order the others were Portsoken (Aldgate), Bishopsgate, Cripplegate, St Sepulchre's (built octagonal overlooking the churchyard and to keep out the bodysnatchers who frequented the Fortune of War opposite), Castle Baynard and London Bridge.

Wood's supporters were few and it was 1827 before they were strong enough to impose a Nightly Watch Committee on the wards in spite of strenuous resistance at first from the majority of the Court of Common Council. Even then most of his supporters thought his plans too radical, and the emphasis of the Committee's first recommendations,* using Wood's earlier plans

* The Watch was to come on:
From 10 November to 10 February from eight o'clock in the evening to seven o'clock in the morning.
From 10 February to 10 May from eight o'clock in the evening to six o'clock in the morning.
From 10 May to 10 August from nine o'clock in the evening to five o'clock in the morning.
From 10 August to 10 November from eight o'clock in the evening to six o'clock in the morning.
The early and late patrols for the changeover were:
From November to February one hour in the morning before the Watch left to eight o'clock, and in the evening from five o'clock until the Watch was set; between March and October this was changed from six o'clock in the evening until the Watch was set, and in the morning from the Watch leaving until eight o'clock. The Committee's final recommendation was that the Day Police should come on one hour earlier at eight o'clock to cover the remaining blank. This was done in 1828.
Other basic recommendations were that no watchman should be employed who was over forty years old, that wages should be two-and-one-half pence an hour (this became three pence), that beats should be changed every night, watch-boxes abolished, and that the watchmen should patrol for two hours and spend one hour in the watch-house.

as the model, was on a uniform system of watching. The proposed changes stung the wards into a fury, and at meetings of the Court of Common Council on 4 and 11 October they tabled amendment after amendment to stop them from being accepted. These attempts failed, and the formal petitions of protest from Dowgate and Aldersgate Wards were similarly rebuffed. To implement the changes the Committee had to include them in the next year's Watch Act for 1827–8. This was instantly challenged by the wards in a final effort to restore the *status quo*. They tabled a motion 'That the Watch Act for the year ensuing be framed upon the basis of the Watch Act for the present year'. For a moment it seemed as if the motion was carried until the Committee's supporters forced a division. The voting was fifty-six for the motion and seventy-three against. In fact they had a majority of seventeen.[45]

The Committee had noticed that in some of the wards the number of watchmen was 'as great as in the reign of Queen Anne, when the darkness of the Streets obliged them to be stationary'. On their recommendation these were reduced from 725 to 749 men; with the ward constables, numbering 478, and the Day and Night Police, the City had more than 1200 men to protect it, or about twenty per cent of the total police of the metropolis.

In spite of this reorganisation, the same disunity prevailed. In this the City was no different from the parochial authorities for the rest of the metropolis. Their organisation, too, made them part of the proverbial 'rope of sand'. Each parish had its own watchhouse, its own watchmen and its own organisation and methods for protecting property and enforcing the law. Frequently they were further subdivided into districts which, again, acting independently of each other, tended to isolate them still more. The only truly cohesive force at this time was the Bow Street Horse and Foot Patrol. Because of the frequent highway-robberies in certain parts of the metropolis this had been formed in 1805. In 1828 it consisted of a mounted branch of 2 inspectors, 4 deputy inspectors and 60 patrols, a dismounted patrol of 100 men and a street patrol of 127 men, of which only 27 men did day duty.[46] Altogether, excluding the parish watchmen and the Thames police, the Home Secretary had less than 400 men

with which to control a population of more than a million.
Successive committees in 1812, 1818, 1822 and again in 1828
had urged that something had to be done to reform the watch
and police, but all had foundered on the prevailing hostility
towards a central police force. The chairman of the 1822 committee had been Peel. He was convinced, he later wrote, 'that the
country has entirely outgrown its police institutions'. He confessed that he was afraid to meddle with the City but hoped that
it would be possible to take an area within a radius of ten miles
of St Paul's and treat it 'as one administrative district, with
stipendiary magistrates and police organised on a uniform basis'.[47]
But he had to move cautiously. His first move was to press for
an enquiry into the state of the police of the metropolis, thus
indirectly exposing the weaknesses of the existing system. He
gave notice that he intended to move for such an enquiry in
December 1826. But Canning's subsequent appointment as
Prime Minister and his own resignation meant that this had to
be postponed until February 1828, one month after he was
restored to office. Only six of the 1822 committee members,
including Matthew Wood, were co-opted on to his committee
which was heavily weighed in favour of reform. The committee's
main recommendation was that there should be a radical change
in the system of policing the metropolis and outlined a general
plan. The one omission was the City of London because of its
recent changes.

On 15 April 1829, Peel sought leave to bring in his 'bill for
the Improvement of the Police of the Metropolis'. The very
vagueness of his proposals lulled suspicions. At least one member,
when he had finished outlining them, thought that they only
referred to the night police and watch. The term 'watchmen' he
proposed to abandon and their substitutes consider as a species of
night patrol. All parochial police authorities were to be united
under one head, a Board of Police directed by three magistrates.
Under the Act a certain day would be appointed when the
parochial authorities and the watchmen would be abolished and
the new police would take charge.[48]

On 29 September 1829 the first Metropolitan policemen were
seen on the streets of London. Two weeks later, at the Guildhall,
'after Sir Peter Laurie had admonished and discharged a dis-

orderly woman, who had been accused of being noisy in the street, he asked her accuser, a watchman, named Livingstone, where his beat was? The watchman said it was from St Dunstan's Church to Temple Bar. Do you find any increase of bad characters on your beat? Watchman (smiling): Yes, I believes I do; the New Policeman drives 'em into the City. Sir Peter: Then you should drive them back again; it would be better than taking them up. Watchman: When there was a quarrel among them the other night, a policeman came up and drove them through the Bar, saying, "Ye shan't stand here; go into the City with your rows." Sir Peter Laurie said that he had heard that a police magistrate had directed the policemen to drive all bad characters into the City. If there was any truth in this, it was an imprudent – an improper observation. He desired the watchman present to drive all the bad characters out of the City. The thing must be put down. Subsequently some vagrants were brought up, and Sir Peter told them to drive them out of the City instead of apprehending them in future. "We can play at tennis-ball," said the Alderman, in an under tone.'[49]

The Last of the Charleys

The revision has commenced at the source of the evil – the
watchmen. . . . That they are corrupt, venal, and inefficient,
arising from their inadequate pay, their advanced years, a
reciprocal jealousy as to their parishes, and a want of uni-
formity, or central control, is too unfortunately elucidated
to require any comment; and that a change was necessary is
proved by the abandoned character of the majority – their
levying contributions on the wretched street-walkers – their
keeping brothels – and their seldom, if ever, bringing a thief
to justice.

The Times, 4 May 1829

CRITICS of Peel's bill 'for improving the Police in and near the
Metropolis' were hostile to the exclusion of the City. The Earl of
Malmesbury growled that thieves 'would assemble in London as
an asylum. When they threw a dog into the water, the fleas all
got into the head to avoid drowning, and in the same way all the
thieves would get into the City to avoid hanging.'[1]

In private Peel confessed that he was afraid to meddle with the
City. But ignoring the advice of his own committee of inquiry
that the City should be excluded as it had recently improved its
own police, he included it in the draft bill in the new police area.
This was a necessary move tactically, as there was strong opposition in both Houses of Parliament, from both Tories and Whigs,
to the formation of a paid professional police force. To pass the
Bill through both Houses and to secure the tacit consent of the
two parties to a measure which was to most members both
repugnant and incompatible with the Englishman's love of
liberty, Peel had to silence not only the critics in his own party
but the Whig opposition as well. He knew that the Whigs, as

political allies of the City of London, would support the City's
representatives in opposing any measure that tried to wrest from
the City's hands the control of its police. But by including the
City in his draft bill and placing it within the metropolitan
police area, he hoped that the Whigs would agree to his subsequent offer to exclude it, as in fact they did, in return for the
minimum of opposition to the rest of his bill for a metropolitan
police force.[2] He confessed, ten years later, that he 'did then
(under the pressure of circumstances which I could not control,
and to secure the introduction of a system which was denounced
as rash, experimental and dangerous) – I did consent that the
City of London should not be included within its operation'.[3]

In the House of Lords the Duke of Wellington stated that the
City would remodel its police on similar lines. The Nightly
Watch Committee referred this thorny subject to a sub-committee
of prominent radicals headed by Wood and Venables who, once
more, on 24 March 1830, recommended that the Nightly Watch
and Police should be merged into one force, this time of 480
constables (one out of every ten to be a conductor or sergeant),
twelve inspectors and three superintendents.[4] The committee
found that the constables' substitutes were themselves hiring
substitutes whose true identities were often unknown to the
marshalmen so long as they answered to the correct names on
the lists; they confirmed, too, that many watchmen were
hopelessly unfit for such work and often had been working hard
in the docks and other places by day. Wood wanted the 'whole
troop' paraded and inspected; they were ordered to muster in
the Guildhall yard but 'the wards resisted it, they would not
show them up in the Guildhall, to show what sort of a regiment
they were'.[5] In some instances men of sixty and seventy had been
hired 'because they were paupers, because they would become
burdens to the parish'; others were cast-off servants and porters
hired 'to oblige a powerful neighbour who has a servant that he
wants to provide for, by appointing him one of the watch'.[6] The
ward deputies and common councilmen had, besides, a pecuniary
interest in retaining this 'enormous patronage' in their own
hands; they began some wardmotes by electing and fining those
they knew would not take office but, instead of using the money
to hire substitutes as they were supposed to do, they then went

on, until found out, to elect by illegal means more than the traditional number of constables, choosing men who could not pay the fines but whom they could compel to take office; this enabled them to pay the fines into the watch rate to subsidise other expenses 'for keeping pumps in repair, advertisements in the newspapers of votes of thanks to aldermen' and expenses for eating and drinking which, though not heavy, were a constant source of annoyance to the ratepayers. If, at the end of the year, the watch rate showed a surplus, the practice was to give a percentage to the deputy who had so carefully husbanded it by paying, among others, the substitutes less in wages than he had received in fines.[7]

The sub-committee was anxious that this patronage should be vested instead in a Chief Officer with powers similar to, and with the independence of, the Metropolitan Police Commissioners.[8] His appointment was bitterly opposed by the wards, by the deputies and common councilmen, who insultingly objected that the appointment of a Chief Officer 'would occasion an unnecessary expense, and would give to that officer an undue and improper influence; and it is utterly impossible that such an officer can ascertain in a correct and proper manner the true character and requisite qualifications of the persons proposed to be appointed by him'. With great difficulty the sub-committee could only get their tentative agreement to the appointment of a Chief Officer during pleasure and subject to annual election; worse still, the wards insisted that he was to be no more than a 'method of communication' between the force and their own commission or committee of fifty-three consisting of the Lord Mayor, all the aldermen and the common councilman from each ward. For the sake of other possible reforms the sub-committee grudgingly conceded this point and recommended it in their report to the Nightly Watch Committee who not only rejected the report but formed the same day a new sub-committee who firmly vetoed any changes. *The Times* snapped, 'There still exists, however, notwithstanding the glaring deficiencies of the City system, the strongest prejudice in favour of the drivelling Dogberries who have in many instances aided and abetted in the plunder of the dwellings under their protection.'[9] As a sop to the reformers they made the Under Marshal the Chief Officer of police but ensured

that he would not usurp their authority, or indeed have any
over the watchmen, by insisting on the disbanding of the only
force through which he could now issue orders and maintain
supervision, the Court of Aldermen's Night Patrol.[10]

This insane measure effectively severed the one remaining link
between the police and watch. For the next eight years they
moved in separate orbits. As late as 1837 complaints were still
being made that robberies were mostly committed in the morning and evening periods when they were not on duty. The wards
were, in fact, left 'without any communication with each other,
without any co-operation or general system, or any efficient
controlling head, so that, to use a figure of speech, they may be
called a rope of sand'.[11] The boundaries were sharply defined.
One man complained that when he 'pointed out to a watchman
a man and woman on the opposite side of the street in a very
indelicate situation; he said, "Oh, that is not in my beat, there
is a watchman on that side"; I said, "Do you mean to say you
must not go over to prevent that?" he said, "Oh no, unless it is
a riot, or something of that kind".'[12]

The Day and Night Patrols were merged and they became a
Day Police only. In 1832 the number of men was doubled,*

* There was a thorough reorganisation. Besides the Marshals and marshalmen, the number of men before reorganisation was 50, consisting of 1
inspector, 6 police officers, 11 station men, 22 Day Patrol, 8 Smithfield men
and 2 men for the Guildhall and Mansion House Justice Rooms. In 1832 this
was slightly more than doubled to 82 constables, 10 sergeants (following
military practice they had two buttons on each sleeve – there were twenty-two
buttons on the coat!), 3 inspectors, 6 station men and 4 police officers, 2 at
each of the Justice Rooms, with 2 men to assist them. The Under Marshal,
William Wadham Cope, was nominally in command but most of his duties
developed on the Superintendent, John Cowtan, the former inspector of the
Day Patrol. A clerk and a surgeon were appointed too.[13]

Wood was actively concerned with the reorganisation and his committee
closely followed the advice of the metropolitan police commissioners on conduct
and pay. The men were given a monthly boot-allowance of 1s 6d and, following metropolitan police practice at this time, they were issued with white
trousers for summer wear. Pay was assimilated as closely as possible – 30s for
inspectors, 22s 6d for sergeants and 19s each week for constables. The veterans
of the Day Patrol, some of them with more than thirty years' service, had
their wages reduced from 28s a week; they immediately protested that 19s
was 'insufficient to place them above want'. A compromise was reached. Those
that were not promoted but with more than four years' service were allowed
an extra 3s 6d a week (45s 6d a quarter) and those with less 2s (26s a quarter).[14]

In September 1832 the wards standardised the watchmen's clothing. Each partly to relieve the plight of the ward constables who by this time had openly rebelled and bluntly stated that it was none of their business to catch thieves. In some wards this had become a political issue. The number of constables had been fixed by tradition at 244 and this was never varied in spite of the constant rebuilding and shifts in population. For instance, Bread Street Ward, which was a small ward, had thirteen constables, while Coleman Street had only six as there were in the days when the 'inhabitants of Coleman Street were confined within the walls, within Moorgate; but since Moorfields, which went without the walls of the City, has been built upon and inhabited, it has become a very large ward; but the ancient number of constables is still preserved'. In Bridge ward a great number of houses had been pulled down to make the approaches to the new London Bridge and consequently the number of inhabitants was very small; this meant that with monotonous regularity the same persons were compelled to take office over and over again. Extra constables were hired to help them on execution day, at the sessions and other public events, and swelled their numbers to 400; understandably, the Marshals preferred to use them as they were paid and therefore more manageable.[15]

The wards and the aldermen were in common agreement that the office of ward constable could be suspended if the police and watch could be merged to form a Day and Night Police. Apart from the natural difficulties of control, the financing of such a force was a stumbling-block of equal obduracy as it meant involving Parliament, which the wards were reluctant to do. The Day Police was financed from the City tolls and the Smithfield dues but 10. Geo. *c*. 22, the 1737 Watch Act, expressly confined watch-rate expenditure to a nightly watch; this could only be changed by Act of Parliament. In 1832 the Court of Common Council were manoeuvred into submitting such a bill. The

---

man was given a blue-cloth greatcoat with white buttons with the City coat of arms and marked on the collar with his number and the initial of his ward; the Night Superintendent had yellow buttons and a star on the collar. They were issued, too, with capes of canvas painted dark green and hats of glazed leather with their number and the name of the ward painted on, a black leather stock, small rattle and a short staff of wood with a leather thong attached. Some, but not all of them, were issued with lanterns.

Aldermen offered to merge the constables and the police with the watch and leave control in the hands of a committee on which they were represented but outvoted two to one. In return, however, they insisted that the wards must agree to their extending their authority and control as magistrates to the watch. But to get the bill into Parliament they had to concede even this. The Common Council objected to the words that the watchmen 'should obey all such lawful commands as they may from time to time receive from the Lord Mayor, or any of the Aldermen or Justices of the said City for conducting themselves in the execution of their office'. They argued that this would give the aldermen a control over the watchmen they had never before possessed. But without this clause there was no guarantee that the committee would have the watchmen sworn in, or the constables and policemen either. It was only because the latter two had been sworn in in the past that the aldermen had been able to compel them to obey them as magistrates. For this reason the wards had never let the watchmen be sworn in. If, then, the aldermen yielded to their demand, and the police and watch were not sworn in, their own authority would be limited exclusively to the committee on which they were outvoted two to one. But, if they did not concede this point, the Bill would not be submitted to Parliament. The aldermen agreed to strike out the offending words. It was on this understanding that the Bill was presented to Parliament.[16]

Without the consent or knowledge of the Court of Common Council, Matthew Wood (according to him it was at Lord Shaftesbury's insistence) then inserted a similar clause that the police should 'be subject to the jurisdiction of the magistrates and Justices in such and the like manner as other Constables are by law subject'. Had the aldermen had any assurance that the men would be sworn in, this would have been completely unnecessary. As counsel pointed out, 'It is of no use to mince the matter by a diversity of words, the fact of their being sworn constables places them under the direction and control of the aldermen as magistrates.' Wood made other changes too, making it impossible for the wards to revert to the old system, once the bill had passed, even if they wished. His changes put the aldermen firmly in control.

The Court of Common Council was unexpectedly convened just before the Bill had its third reading in Parliament. Thirty-six common councilmen complained to the Lord Mayor that they had 'reason to believe that without the knowledge of the Corporation of London and contrary to a distinct understanding, a Clause has been clandestinely introduced in the Day and Night Police Bill, placing the Night Police under the jurisdiction of the Aldermen which has heretofore been vested in the Common Council . . .'. Matthew Wood was bitterly attacked. One common councilman shouted that he was warned against trusting him with the Bill 'for so sure as he did he would manufacture it as he pleased'. Others rounded on the Court of Aldermen. 'Thus by this clause all self-governing power was at an end. It was transferred from the Court of Common Council to aliens, imbeciles, and men who had neither local habitation or a name in the city, and who would now be placed as protectors over the lives and property of the citizens.'[17] They ordered the Remembrancer to apply to 'some noble Lord' to expunge the words in the committee stage in the House of Lords; failing that, he was to take the necessary steps to stop the Bill from passing. The Court of Aldermen promptly counter-attacked and petitioned the House of Lords not to pass any Bill which did not contain the clause. On 3 August 1832 the Remembrancer reported that he had been unsuccessful in his mission, none of the peers he had spoken to would help him, and from their manner he saw no reasonable chance of success. The Bill was withdrawn.[18]

An amended version of Matthew Wood's bill, as *The Times* called it, was brought up for consideration the following year, 1833. Mr Legge of Bread Street ward 'admitted that it might be politic to have a day police, constituted of young men, such as were employed in the metropolitan police; but he utterly disapproved of the idea of placing on the night police men under 45 or 50 years of age, for his experience told him that at night young men were thinking of something else'. It was different with the man of 45 or 50 'whose passions had cooled'.[19] The Bill was thrown out by a large majority.[20]

The following year they again snubbed Wood's plan to merge the police and watch. He was the radical MP for the City and four weeks later, probably just for the nuisance value and as a

vent for nearly twenty years' frustrated effort, he brought in
'A Bill for more effectively enforcing the due execution of the
Office of Constable in the City of London and the Liberties'.[21]
The Court of Common Council was quick to point out that the
Bill was a very different bill from the preamble and would in
fact do away with the nightly watch and open the way for a
police force. They requested Wood to postpone the second reading
and took steps to isolate him. They handed in a resolution to the
Court of Aldermen advising them to withdraw their support.
In less euphemistic terms they ordered the Remembrancer to
abandon all proceedings in the Bill and likewise bills of a similar
tendency not originating with the Court of Common Council.
His final instructions were to oppose Wood if he persisted in
going on.

Similar efforts were frustrated in 1835, 1836 and 1837. But
each time support for the hard-liners fell and the majorities
dwindled. On the last occasion on 7 December 1837, they had
a majority of only four. Seven weeks later the radicals asked the
Lord Mayor to convene a special court. For the first time they
outvoted their opponents and they promptly voted down a
motion not to apply to Parliament. The bulk of Wood's supporters were necessarily common councilmen, and though they
were agreed that the police and watch should be merged, they
were not convinced or willing to have control vested in a Chief
Officer or Commissioner. Instead they vested control in the
Court of Common Council, in a committee of more than seventy
persons, with the aldermen represented but outvoted two to one.
It was 1832 in reverse. The Court of Common Council drafted a
bill in its own favour, approved it one week later, on 1 February
1838, and brought it into Parliament. The aldermen insisted that
it should be either changed or withdrawn. At this point the
unexpected happened. The Home Secretary, Lord John Russell,
wrote to Venables saying that he thought it only right to inform
him that the Government was of the opinion that the City Police
ought to be under the Metropolitan Police Commissioners and
that 'Her Majesty's Ministers therefore intend to propose a
measure for accomplishing this object'.[22]

The City closed its ranks. Russell spoke with deputations from
the Court of Aldermen and the Court of Common Council on

2 March 1838.[23] He agreed that a copy of the Bill should be sent
to him and used as the basis of a discussion between himself,
Wood, the Lord Mayor and the Remembrancer on 9 March, one
week later. At this meeting Russell insisted that the force should
be controlled by a Chief Officer and not by a committee. He
promised to support a bill to this effect but withdrew his offer a
few days later when he was told that the Select Committee,
which was sitting, would recommend a merger. Instead he committed himself to bringing this about and told the City delegates
that they could frame their own bill as they pleased. Wood urged
him not to oppose it. The backlash of City opposition to the
government bill might destroy both. Russell was apologetic but
hoped that Wood would support him in this. His tone convinced
the City that they would not now get their bill through, and so
they withdrew it. It was implemented without parliamentary
approval. Upon the basis of this bill they formed a force of 500
men.[24] All doubts as to whether the watch rate could be levied
and used for a police force were quietly suppressed.

In theory recruiting to the newly formed Day Police and
Nightly Watch as it was called was restricted to men under 35.
But as a short-term measure the regulation was waived, and out
of the force of 500 men more than 200 were over 45;* some of
them were former watchmen, nearly 400 of whom had to be
pensioned off with donations and weekly allowances; those with
less than five years' service got nothing (see Appendix 4). The
public was unsympathetic and a contemporary song 'The Charley's
Tear' suggested they

> Go, watch the lads in Fetter Lane,
> Where oft you've made them fear;
> The hand, you know, that takes a bribe,
> Can wipe away a tear.[25]

---

* On 30 January 1839 Superintendent Whitair reported to the Day Police
and Nightly Watch Committee that since 25 December 1838 he had discharged 41 men for drunkenness, 12 for insubordination and negligence, and
7 had resigned. The vacancies had been temporarily filled by old watchmen
until new men could be appointed. There were: 96 Day Police; 148 watchmen; 256 new men.

The pensions lists amply testify as to their age and physical weakness. They were sufferers from asthma, defective sight, 'very bad Health', one man was crippled by 'Chalky Gout' and then there were exceptional cases like seventy-three-year-old James Towell, 'Paralytic and very Infirm', who had been unable to work since 1834 but who for five years had drawn watchman's pay. The weekly allowances they were now given covered little more than the rent of a room in the City. Pensions of £8 a year had to be occasionally supplemented by the ward and a few charitable inhabitants. A few ex-soldiers had pensions of 5*d*, 9*d* and 1*s* a day from Chelsea Hospital. Others like James Jackson tried to sell watercress, though he was nearly blind. But most of them were too 'old and infirm to earn anything' and soon were in 'great distress'.[26]

On 5 February 1839, the Under Secretary of State applied for leave to bring in the government bill 'For further improving the Police in and near the Metropolis'. Clause 1 made the City of London part of the Metropolitan Police District. The wards had been steadily agitating against it for some time and on 21 March presented a petition to their young sovereign Victoria. Her stiff and noncommittal answer angered them so much that they entered in the Journals 'their extreme regret that Her Most Gracious Majesty should have been advised by Her Ministers to return An Answer to the Address of this Court, so deficient in the usual courtesy hitherto observed on like occasions, and without in any manner noticing the important topics contained in the Address'.[27]

Parliament, the Select Committee and certain sections within the City itself were in favour of the measure. But inexplicably Russell changed his mind yet again. Whether this was because of some private bargaining with the City or because, as he said, that if the merger 'were forced on the City the commissioners of police would not have that authority or be so well received in the City as was requisite in order to secure to the public the full benefits of the act', is not clear. He intimated to the Police and Nightly Watch committee that he would not object to seeing a small deputation.[28] Wood, Venables and three others met him for two conferences. He agreed that the City should keep its own police and bring in a private bill in opposition to his own. He promised to support it through Parliament; but he insisted yet again that a Commissioner had to be appointed.

The period had expired for bringing in private bills and the City had to petition for leave to bring in their 'Bill for regulating the police in the City of London'. Russell submitted a copy to the Metropolitan Police Commissioners on 18 April 1839 and Mayne, who was the lawyer, answered the following day.[29] His scribbled criticisms were scathing of the limited powers to be given to the Commissioner who was deprived of

> any independent authority. He cannot dismiss or even suspend a police constable but with the sanction of the Lord Mayor; with such restricted powers he could not enforce obedience to the orders nor even ensure respect or attention, as the nominal ostensible head of the police. The effect of making the Commissioner removeable by the Common Council will be that they will practically have complete control of the force. The restriction that the Commissioner is not to suspend or dismiss any policeman without the sanction of the Lord Mayor will, I think, paralyze his authority.

A private bill, such as the City's was, should have gone through unopposed. On this occasion there was bitter opposition from the chairman of the Select Committee, Benjamin Hawes, who forced a debate and threatened to divide the House, even if he stood alone, if the Bill was not drastically amended in committee. He objected most violently to control being with the Court of Common Council, the non-existent powers of the Commissioner and that he, unlike the Metropolitan Police Commissioners, should be able to sit in Parliament. This was a shrewd blow at the Member for Southwark, Daniel Whittle Harvey, who, so The Times informed its readers, was canvassing 'with considerable success, for the office of Chief Commissioner of the City Police'. On 7 May 1839, it thought that he would be appointed with a salary of '£1000–1200 a year, which coupled with the patronage, will be no bad berth'.

Harvey was the Member of Parliament for Southwark. Before the Reformed Parliament of 1832 he had been the member for Colchester. He was a friend of Matthew Wood. Like him, he too was thought by many to be no more than an 'eminent mountebank'. In his time he had been an attorney, a land speculator

and a newspaper proprietor. At various times he had owned
several newspapers, including the *Sunday Times* which he had
taken over after the first few issues as the only way of settling a
debt. Much of the hostility that had accrued to him was directly
traceable to his early career. To get a 'slap at Harvey' who, in
those years, 'was at all in the ring, without waiting for an
invitation to combat, was thought by the generality of folks, as
fair sport as hunting the fox or hare is'.

In 1807, when he was twenty-one, he had taken possession of
his maternal estate in Kelvedon in Essex and had set up practice
as an attorney. Also, in partnership with his father, a wine and
hop merchant, he had speculated in the buying and selling of
estates. Business had come in upon him in a flood-tide and his
double success had quickly antagonised other attorneys with whom
he was in competition in both fields. His bitterest opponent was
Thomas Andrew, a 'violent' and 'vengeful' man, who for some
years locally had 'reaped all the benefits from an extensive
unopposed practice'; he had 'been employed by his friends and
connexions from choice, and by those who were not so, from
necessity; any infringement, therefore, upon his hitherto un-
disputed province could but excite his liveliest apprehensions,
and in some small degree perhaps irritate his passions'. As
Harvey ruefully admitted later, 'No man was more calculated to
rouse these feelings than myself.'[30]

Andrew was considerably Harvey's senior and 'could ill brook
to see a stripling, just out of his articles, carry away all the business of the neighbourhood'. Elated by success Harvey made little
or no effort to soften his natural arrogance and the two men
seldom met without 'some display of warmth' on one side or the
other. They became professionally embroiled on opposite sides
in a local dispute between Harvey's carpenter and widowed step-
mother. The latter was represented by Andrew. In his dealings
with Harvey he lied about the value of some personal effects.
By chance Harvey found out. He was furious and would not
have any more personal dealings with him. He said nothing to
anyone else. But Andrew thought that he might try to ruin him
professionally, as he would have done if the situation had been
reversed, by reporting him to his Inn. To negative this imagined
threat he took the initiative and began to spread the story that

Harvey had stolen from his office a document highly damaging
to his (Harvey's) client, and later that he had defrauded a client
of some sale money. Harvey soon heard the rumours and contemptuously tried to shrug them off at first but eventually he
was forced to sue Andrew for slander. This case was the most
important of the three personally disastrous court-actions he
fought between 1808 and 1814. Andrew was only indirectly
involved in the other two but both were instigated by him. He
was so determined to ruin Harvey that he even offered to pay
the costs of the man Harvey was accused of defrauding, John
Wall Frost, if he would take him to court. Frost was the local
apothecary, and also the local eccentric. He pulled faces at the
gentry, he would pick up a sow by legs and smack 'its hinder
parts to make it go to brawn' and he would change his coat for
a red coat whenever he went to the privy. In later life he became
an alcoholic and called himself the Duke of Wellington.

Andrew bribed and perjured his way through to his three
successful verdicts. He was also unusually lucky. His own trial
for slander was held on St Patrick's day. Stationed nearby was
an Irish regiment. In honour of the saint the soldiers got drunk
and attacked the townspeople with clubs. They broke into the
courtroom where the trial was being held and successfully
panicked the jury, as well as Harvey's counsel who climbed onto
the table in his haste to get out. The coolest person in court, it
was reckoned, was the judge who was eighty-five years old. He
broke off the hearing, but when it was resumed fifteen minutes
later the hubbub was such that the shorthand writers threw
down their pens in despair as neither they nor the still-terrified
jury could hear the closing speeches and the judge's summing-up.
Harvey and Andrew by this time were little more than objects
of resentment to the terrified jury who felt that neither of them
had had 'any business to come with their disputes to keep them
to such a late hour'. In spite of the evidence and in their haste
to get home they gave the verdict to Andrew.

Andrew was understandably elated by the decision and printed
his own account of the trial. As the shorthand writers had missed
counsels' closing speeches and the judge's summing-up he rectified these omissions by writing them himself. He also rewrote
passages of evidence damaging to himself, and biased the whole

trial against Harvey. Gradually this printed version came to be accepted as an authentic transcript of the trial in spite of Harvey's repeated protests on its accuracy. It was some years before he found out about Andrew's involvement.

Fortunately the evidence negatived the verdict. Locally nobody doubted his innocence. Not even his political opponents in the Colchester elections in 1812. And they, they later admitted, were prepared to go to great lengths to get him for 'he had lashed all the [legal] profession very much, and made them his opponents personally, and there was no man who opposed him that would have hesitated to give him a strong turn; there was great personal feeling towards him'. His contempt, though, was for lawyers and not for the law. His opinion of most barristers was scathing. Some years later he compared them to cabmen: 'They hailed a cabman – they got into his vehicle, gave him a couple of shillings for the drive, and they cared not about his character. Well, so with a barrister. A party held up his hand, gave him a guinea or two, and secured his tongue – oftentimes giving him the larger fee, because the tongue was the fouler.'[31]

The implications of the trials were not immediately obvious until some years later. In 1819 he stopped practising as an attorney preparatory to being called to the Bar to enable him to take up the post of Recorder of Colchester which was being held for him by his friends in *locum tenens*. He was already the Member of Parliament for Colchester and, in between eating mutton and potatoes and beef and pudding in the Temple, he attacked the heads of his profession in the House of Commons, the Attorney General and the Solicitor General, for tolerating and profiting from abuses in the Court of Exchequer.[32] His splenetic tongue roused a great deal of bitterness and when he applied in 1821 to be called to the Bar the Benchers of the Inner Temple refused to call him, after he had waited two years, giving as their reasons for rejecting him Thomas Andrew's old slanders. One of the Benchers had written to Andrew, who had sent them his printed copy of the trial and other papers emanating from the same tainted source. Harvey denied the charges and appealed to the Benchers to hear his witnesses, including Frost, who could refute them. This they would not do. They insisted that Harvey should make his defence on documentary evidence only. This he

3. 'The Last Day or the fall of the Charleys'

4. 'The Last of the Charleys ! ! ! !'

5. St Sepulchre's watchhous Giltspur Street

6. William Anthony,
   one of the last of the
   London Charleys

could not do. Some of the papers had either been lost or mislaid and others, through personal hostility, were deliberately withheld from him. His appeal was rejected.

The blow wrecked the career he had mapped for himself. The Benchers' sentence, he later said, proved to be 'most afflictive in its nature and ruinous in its effect – a sentence, which went in its design, and so far as they could effect, to brand my name with ignominy to the last hours of my life'. For the next thirteen years he stubbornly pressed for an inquiry into his rejection and into the Inns of Court. Ceaselessly he attacked 'those narrow minded monopolists of an absolute remnant of monasticism' the 'cloistered nest of wigged benchers in the Temple'. In 1834 he achieved his aim. A parliamentary inquiry was ordered into his case. The Select Committee was chaired by Daniel O'Connell. Thomas Andrew was dead but the feud with his family was as bitter as ever, except with his brother who had confessed on his deathbed to his shameful part in ruining Harvey. Only a chance remark by one of the witnesses led to the committee exposing Andrew's widow who, even as the committee was sitting, was trying to destroy evidence and witnesses favourable to Harvey. The evidence cleared him completely. In spite of this the Benchers adhered to the original decision and refused to call him to the Bar.

He continued to practice as an attorney but his polemics were mostly confined to Parliament and to his newspapers. In 1823 he had taken over as the only way of settling a debt the ownership of a fledgling newspaper the *Sunday Times*. The seventeenth issue, published on 9 February 1823, was seized in the 'iron fangs' of his old enemy the Attorney General for publishing a libel on the King – that George IV was mad like his father. *The Times* and several other newspapers had already published the same libel but only Harvey was prosecuted. He was fined and sentenced to three months' imprisonment in the King's Bench Prison.[33]

From 1826 to 1835 he was the Member of Parliament for Colchester. In 1835 he changed his constituency and became the member for Southwark. His platform chairman was James Greenacre, who quickly became a *cause célèbre* by leaving his mistress's head in the Regent's Canal, the trunk in the Edgeware

Road and the legs in Coldharbour Lane. As a speaker Harvey was reckoned by some only second to Burke; but his political independence put him at the mercy of both parties and there was 'one law for party men and those who were highly connected, and another for those who had no such connexions'. In February 1839 determined efforts were made to oust him from his Southwark constituency. His temporary acceptance of the post of Registrar of Metropolitan Public Carriages was held to be an office of profit under the Crown and therefore a bar to his seat in Parliament. Fresh writs were issued for an election in his Southwark constituency. *The Times* commented,

> The Government have managed this with dexterity. They probably have no great desire to keep Mr. Harvey in the House, as he is sometime sadly inconvenient to them; indeed their appointment of him to the conductorship of the omnibuses was obviously made with a view to get him out of the way; for though he has little ability for doing business, he has a remarkable and comical knack at spoiling it; and he often contrives, on saying, droll, quaint things, to make them and their measures excessively ridiculous. But then, on the other hand, they dare not irritate by openly opposing him, for he would presently be teasing them again with his caustic, or, at all events absenting himself on some pinching division. The best way, therefore, was to get rid of the awkwardness of voting at all upon his title to sit, by throwing the responsibility on a committee. Then, whatever may happen, the Ministers are clear; they can lay all blame to crooked law and the musty precedents, and rub down Mr. Harvey with a little more 'friendly commiseration'.[34]

He was a popular figure with the Southwark electorate and he was quickly re-elected. He once more took his seat 'jammed in between the two great parties'. Shortly afterwards he began to canvas for the Office of Commissioner of the City of London Police. His motive for wanting it was unquestionably financial. His creditors were pressing him hard. Yet he should have been a rich man. For many years his annual income from his practice had not been less than £2500; his wife had brought him a dowry of £30,000 and there had also been the undisclosed earnings from his newspapers and from his speculations. However, most of his fortune had been squandered on buying his way into Parliament. At Colchester in 1812 his election expenses were an estimated £40,000; a rich relative paid the £26,000 it cost him to win the seat in 1818. Equally ruinous to him had been the collapse of the Rochford and Billericay Bank in 1814, owned by his father and his uncle John. He had raised nearly £30,000 on his own credit. When he had paid every creditor only £800 was left. Only the previous month £4500 damages had been awarded against him for his involvement with a bankrupt firm. His expensive mode of living was a further drain on his resources.

He made it clear that he would not give up politics if he could not combine the office of Commissioner with his duties as a Member of Parliament. His chief supporter was Matthew Wood. The most influential members of the Corporation publicly pledged him their support at a meeting at the Guildhall Coffee House on 14 June 1839. His only rivals were military men with the exception of the Commissioner of Police in Liverpool, Maurice Dowling, who was a former metropolitan police superintendent. As soon as his candidature was known both the Tories and the Whigs combined to insert in the recently drafted City of London Police Act a disqualifying clause barring the Commissioner from having a seat in Parliament. Other amendments were equally controversial. In spite of the City's furious protests thirty to forty clauses were transposed from the Metropolitan Police Bill to give it greater uniformity. An amendment that the Lord Mayor, Aldermen and Commons assembled should have the power of suspending the Commissioner, instead of confining it to the Lord Mayor and Aldermen only, was rejected. The Government explained that this had been discussed in committee and it had been agreed that a popular body such as the Court of Common Council should have some say in the appointment of the Commissioner, but with regard to his dismissal it was thought unfair to the Commissioner that the retention of his office should be dependent on the will of such a popular body as the Court of Common Council. His rules and orders did not have to have their approval either, only the approval of the Lord Mayor, the Aldermen, or any three, and the approval of one of Her Majesty's principal Secretaries of State.

A furious debate raged over the disqualifying clause. Everyone

either knew or had heard that it was aimed at Harvey. Disraeli*
was one of those who argued that acceptance should not dis-
qualify him from a seat in Parliament. Finally it was Peel who
smashed their arguments. He explained that the Metropolitan
Police Commissioners were similarly debarred, and that if the
City Police Commissioner were to be otherwise privileged then
he must become their spokesman on police matters and they must
become eventually his subordinates. The most telling part of
his argument was a word portrait of Harvey, though he did not
mention him by name, combining the roles of policeman and
politician:

> Suppose the Commissioner who held a seat in Parliament should be
> a clever debator, who took every opportunity of attacking the
> Secretary of State. Suppose that whenever he spoke upon the police,
> he turned into ridicule the views of the Secretary of State with
> respect to that body and called them narrow and confined. Supposing
> that the Secretary of State was unable to engage with that gentleman
> in debate, and found himself unsuccessful, what would be the
> consequence? Would the Commissioner feel his authority lowered?
> The Secretary of State would say, this man is constantly attacking
> me, but I cannot remove him, as people would say it was on account
> of his popularity; and thus in what relation would he stand to the
> others? Persons will always place most reliance upon such a person
> in consequence of his not being a political partisan. . . .[35]

The Bill was passed with the disqualifying clause.[36]

Harvey half-expected this blow. But the blow he did not expect
was dealt by a punitive Court of Common Council, angry at his
appointment and their own loss of power which was now limited
to equipment, clothing and finance. They slashed his salary by
one-fifth, from the expected £1000 to £800 below which they

---

* For a short time Disraeli belonged to the Westminster Reform Club which
met at 24 Great George Street, Matthew Wood's home, and of which Harvey
was a member. A. G. Temple, *Guildhall Memories*, p. 26, recalls: 'I once
heard my father say that it was Daniel Whittle Harvey, the Commissioner
of the City Police, and for some time Member of Parliament, who, on the night
of Disraeli's maiden speech in the House of Commons (7 December 1837),
followed him out and overtook him, downcast and depressed, in the lobby, and
placing his hand on his shoulder said "Never mind, don't be disheartened, you
are destined to be a great man".'

could not go by law. Harvey would have withdrawn his candidature but his friends told him that he had committed himself too far and that he could not with honour withdraw. On 11 November 1839 he was sworn in as Commissioner of the City of London police.

The City Marshal, Neville Browne, and the Under Marshal continued to hold office, but the duties of both were confined to the purely ceremonial and to attendance upon the Lord Mayor. In 1852 Frederick Browne succeeded his father as City Marshal, and the Under Marshal's office was abolished. The marshalmen's offices were similarly allowed to lapse as they fell vacant. The last marshalman died in 1851 aged eighty-one.

11. *The City Marshal*

II. The Commissioner

THE GREAT CITY POLICE

12. *Gog and Magog as City Policemen*

7

The Early Victorian City of London

Hats off – down there! you in the white hat and crape – you in butcher's mourning – bonnet him – silence! Yes, says the Brahmin, the ceremony is about to begin; the national games are about to commence. He then inquired how many were that morning to be rewarded? He is answered
'Vy, my cock, there's strings for six.'
The Groans of the Gallows[1]

IN the eighteen thirties and forties travellers were told that the best way to approach the City was from Southwark. From London Bridge they could get their first glimpse of the City skyline with the giant dome of St Paul's riding high above the houses and spires, some of which, like St Bride's, looking like an extended telescope, or the flying buttresses of St Dunstan's in the East, were instantly as recognisable as the dragon on Bow steeple. By peering between the gas standards on the parapet they could see into the Pool below where a forest of masts rode at anchor on the eddies, currents and waves that would soon carry them out of the Pool once more, back past the colliers at Cuckolds Point, and out to sea. Nearly 3000 men worked on the 300 sailing ships moored in the docks each day, loading and unloading cargoes. The tobacco warehouses covered nearly five acres of ground; in the north-east corner, damaged tobacco was burned in a kiln and the smoke carried off in a tall chimney facetiously known as 'The Queen's Pipe'.[2] The bridge was a favourite loitering-ground for pickpockets, and travellers gazing over the granite parapet had to be warned to keep a tight hold on their handkerchiefs and pocket books. Similarly they had to be warned not to drink from

the Thames which was daily poisoned with gas washings and the
tribute of a 'thousand foul sewers' though flounders, eels and
whitebait, the former small but sweet, managed to survive and
could still be caught with fishing-tackle from nearby Crooked
Lane.[3] Once fish could be caught in the rapids beneath the
bridge but these had disappeared when the old bridge was
demolished and the new one opened in 1831. The current was
faster now; the smaller number of arches meant that the bridge
no longer acted as a dam and, for the first time, high tides had
begun to breach the upper reaches of the river between Lambeth
and Vauxhall.[4] However, London oysters and London porter
could still be enjoyed at the Cock Tavern in Fleet Street, and the
famous chops and stout, though in summer connoisseurs preferred the stout of the Rainbow opposite on account of the cool-
ness of the cellar. Merchants trading to the East Indies used the
Jerusalem Coffee House and the stockjobbers Jonathan's in
Change Alley. 'Jose' in Finch Lane was highly rated for its
chops, steaks and mealy potatoes, and for eighteen pence capital
dinners could be had every day between one and four at the
One Tun Tavern in Billingsgate, which served not only three
kinds of fish but joints, steaks and bread and cheese.

The coal-whippers' beer, however, was often as 'grey as a
badger', sometimes white, and frequently had to be drunk
through a handkerchief to 'keep the dregs and the offscourings'
from the mouth.[5] One pot had to be drunk with a preliminary
glass of gin or rum, and nine more carried on board the colliers
the publicans had hired them to work; sometimes the publicans
made them stand 'like a regiment of soldiers to drink it, with
pots in their hands'; others credited them with more beer in
proportion to the number of tons they unloaded. No 'milk' scores
were tolerated if the man wanted to work. And when these had
been paid from the day's wages each man, if he wanted to work
again, had to chalk up a fresh score before he went home. Some
publicans compelled them to buy as well exorbitantly priced meat
and bread – one man took 17s 6d out of every 25s earned, for
'meat and the Devil' he said. The men complained bitterly that
to get work they had to be drunkards and have their children
'reared up in public-houses from the time they have been able
to crawl, and taught to drink and break the laws in every way;

they have been brought up as thieves, and the females brought up as prostitutes, through the same cause . . .'.[6]

To disperse them and others like them, and to stop the late-night gambling, the City imposed in 1826 a uniform closing-time of eleven o'clock on all the taverns except for market taverns like the Green Man and Bell and the Newcastle in Billingsgate, and the Bull and Butcher, the Bull's Head, the Golden Lion and the Barley Mow in Smithfield. Monday was the market day for fat cattle and sheep. But by nine o'clock on Sunday evening Holborn and the surrounding streets were choked with vast droves of sheep waiting to come in. Exclusive of the pig market near Long Lane but taking in the streets and pavements as well, the space between the houses and St Bartholomew's hospital and church was three and three-quarter acres. Into this space was crammed on average 3000 cattle and 30,000 sheep. At eleven o'clock large droves of cattle from Essex and Norfolk came bellowing in by torchlight; 'from eleven till four o'clock in the morning there is one uninterrupted scene of noise and confusion, which is greatly aggravated by the exclamations of the drovers endeavouring to keep the cattle in order; coming from the narrow streets, of course they scatter, and the cries of the cattle, and the screams of the drovers are so great, that it is a well-known fact, that any individual coming from the country is unable to sleep for several nights . . .'[7] The cattle were formed into off-droves of sixteen to twenty beasts at a time, perhaps only after an hour's violence; to make them 'hide their noses, and form themselves into a ring', heads in tails out, so the butchers could feel their rumps, they were consistently beaten over the head, sometimes blinded by the blows, and goaded from behind. By the time they were beaten out of the market by the butcher's drovers, they were maddened enough to run 'at any thing, or over anything, or through any thing . . .'. The slaughtering was done in shops. Meat from the 'very old cows, skin and bones and worn-out bulls' was sold as cag-mag at twopence a pound. As late as 1849 there were 138 slaughter-houses in the City.[8] Aldgate was generally awash with blood with snarling dogs fighting for scraps on pavements clotted with blood and filth. Fifty-eight slaughter-houses were in vaults and cellars. 'A great part of Leadenhall is excavated, and the slaughter-houses are underneath. You descend a flight of steps, several feet, twenty feet, perhaps, and you go into a dismal dungeon which is almost dark; there is a little light only from the place that you enter, and around the floor of this place, covered with blood and filth and garbage, are the poor sheep lying in different places till they are killed.'[9] According to a surgeon who lived at the corner of the market, the butchers there were emaciated in appearance 'more from the effects of drinking gin than the effluvia of the market' which, at least, unlike many parts of the City, had sewers to carry off the blood and offal. He objected to the stench that came from the Spread Eagle and other places in Gracechurch Street when they pumped their cesspools into the street, Mondays and Thursdays, and left them to run down to the river; when this was done he thought it fortunate that most of the inhabitants were in bed.[10]

Between 1756 and 1832 less than ten miles of sewers were built in the City. In the next ten years this was doubled.[11] The work was partly hampered by the need to trace the network of private sewers that had existed before. Some like the Walbrook, more than 400 years old, were known but most had simply been forgotten. In 1836 an anonymous letter-writer walked up one of these forgotten sewers to keep an appointment in the bullion room with the startled Directors of the Bank of England. In one graveyard somebody, probably the sexton, had used a sewer as a vault and in another the beadle of the parish had been buried in the sewer; in Cripplegate churchyard the sewer had been broken open, sealed off with two flat tombstones and six or seven coffins inserted.[12] The new sewers had to be worked up from the river and it was a slow process. In 1849, the City's first Medical Officer of Health, Dr John Simon, complained that there was still some thousands of houses connected to cesspools with the inhabitants thriving in an 'atmosphere of their own decomposing excrements.'[13]

According to the medical evidence the 'line of habitations badly cleansed . . . almost formed the line of cholera cases'. In the space of a few hours 'the sufferer might be lying pulseless and blue, his body shaken by repeated vomiting and purging, his limbs twisted with cramp; and in the existing state of medical knowledge, one half of those who passed into the blue or collapse stage of the disease were doomed'.[14] Simon compared Blackfriars and Dulwich which were then nearly equal in population; in the latter there was not a single death from cholera, in the former deaths were at the rate of twenty-five in every thousand. In one cholera outbreak in the neighbourhood of St Mary Axe 'there were eight houses out of nine where five men lay dead one day, and one died about 12 hours afterwards, and two others' as the witness believed.[15] Defective house-drainage, bad water-supply and intramural burials were blamed.

Efforts had been made to reduce the number of churches. Thirteen only had survived the conflagration of 1666 and of the eighty-four burned down, only fifty-three had been rebuilt. St Michael, Crooked Lane, was pulled down in 1831 to make the approaches to new London Bridge. And when the Royal Exchange was burned down in 1838 further efforts were made to demolish thirteen 'superfluous churches'; these were dropped after St Bartholomew-by-the-Exchange and St Bennet had been destroyed. The graveyards were choked. St Andrew's, Holborn, had become 'an artificial construction, a catacomb above the earth'. Frequently they had to be emptied by breaking up the bodies, burning the wood and selling the lead. A pauper graveyard in Smithfield, ten feet wide by forty-five or fifty long, 'impacted or stuffed, crammed with dead bodies', was emptied and filled three times to the knowledge of one ward official.[16] Typhoid was rampant as the adjoining houses emptied their cesspools and chamber pots into the ground.

Black spots like these would have been swept away by redevelopment if the Corporation had agreed to turn Smithfield into a Grand Railway Terminus. The railway companies wanted to link the City to the six main stations surrounding it – King's Cross, Euston, Paddington, Shoreditch, London Bridge and Waterloo – by building a giant terminus on a site stretching from Battle bridge, Clerkenwell in the north to Ludgate Hill and Fleet Street in the south, from Shoe Lane in the west to Old Bailey in the east.[17] The Corporation was violently opposed to bringing the railway within the City walls. According to one witness they thought it dreadful that people should be brought to business. But fewer people now thought of lodging or living in the City. The great City merchants lived in the west end, or a

little way out of town, and left their counting-houses and warehouses to the keeping of their porters and clerks, most of whom
had suburban cottages. The majority of horse-drawn omnibuses
ran from nine o'clock in the morning until twelve midnight,
and every five minutes in the busy periods; most had two prices,
threepence for part of a distance and sixpence for the whole. On
Sundays the City was deserted and people flocked to places like
Greenwich, Hampton Court and Hampstead; others went by
railway and steamboat to Windsor and Gravesend. In spite of
the City's opposition, the London and Blackwall Railway opened
a station in the Minories in 1840. But because of the risk of
'burning coke flying about among the roofs',[18] no locomotive
engines were used; instead the coaches were clipped to wire
cables, an inch and a quarter in diameter, extending the whole
length of the line, $8\frac{3}{4}$ miles, and coiled at each end on drums
worked by two engines, one of 400 horse power at the Minories
and one of 200 horse power at Blackwall.[19] The signal to start was
given by electro-galvanic telegraph. The carriages then travelled
alternately along either line guided by wires running through
grooved pulleys. The number of passengers was increased by
half when the line was extended to Fenchurch Street.

The immediate effect of the railways was to force the long-
distance coaches into extinction. The famous red and black coaches
of the Swan with Two Necks, the coaching inn for the north, in
Lad Lane, became parcel omnibuses. Edward Sherman of the
Bull and Mouth in St Martin's Le Grand, tried to run them off
the road with his Red Rover and Manchester Telegraph and
failed though his relays of horses consistently maintained high
speeds of 9–10 miles per hour.[20] By 1867 the mail trains were
averaging 24 miles per hour and reaching on certain lines speeds
of 50 miles per hour. Fortunately competition from the steam
coaches, or Tea-kettles as they were called, was stifled by the
punitive tolls of the Turnpike Trusts.

In spite of the fact that the City boundary was no longer
sharply definable by a wall or ditch and had no gates except for
Temple Bar, the boundary was marked nonetheless by toll
collectors who exacted twopence from carts not belonging to
freemen and not bearing the City arms. The toll was payable
whenever the boundary was crossed and could not be evaded by

running halfway round the City to get in at another entrance.
From early morning there was a steady stream of advertising
vans, waggons, carts and laundress's vans into the City. On
average 2000 carts were stopped every day, each 'stoppage in
itself a nuisance; the cause of continual quarrels and frequent
fights between the man in the cart, and the man who stops the
cart by catching hold of the horse to exact his 2d'.[21] Traffic was
further obstructed by hazards such as Temple Bar and the statue
of William IV on the north side of London Bridge, 15 feet
3 inches tall, formed of two blocks of granite weighing 20 tons.
On Mondays and Fridays the streets were almost impassable for
cattle and sheep. In summer the horses' hooves stirred up

13. *The Site of the Fleet Prison*

blinding clouds of dust and in wet weather churned the droppings into mud and slush ankle deep. Tempers were easily frayed and fights were frequent on the coach stands. 'The Coaches and Cabs, are placed abreast, or side by side, four in number behind which, are usually several others, waiting in irregular order, to take the place of one of the first if vacant. When one is hired, a rush is instantly made, and that coachman succeeds into getting into the rank, who lashes his Horses most severely thrusting out his opponent. The Men drive furiously against each others horses, force the Coach poles against them and frequently tear their Shoulders with the Tire of the Wheels or points of the Shafts. The noise and bad language, produced by their frequent quarrelling, add much to this incessant nuisance, which is much aggravated on Sundays by their being less occupied.'[22]

The railways and the Penny Post were changing the face of the country. One hundred and thirty-one houses were pulled down in the old sanctuary of St Martin's le Grand for the headquarters of the Post Office.[23] The new building was erected with a Portland stone façade stretching over 400 feet down King Edward Street, the Stinking Lane of Elizabethan times. The City was becoming more businesslike and sought to conceal its past with euphemisms. Bagnio Court became Bath Street, Hog Lane was called Worship Street and Grub Street was renamed Milton Street. Other more familiar landmarks had gone. The Fleet prison was demolished in 1844. The site was used as the City stoneyard until part of it was built over by the Congregational Hall and the other part was sold to the London, Chatham and Dover Railway Company to extend the line from Blackfriars to Holborn Viaduct. But for some years remains of the old prison lingered on in the long, blank street wall that was left standing and of the iron box that used to be protruded through the grating in the wall with the importuning cry of the prisoners, 'Remember the poor debtors'.

The 'quarry of stone', Newgate, still stood. And in Whitecross Street prison newcomers continued to pay 'garnish'. If they could not pay or failed to deposit some article of about that value with the Steward, then it was customary to 'Cat' some of their property. 'That is for several persons, generally those of another Ward to disguise themselves with their bed rugs and their faces blacked and to go in a body mewing like Cats, and take away some part of his property, as his Hat, Coat, or otherwise'.[24] Unsuspecting solicitor's-clerks who sometimes had to serve them with summonses were greeted with shouts of 'A rat, a rat' as soon as their presence was known. They were likely to be hustled into a room and beaten by as many as twenty persons. Their hands were held behind their back and their eyes were blindfolded to stop them identifying their assailants. One unfortunate clerk was daubed with soot and grease and stood in a ring of prisoners who danced round about him frantically singing 'Sing, sing, my darkies sing'; he was bonnetted by everyone in turn and at the climax a bucket of whitewash was tipped over his head. Few of them had much to steal – an imperfect pack of cards, a cribbage board and dominoes of firewood, a paper draught-board, a piece of steel for a poker, some small quantities of cheese and tobacco (probably smuggled in by the women) matches and a cord to hang stockings in front of the fire to dry, these were the pathetic items confiscated in a search of the Giltspur Street compter. The régime was more strict in Bridewell. Hard-labour convicts worked the treadmill grinding corn for Bridewell, Bethlem and the House of Occupations. Those who were too old or too weak to stand the strain worked with the refractory apprentices, boys under fourteen, committed by the Chamberlain, picking junk and cleaning the wards; the women were employed as well in washing and mending linen and bedding.[25]

On average a fifth of the occupants were vagrants, often picked up from the streets or the alcoves on London Bridge where they sheltered for warmth. Large sums were raised by the wards for charitable purposes. The inquest men would walk 'round the City in silk gowns with furred edges, going into the shopkeepers' shops and merchants' counting houses'; the deputation would present themselves 'headed by the beadle in his gown and with his mace; he thumps at the door, and says, "I have come for a contribution to the inquest." To get rid of them some parties give more and some less.'[26] As winter approached, the vagrants made their way to London, and it was a pitiable sight to see the swarms of young children huddled in streets and alleys. The alleys in Cornhill and Threadneedle Street were notorious for their beggars. One complainant wrote,

I yesterday witnessed in Cornhill the disgusting exhibition of two livid infants, apparently corpses, lying on the knees of a woman, who cast most pathetic and sentimental glances on their visages, and had succeeded in attracting a crowd about her, – this was within ten yards of the Mansion House; and no sooner had I left them than I fell in with another, one of the feminine gender, with a bantling in her arms, not dead, certainly, for at the moment I passed, the mother, if such she were, gave the babe a pinch, and the babe gave a squeal or yell, as who should say, date obolum, which was instanter translated into literal English by the beggar.[27]

Certain parts of the City were notorious for their bawdy houses. In Reynolds Court, Moor Lane, numbers 1, 2, 5, 6, 9, 10, 11 and 18 were bawdy houses as were numbers 1, 2, 3 and 7 Bookers Gardens, Katherine Cree. Others were scattered through-out the City. Everyone knew what they were though there was 'no particular sign upon them, yet, from the door being kept upon the jar, the particular manner in which they are fitted up, the manner in which they are painted, the blinds and curtains, it is very well known what sort of houses they are'.[28] If they were not forced into prostitution then the women and girls might scrape an existence in Rag Fair, the Old Clothes Market, in Cutler Street and Houndsditch. Its more famous predecessor was nearly extinct. The life of Bartholomew Fair was now limited to three days a year. In between the cattle posts and the sheep pens the public could still be tempted with penny shows with 'Ball's Theatre; Ballards Beasts (including a Seal in a tub); Key's Conjuror; Frasier Conjuror; Pike; the Learned Pony; the Pig-faced Lady; the Shaved Bear, the Living Skeleton, the Red Barn Tragedy, the Court of Pekin, the Fat Boy and Girl, the Fire Eater, the Scotch Giant, the Elephant of Siam, the Learned Cats' and the Wonderful Dog who would 'play any gentleman at Dominoes that will play with him!'[29] Some of the carnival element spilled on to the vagrants and there were bitter com-plaints from businessmen of 'Bands of squalling singers, trombone players, organ grinders, bell-ringing and tolling' and more vehe-mently of a female band playing the french horn, trombone and bassoon who not only invaded the privacy of coffee houses and hotels but gave battle if opposed, with their leader, a perfect virago, wielding a brass bowl which she would shy at offending heads.[30]

There were complaints, too, that the Old Bailey had been reduced 'to the character of a theatre, by their setting apart the best places in the court in the shape of a gallery, and to their sanctioning the charge of money for admission, which leads to exhibitions of a most unseemly character. It is notorious that on occasions of the trial of great criminals as much as a guinea apiece is charged for admission into that gallery, and in common sessional cases they are very glad to take one shilling; for the price of admission is on a sliding scale; the greater the criminal the greater the tax upon the prurient curiosity of the public.'[31] Upon the same principle, when there was to be an execution, the rooms in the Magpie and Stump opposite fetched more money if the condemned man had done some very desperate deed. The crowds would begin to assemble at three o'clock in the morning to see the scaffold, Black Meggie, wheeled in front of the debtors' door. There would be the usual muster of thieves and blackguards who would amuse themselves by throwing baskets about and 'bonnetting each other'.

On 16 December 1839 William Lees was hanged for cutting the throat of his wife whose temper, when she was alive and drunk, had been so 'furious and ungovernable that he [had] generally endeavoured to escape from her presence' and from 'striking her as long as he could'. The new Commissioner of the City of London Police, Daniel Whittle Harvey, carried on the tradition of the City Marshal and headed the procession on to the scaffold; he was followed by the sheriffs, the under sheriffs, the Keeper of Newgate and the ordinary who read the Burial Service for the Dead to the condemned man pinioned and walking by his side.

And when the miserable convict appeared on the scaffold some hissing was heard, and just as he was turned off a fellow in the crowd, pulling a bundle of papers from his pocket, immediately commenced bawling out, 'The last dying speech and confession of William Lees, who was this morning executed at Newgate for the murder of his wife, all for the small charge of one penny'. Some of the ruffians present enjoyed a hearty laugh at the oddity of such an announcement under the foot of the gallows, and before the life of the wretched man was extinct. Some few, however, had the good feeling to cry 'shame'.[32]

The Guinea-a-week Men

Mr Croker to Mr Peel
  '*Your 3s. a day man is to be on duty, that is, in requisition
  for duty, the whole twenty-four hours; his duty is in the night,
  and without shelter in bad weather, or society in fine; he must
  reside where he is ordered; he can have no recreation; in short,
  as they say of a broom that it is dirty to keep other things
  clean, your constable must live in a state of perpetual trouble,
  labour, and disquiet that other folks may enjoy their rest. Can
  this be expected from competent persons at 3s. a day?*'

Mr Peel to Mr Croker
  '*No doubt three shillings a day will not give me all the
  virtues under heaven, but I do not want them. Angels would
  be far above my work.*'[1]

                                    The Croker Papers

'MEN, dwarfs in height, and old in years, of divers bodily
deformity, mentally weak, and with little or no character, had
no hesitation to apply' to Harvey's call for more recruits in
1861.[2] Between 1840 and 1861 the force strength had been
increased from 500 to 627 men. But behind those figures lay the
appalling waste of twenty years. In the same period Harvey had
recruited 3136 men, and out of 1815 men recruited in the first
ten years he had a mere 136 left.[3]

The fault lay initially with Peel in 1829 when he fixed the
wages of his metropolitan policemen at the extremely low rate
of three shillings a day. He wrote to Croker that out of his wage
of a guinea a week one of his constables should be able to find his
'(1) lodgings, (2) medical attention, (3) very comfortable subsistence at his mess, (4) clothing' and save ten shillings a week,

if he was a single man. This was mere supposition. If he had extended his analysis to the married men it would have borne even less relation to the facts. According to the author of *Hints for Practical Economy* a family of four could just eke out an existence on a guinea a week; below that they were living on charity. He wrote, 'It would appear a very ungracious task to attempt to exhibit a lower scale; for, though every reader must be conscious that thousands or millions are compelled to live on a very much reduced rate, yet he will be utterly at a loss to know how it is accomplished.'[4] The effect on the Metropolitan Police force was disastrous, and pay was largely responsible for the high wastage rate in the early years. Within four years only a sixth of the original force of 3000 men was left.

The implications for the City police were far more serious. The wages of the former Day Police had already been slashed by nearly a third to make them standard with the Metropolitan Police (see p. 118). Harvey's first act was to have the Court of Common Council empower him to make an increase in wages by making a distinction in wages between those who did their duty and those who did not. He broke the constables' wages into five classes of pay, excluding probationers, with minimum and maximum earnings of 17s 6d and 22s 6d a week (see Appendix 5). Whether a man moved up or down the scale depended entirely on his conduct and behaviour. The men's wages consequently were in a constant state of flux.

The extra money went on rent. The policemen were bound by their conditions of service to live within the City. The amount of housing available, however, was steadily being eroded by the building of offices, street widening and the railways. They were forced to compete with porters and others, similarly tied by their trades, for rooms in small, densely overpopulated courts. The inquest of Farringdon Ward Within was shocked by what it found in that part of the ward

bounded on the north by Ludgate Street, on the south by Earl Street Blackfriars, on the East by St. Andrews Hill, and on the west by Water Lane and includes Holiday Yard, Ireland Yard, Glasshouse Yard and a great many yards and courts adjoining. And all these yards and courts consist of buildings or houses which with fewer

exceptions are in a state of decay in a greater or lesser degree. It can
scarcely be said that they possess any other accommodation than a
roof – none that Christian feeling would assign for a fellow creature:
yet these wretched places are let in tenements consisting of a single
apartment each, for sums varying from two shillings and sixpence
to four shillings weekly, a most enormous rent in proportion to the
value of the property especially when it is considered that the tenants
are the poorest of the poor. And the occupiers, who are mostly
persons whose subsistence mainly depends on casual employment in
the City are compelled to pay this amount of rent; for when, through
any misfortune, any of them suffers their rent to go behind for a
few weeks, what little household furniture they may possess is liable
to be instantly wrested from them by a summary legal process, and
too often they are treated by their landlords with a ruthless severity
that people in better circumstances cannot conceive.

Many of these houses are densely crowded some of the rooms
containing six seven or eight persons, old and young, and even this
manner of living is rendered doubly unhealthy by the buildings
being destitute of drainage and sewers and by the consequent
accumulation of filth in the vicinity, which however cleanly disposed
any one family may be, cannot easily be removed; and also by a very
scanty supply of water, as that very necessary article is only to be
obtained for two hours on three days in the week and then it has to
be fetched a considerable distance from some of the houses under
circumstances of difficulty and annoyance.[5]

In 1861 the men, including the sergeants and inspectors, were
paying on average for one room 3s 7d, two rooms 4s 8½d, three
rooms 6s 5d and four rooms 7s 9d. The majority of constables
could not afford to occupy more than two rooms, and more than
eighty constables were living with their families, each numbering from one to four children, many of them over ten years of
age, in one room and paying in many instances for that room
four shillings a week rent. The men justly complained of having
to live in badly ventilated rooms in which they had to wash and
dry their clothing besides live and sleep. There was often the
added humiliation of sharing the house with thieves who would
annoy them and insult and humiliate their wives and children.[6]
The rooms were frequently sub-let by the other tenants so that
stowed away under one roof there could be about 100 men, women

and children. The overcrowding was so bad that Harvey eventually would not accept recruits with more than two children. One of the worst areas was Gun Square near Seven Step Alley in Bishopsgate. One woman and her family sub-let and shared the same room with nine tailors. Fights were not unusual and when the tailors got drunk 'the poker, the goose, and the other familiar instruments' would be brandished and there would be the cries of 'murder'. A policeman stated that

> the condition of the houses in Gun-square and Seven Step-alley, was the most extraordinary that could be imagined. The difference between the sexes appeared to be no difference at all. There they were, old and young, men and women, married and unmarried; every room was crammed with occupants, so that when a dispute took place in any particular building, such crowds flocked in from other habitations that it often appeared to be a miracle how the walls could stand together; and what was most surprising of all was that every inmate seemed to be fighting, and when the struggle was at end not a drop of blood was to be seen.[7]

There were equally bad areas by the river. The water off Whitefriars had its own peculiar colour and flavour called 'Blue Jack' from waste water let into the river from the gasworks in Tudor Street. The inhabitants complained of nausea, headaches, sweating and burning of the throat.[8] The overcrowding and lack of sanitation caused the City to be scourged more than once with cholera. But even cholera, or the fear of it, could be turned to advantage by a clever thief. Elizabeth Newan was stopped when a policeman saw her running through the streets at three o'clock in the morning with a bundle under her shawl. She was charged the next morning with robbing a seaman, Jack Flaherty, of his clothes. The sailor came into court with his legs thrust through two sacks tied together and wearing an old piece of canvas which, he told the magistrate, he had borrowed off 'a gentleman named Mr Moses Lazarus, who was kind enough not to think of leaving him until he should procure some money from his captain'. He told the court that the woman had borne down on him the night before and given him a hearty invitation to her apartment in the neighbourhood of the Whitechapel slaughter-houses. He fancied a stretch upon the straw but she told him that

the flue from the feathers would spoil his new clothes. He felt
her pulling at his stockings but he was too sleepy to mind. When
he woke the next morning the sun was coming in through a
broken window and the woman and his clothes were gone. He
bawled out for half an hour and at last an old woman appeared
and told him that the lady had gone for a doctor. 'For a doctor!'
said he; 'Who wanted a doctor?' 'Why, she said you was taken
bad with the cholera,' replied the old woman, 'and as my missus
and me knowed that a poor man died blue in that bed two
nights ago, we thought you might have cotched it, so we let her
out.'[9]

The policemen, especially the married men, seem to have had
little resistance to disease, possibly because they were suffering
from malnutrition. The single men generally lived off rump
steaks and mutton chops, and the married men off bread and
potatoes. The size of family obviously restricted the diet. The
breakdown of budget in 1853 for a first-class constable,
P.C. Andrews, earning 22s a week was: rent 4s 6d; bread 5s; flour
1s; tea 1s; sugar 8d; potatoes 1s 4d; butter 1s 4½d; pepper and
salt 2d; cheese 9d; wood and coals 1s 4d; candles 4d; milk 3½d;
soap 4½d; schooling 4d. This left 3s 6½d for meat, clothing and
medicine for himself, his wife and five children.[10] Beer was
drunk in preference to water drawn from a fly-blown water-butt,
or one of the City pumps. In the cholera epidemic of 1849, the
scourging of the houses near St Bride's church was attributed to
the poisoning of the well by liquid seeping into the springs from
the graveyard.

Illness could at any time overwhelm the married man's shaky
finances and plunge him hopelessly into debt. If the illness was
not attributable to his work he was fined one shilling for each
day he was sick. The sick rate was consequently higher among
the 135 single men than the 436 married men, the ratio per
thousand being 1450 to 1440; the surgeon explained 'the single
men would lose 1s per day, and the married men as well' but
'the single man would feel the loss less than the married man,
and consequently the inducement would be greater on the part
of the single men to throw themselves on the sick list'.[11]

Their hours were equally pernicious. The men worked three
shifts. The two day-shifts were split so that the men would

always look smart in public. The first shift worked from 6 o'clock to 10 o'clock in the morning and from 2 o'clock to 6 o'clock in the afternoon; they were relieved by the second shift who worked from 10 o'clock in the morning until 2 o'clock in the afternoon and from 6 o'clock to 10 o'clock in the evening.* The night-duty men worked from 10 o'clock in the evening to 6 o'clock in the morning; they had to wake the men living on their beats; they worked nights permanently. They could ask for a change of shift but the surgeon's instructions, and presumably the inspector's as well, were 'to regard a man who feels himself incompetent for night duty as unfit for the force'.

Long hours, poor food and bad housing steadily weakened these men who, when they came into the force, were looked upon as men 'possessing a high standard of health, and capable of undergoing a more than ordinary amount of physical exertion',[12] and undermined their resistance to the tedious hours of patrolling and the sudden extremes of weather for which they were ill-equipped. There were frequent complaints of the clothing and equipment. Truncheons broke, capes cracked and peeled, the nap wore off uniforms 'leaving a whitish bareness only to be seen' and the seams were constantly giving way. On one occasion, when they were delivered, the uniforms looked better than the samples but even this proved illusory. When the men tried 'on the clothes for which they had each been measured a general complaint arose that the trousers were cut scanty, and that those appearing long enough in the legs did not cover their loins. As the men wear no waistcoats they complain of want of warmth to their bodies'. Over 200 men had ill-fitting clothes. 'Coats too large, coats that would not meet, bad embroidery, short trousers, and in some instances the new clothes were brought in a bundle as the fit was so ridiculous the men could not walk through the streets with their new clothes on their backs'.[13]

In the first year each man was issued with one dark-coloured greatcoat, one blue coat with one embroidery, the City badge, on his collar, two pairs of trousers, two pairs of boots or boot allowance, one cape, one hat, one hat cover, one stock, one button brush and stick and one armlet. Armlets were worn by constables

* These hours varied from time to time.

on the left wrist and by sergeants above the elbow; later it was transferred to the right wrist for sergeants when the chevrons on the sleeve made this impossible. In the second year he was issued with one blue coat, one embroidery, two pairs of trousers, two pairs of boots, or boot allowance, and one armlet coloured red and white, the City's colours.[14]

The top hats had polished-leather crowns which made the hats bright and clean to look at but hot and extremely unpleasant to wear. The men changed to hats with beaver crowns. These were comfortable to wear but they soon looked shabby and acquired a rusty appearance. In street fights they were easily pierced with stones and heavy pieces of wood, or stolen because they could not be identified, unlike the leather hats which also offered more protection to the head. Harvey changed back to them when the contractors found out how to ventilate them with two perforated buttons on either side of the crown.[15]

The surgeon blamed the numerous cases of rheumatism on the poor quality capes. When they were not being worn they were carried in straps by the side; but because they were tightly buckled they became easily chipped and cracked. They retained water and became cold and clammy to wear. They protected the shoulders but not the knees and thighs and were compulsory wearing in summer instead of the greatcoat. One disgruntled policeman complained to *The Times*, 'From 1st October to 1st May the policeman must wear his greatcoat, let April be ever so scorchingly hot; and from the 1st of May until the 1st of October, he may not put it on, though the rain pour down in torrents, as within the last six weeks it had frequently done.' He grumbled, 'Surely the Commissioner should not stop at a partial measure. If he regulates the clothing, he should regulate the weather.'[16]

Men rarely stayed more than four years. In twenty years Harvey recruited 3136 men; in the same period 2562 left – 600 were dismissed, this was more than the whole force, 104 died, 125 were pensioned off and 1733 resigned for better jobs. Because of the demands for men, Harvey continued the old practice of hiring 'supernumeraries, persons, for the most part, engaged in other Occupations, and not being sworn, nor wearing the Clothes of the force, elude the obligations of the Law, and their obedience

to the Chief Office. . . .' They were hired on a casual basis when
policemen were sick or absent for some other reason. Harvey
quickly became infuriated with men handing in their resignations and leaving their work to them, and on one occasion hauled
a night-duty man before a magistrate, as he was entitled to do
under section 15 of the City Police Act, and charged him with
neglect of duty. The constable explained that 'he met some
friends at the west-end of town, and while they were chatting,
and he was waiting to hear the clock strike 8 it struck 9. He knew
a supernumerary would be instantly sent on his duty, and it
would be useless to give himself any trouble about it'. He was
shocked at the totally unexpected sentence. The magistrate told
him that he could be 'fined £10, or to be sent to the treadmill for
a month; but, considering his previous good conduct, he should
adjudge him only to be imprisoned in the House of Correction,
without hard labour, for one week'.[17]

The supernumeraries were useful to Harvey. Certain bodies,
like the Middle and Inner Temple, would not let the police onto
their property, though this might have been due to personal
hostility to Harvey himself. Others, like the Bridge House
Estates, would not disband their private watch-forces unless a
fixed number of constables was permanently stationed on their
property, in this instance, Blackfriars Bridge and London Bridge.
The supernumeraries were useful for this kind of work but still
left Harvey short of men. His numbers were continually being
bled through sickness – the daily number of sick was never less
than twelve and in winter averaged between thirty and forty –
and by the Corporate demands for men for the markets, for the
justice rooms, for special duties and for the Central Criminal
Court. He asked for an extra forty-two men for a Reserve to
draw on, but this was agreed to only on condition that the supernumeraries were suppressed as they were not sworn in and were
therefore beyond the aldermen's control as magistrates.

They were disbanded temporarily, but in 1845 Harvey began
to press for their revival. He wrote to the chairman of the Police
Committee, Thomas Wood, that his men generally found 'great
Robberies' to take place on premises entrusted to men whose
characters were unknown, or to the 'indifferent and uniform rest'
of the private watchmen; they had traced to these causes con-

siderable losses. Since many public and private institutions were
willing to pay for the exclusive services of constables he suggested
that the supernumeraries should be sworn in as special constables
appointed by, and amenable to, the police and under their
supervision. It was a way not only of cutting down crime and of
supplanting the private watchmen but of gaining access to areas
which, because they were private property, had formerly been
outside his control. Harvey also saw it as a way of pensioning off
the growing number of men whose disabilities would soon force
them to retire.[18]

The scheme was approved on condition that all appointments
and dismissals were notified to the Police Committee, that the
hirers paid one-quarter or one-half year's salary in advance and
that they paid for the hire of the uniforms which had to be worn
by the supernumeraries in private service and returned by them
when their employment ceased. The policemen Harvey selected
for this work, the potential pensioners, had to continue their
contributions to the superannuation fund; they were considered
in actual service, and therefore entitled to the benefits of the
sick fund which was denied to men who had not been in the
force. But in their case the requirements of height and age
were waived.

In 1840 'Constables had to be under forty years, to stand
five feet seven inches without shoes, to read and write and keep
accounts; to be free from any bodily complaint, of strong constitution and generally intelligent'. He was also expected to possess
a decent suit of clothes and a hat. By 1861 recruiting was restricted to men under thirty-two and not below five feet eight
inches in height, though if the recruit had served elsewhere as a
policeman for more than twelve months, he might be accepted
if he was not less than five feet seven inches. In the first seven
years Harvey personally interviewed over 3000 men. His choice
was restricted not only by the physical and mental qualifications
of the candidates but by his self-imposed ban on men with more
than two children. His advertisement in 1861 brought him 570
applications for 43 vacancies; more than half of them were not
even worthy of consideration, and out of the remainder he could
find only thirty-eight, leaving him with five vacancies still. The
great disparity between the number of applicants and the

number selected he attributed to 'the eager desire of men out of employment to obtain it, without any regard to the conditions imposed' and the poor mental and physical condition of the rest.[19] The medical examination was similar to that for the Army. The surgeon quoted Xenophon to the Police Committee: 'Look to the feet, observed the Celebrated Greek, in your choice of a horse; should these be faulty reject the animal at once, whatever other good qualities it may have.'[20]

Because of the poor physiques induced by their environment, men were rarely recruited from Whitechapel, Spitalfields and the poorer parts of London.[21] Like the Metropolitan Commissioners Harvey recruited chiefly from the army. The partial militarisation of the police force made the transition an easy one. Companies of privates or constables lived in quarters or barracks, they mustered for parades, they were inspected, they saluted, they were marched to their beats by sergeants, they had cutlass training, they were drilled and for minor offences had punishment drills; later, the sergeants wore chevrons, the higher ranks had captains, and the military-styled helmet replaced the top hat. The new recruits were 'licked into fitness' by Inspectors Adam Spary and Joseph Todhunter to give the force its 'military turn'.

Todhunter had been a Metropolitan Policemen before he joined the City Day police in 1837. Before that he had had a stake in the City Theatre.* His boxkeeper told him on one occasion that a young girl sitting in the boxes by herself was the sister of one of the actors named Palmer. Todhunter subsequently found out that this was false and that her true name was Bird. He introduced himself to Elizabeth Bird and the following day he took her to Richmond and spent the night with her at the Roe Buck Inn. He confessed, 'I having but little opinion of her respectability and virtue, was of course anxious to get rid of her the following day', but she persuaded him to stay. And when they returned to London three days later they lived together for six years as man and wife. Eventually he left her because he complained, 'My clothes were daily taken to pawn by Elizabeth Bird but as often as I redeemed them, so often were they

* Whether this was the theatre in Norton Folgate, Bishopsgate or in Moor Lane is not clear.

pledged. . . .' He gave her £7 to clothe herself and two weeks' notice of his intention to leave her. He left her at the beginning of April 1840 and on 6 June he married a woman he had courted ten to twelve years before. But on his honeymoon his wife found out about Elizabeth; she quarrelled with him, he quarrelled with her parents, and for a time they parted by mutual consent. Todhunter took rooms in Fore Street and went back to live with Elizabeth Bird who was threatening suicide, possibly because she was pregnant. However, he was soon reconciled with his wife and left Elizabeth for the last time. But while they had been living together Elizabeth had stolen his marriage certificate. Two years later Todhunter was asked to settle a bill from this period and he, thinking that Elizabeth might have since been posing as his wife and that this might be the first of a series of claims on him, mistakenly sent a constable to find her and to arrest her for false pretences. Elizabeth and her mother complained to the Commissioner,[22] but because Harvey did not sack Todhunter it later led to the charge that he condoned immorality.

Harvey did not want to be an 'Inspector of the force'. But to see how the men worked and behaved he frequently roamed the City in a hired cab – 'I may say that it is idle for me to walk for the moment they see me out there is a lantern to tell it from one end of the City to the other.'[23] He told the Police Committee, 'I frequently see men talking – I frequently see acts that I consider very improper, but I never mention it to the men because I think it would be very unbecoming for me to assume in the slightest degree the character of an accuser upon an offence or irregularity of which I had to be the judge'.[24] He thought insubordination one of the 'heaviest' offences and nine times out of ten it was punished by him. Trivial offences like gossiping, general neglect of duty, drunkenness and occasionally insubordination were left to the superintendent and the inspectors who could punish them with fines ranging from sixpence for mustering dirty to ten shillings and a day's wages for insubordination. This was equivalent to losing more than half a week's wages. Every man could appeal against his sentence to the Commissioner. Occasionally the superintendent would fine them for 'vexatious' appeals – 'An appeal without any ground; an appeal where a man will not submit to the authority of his inspector;

where he merely comes up on speculation; and where in fact he evinces a disposition to browbeat his officer.'[25] Harvey reckoned that without it there would be an appeal against every decision. But even then the men still had the right of appeal. As soon as a man said 'I shall appeal', an appointment was made for him to see Harvey who would not read or hear anything of the case until both parties were standing on the Brussels carpet in front of his desk – a mahogany table with a green cloth, slope, black ink-stand and glasses. He took no notes. And neither the accuser nor the accused would leave until the evidence had been heard and he had given his judgement.

Similarly the men could be rewarded with gratuities for meritorious acts; but this was only with Harvey's approval. He was mindful the whole time of the old tendencies of the watch to 'shove off justice' with bribes. His men were soon accused, anonymously, of similar tendencies, of being 'upon the best terms with the omnibus drivers and cads', of drinking in public houses, of lounging and gossiping in the streets and of 'being in daily conversation and familiarity with the women of the town'.[26] A strict discipline was obviously necessary to counter the inherent risks in this too-easy familiarity.

Each man was timed over his beat. He was given a beat card which told him the order in which he had to walk the streets and the time he was allotted for each so that any person, simply by applying at the station house, could find out to within a few minutes the time his house ought to be passed. He was only to talk when necessary, keep an even temper and was forbidden to smoke, to drink, to call the hour or carry a stick or umbrella. He had to report broken gas-lamps, see that rubbish was carted away, the footpaths swept, prevent and detect crime, keep the footpaths clear of carriages and cattle and stop waggons and hackney coaches from loitering and omnibuses from creeping. He was threatened with dismissal if he was found talking with female servants or other women.

Sooner or later he met the beggar, Samuel Ward. According to a magistrate, whenever he was missing from the streets he was in some bridewell. He would lie on the pavement between two long crutches with his feet, about half the normal size, wrapped in white cotton to attract attention. He was always polite to the police and would touch his hat, not only to the inspectors, but to the men who were marked for promotion. At one time he had been a constable of Lime Street ward and had been especially appointed to break up the numerous pickpockets that flourished there. Instead, he had imitated Jonathan Wild, followed the more lucrative role of receiver and encouraged the thieves by purchasing their plunder. He was charged with having disgraced the office of constable and was convicted and sent to prison for three months. Soon after his discharge from prison he went to work on the barges on the Thames. He fell asleep one night in one of them and his feet became frost-bitten. He lived by begging.[27]

His career in some ways was a warning to them all.

'Mother Wood, the popular procuress.' Matthew Wood, dressed as an elderly woman, is standing in the porch of his house in South Audley Street holding a bottle inscribed 'Popularity'. The allusion is to his championing of Queen Caroline. He is compared to a notorious brothel keeper of the same name.

MOTHER WOOD, the Popular Procuress.

James Whithair, Superintendent of the Day and Night Police 1838–1839

9. *Daniel Whittle Harvey, Commissioner of the City of London Police 1839–1863*

10. *P.C. Parsons, 1850*

9

Beggars, Swell Mobsters and Shofulmen

Sarah Smith, 38, no home and her three Children, George 7, Elizabeth 4 and John an Infant, completely destitute, found by P.C. 646 John Staples, on the step of the door No. 20 Wormwood Street. The Woman and her Children natives of London. Sent to the Relieving Officer, refused by Mr Roberts any relief, on the ground that they had been found one door out of his union. Sent to the Relieving Officer, Seething Lane who gave an order for Stepney Green Workhouse.

Police Report, 1842[1]

THE main problem facing the City Police was the casual poor, a category which consisted not only of those who through want of work, illness or other personal misfortune were compelled to seek assistance from the unions, but also those who could be classified only as idle tramps and professional mendicants. In 1839 the City of London Union relieved 356 casual poor. This rose steeply from 2403 in 1840 to 43,575 in 1844 and again in 1847 to 41,743.[2]

By 1848 the windows of the Mansion House had been smashed so many times that a special lookout had to be hired to watch for the beggar women who daily milled about outside and who had even been known to carry from long distances baskets of paving-stones to hurl through the Lord Mayor's windows, and the windows of the banks and counting-houses nearby. They still smashed them, even when they were wired up, by jabbing through the wires the steel busks from their stays. Police constables had to be stationed outside the unions to maintain order. And both they and the union officers were regularly 'thumped, bonneted, kicked, pinched and shoved' by the beggar

F

women, particularly by Irish viragoes who called beating the
former, 'polthoguing' the police. In court they would vow
'vengeance against the plate-glass windows, the union officers,
the police officers, and the Lord Mayor and his brother aldermen'. In every case the intention was the same, to be committed
to prison.

By the New Poor Law Act of 1834, poor relief had been taken
out of the hands of the parish as a unit and had become collec-
tively the responsibility of a union of parishes working together
under the direction of a Board of Guardians controlled by the
Poor Law Commissioners. The ninety-eight parishes within the
walls were formed into a City of London Union and the parishes
without the walls, an East London Union (four parishes) and a
West London Union (seven parishes) the last two with work-
houses in Aldersgate Street and St Andrews Court, Holborn.[3]
However, the workhouse for the City of London Union was at
Peckham and most of the applicants to the office in Cannon
Street were relieved with bread only. The other unions complained that, as a result, these casuals, in Harvey's words, were
being 'thrown off' to them to relieve. But even by grossly overcrowding their own casual wards they could not sleep them all,
and at least a third of the applicants had to be turned away every
night to sleep in the streets. Some went away, some waited a
few hours and then were admitted, some were driven off with
buckets of water and some, the most desperate, lay down on the
'rough stones, rendered most offensive by the droves of Cattle
which pass to and from the Yard in which their applications are
made for admission into the Workhouse, and where they remain
for hours still hoping to be admitted'.[4] In the morning, those
that had been taken into the casual wards were turned out and
joined the others on the streets to beg. About seventy-five per
cent of them were reckoned to live by professional begging and
thieving.

The beggars, like the thieves, had their own 'cant', with the
'cant' words rhyming with the words expressing the similar idea.
'This way's the caper. Suppose I want to ask a pal to come and
have a *glass* of *rum* and smoke a *pipe* of *tobacco*, and have a
game at *cards* with some *blokes* at *home* with me. I should say,
if there were any flats present, "Splodger, will you have a Jack-

surp*ass* of finger-and-*thumb*, and blow your yard of *tripe* of nosey me *knackert* and have a touch of the *broads* with me and the other heaps of *coke* at my *drum*".'[5] Some like the disaster beggars, shipwrecked mariners and the like, had mendicant pedigrees stretching back to Elizabethan times at least; the basic patter was the same but the variants now included blown-up miners, burnt-out tradesmen and lucifer droppers.

As soon as a 'lay' was 'grannied' (known) the professional beggar would move on to another. In fine weather he might take to 'screeving' (writing on stones) with a white cap fastened beneath his chin, to accentuate his pallor as if he was just recovering from an illness; on the stones he might chalk 'Illness and want'; sometimes he might pick his teeth until they bled, or spit and cough as if he had asthma. In wet weather, when it was impossible to 'screeve' he might dress 'tidy and clean' for the 'broken down tradesman or reduced gentleman', or go out with a woman and children on the 'clean family lurk' and stand by the side of the pavement, the wife in a clean cap and milk-white apron and the children in long clean pinafores 'white as the driven snow'. 'To succeed in this caper there must be no rags, but plenty of darns. A pack of pawntickets is carried in the waist-coat pocket. That's to show that they've parted with their little all before they came to that.'[6]

Children could be hired for as little as fourpence or sixpence a day, and in one week might have twenty 'mothers'. One complainant wrote,

My business causes me to traverse Crosby square, South Sea passage, and the neighbouring 'short cuts' many times a day. Every time numerous mendicants have to be repulsed. There appears to be a set for morning operations, and another set for the afternoon, also a general change and return every month or so, as if they relieved guard systematically. In South Sea passage (which is much frequented by merchants, and is full of corners) a mendicant tableau may be viewed every 20 feet. Directly a policeman appears near one end a sentinel runs through to signal each detachment, and the brigade starts out at the other end, to dodge round the neighbourhood and return.

I once watched a woman enter with children decently clad, in a few seconds her skirt folded up showed a torn and muddy under skirt.

The children's bonnets, shoes, socks etc., were taken off, the woman's shawl made a seat, and in crouching attitudes they looked miserable enough. In the dusk of evening there is often a meeting for consultation or sharing of profits.

For the last five years one woman had made a fortnightly round, singing the same melancholy ditty, with six children that are kept at the same height – of course by hiring. On speaking once to a policeman respecting a woman who was dragging a famished child through the streets on a wet cold day, he told me she was one of six old hags who went out in rotation every two hours with the child, whilst the other five sat drinking in a neighbouring pot house.[7]

Mayhew quoted ninepence a day for one child or one shilling for two if no food was given, or two for ninepence with food and Godfrey's cordial, a well-known mixture with a laudanum base for quietening babies.[8] Larger children were likely to blow their cover and 'crack the pitch'. Syrup of poppies was also used to make them 'lie asleep in the arms, in the laps, or at the feet of their infamous parents' or hirers. Inevitably the continual dosing and the permanently comatose state they were left in killed them. The 'shallow' (half-naked) lay as this was called was popular with women probably because of the low earnings in prostitution. Comb-sellers and foreign prostitutes joined with out-of-work milliners, laundresses and domestic servants to swell the already overcrowded ranks of the oldest profession. As one woman told a magistrate, 'The streets a'nt worth anything now at all, and so all the girls that walk them for their bread say. There's too many of us, and so we are all a cutting each other's throats: that's the fact.'

For threepence a night they could sleep in low lodging-houses with 'street singers, dogs meat men, crossing sweepers, pie men, muffin sellers, dealers in lucifer matches, watercresses, fruits and sweet meats, cabmen, dustmen', smashers, coiners, 'purchasers of begged and stolen goods', thieves and prostitutes. 'Gas lamp over the door, opposite the public house', some lodging-houses boasted.[9] Harvey reported as late as 1862 that there were seventy-seven of these houses given over exclusively to thieves and prostitutes.[10] The line of these low lodging-houses followed exactly the line of cholera cases – Field Lane, Plough and Plum-tree Courts, Harp Alley, Church Yard and Cockpit Court, Crown

Court and Hanging Sword Alley. The windows were generally stuffed with rags, and ash heaps stood outside against the crumbling walls. At the bottom of the house would generally be a low cellar, full of filth and rubbish, and above it separated by some thin boards would be the common sitting-room; the bedrooms overhead were reached by a ladder, and at night everyone would just tumble in to the few beds that had been pushed together. The evening was spent playing cards or dominoes; someone might cast some coin from metal in a tobacco pipe that had been thrust between the bars of the grate and pour it into a plaster mould standing on the hob; on the other hob might be a teacup of counterfeit shillings of William IV. Some of them might be passed by ringing the changes, by handing one of them

14. *The Field Lane Lodging-House*

back with some genuine change for a larger coin. But the risks were hardly worth while. An original twist was to sell them. Two utterers stood in Giltspur Street selling counterfeit sovereigns for sixpence each. They calculated that most people were familiar with a variant of the story of the man who, a few years before, for a wager, had stood on London Bridge selling genuine sovereigns for sixpence each. He had been ignored by almost everyone. They reckoned that there would be few people who would not risk an equally small stake on a similar gamble. The counterfeits were like the sovereign in size and colour and in the beading on the edge round the Queen's head, and the edge was milled. But on the reverse, instead of Britannia, was the figure of a man on horseback over a dragon with the words 'To Hanover', and the date 1837. The deviation was so considerable that the two men could hardly be indicted for uttering counterfeit coin, and yet the resemblance was so close in size, colour and general appearance as to deceive most people. The men argued that they were doing it for a wager. They were fined ten shillings each for obstruction.[11]

Vagrant and destitute boys were soon corrupted by the atmosphere of the low lodging-houses. They were laughed at for genuinely begging. 'The others say, "Begging! Oh, you cadger!" So a boy is partly forced to steal for his character.'[12] They were taught how to take a handkerchief from a coat without shaking the bell attached to it; until they could do this they were not well trained. Another way was for the trainer to walk up and down the room with the boys walking behind him trying to take the handkerchief out of the tail of his coat. As soon as they were proficient they went on the streets. Every day, between ten o'clock in the morning and two o'clock in the afternoon, they could be seen loitering about the Mansion House and Cheapside. Those who were fresh out of prison or the workhouse were instantly recognisable by their cropped or shaven heads. In theory this was done to free their heads of vermin. But, in the case of the West London Union, it was shown that the barber was given a basic fee of 7s 6d a week for looking after 300 to 400 heads, and further fees of a penny for haircuts and sixpence for shaving heads. Whether he shaved or cut was left entirely to his discretion. Needless to say, he shaved every time. And girls as

well as boys in the West London Union had bald heads, except
for the slight ring of hair he left them to poke from beneath the
concealing bonnets and caps.[13] The boys wore, whenever possible,
men's cast-off clothing, often many sizes to big for them, to help
to convince the magistrates that they were older than they were;
this was to escape the whipping that could only be inflicted on
boys under fourteen.

> Many of them are only 6 or 7 years of age, others 8 or 10. Som
> have no jacket, cap, or shoes, and wander about London with their
> ragged trousers hung by one brace; some have an old tattered coat,
> much too large for them, without shoes and stockings, and with one
> leg of the trousers rolled up to the knee; others have an old greasy
> grey or black cap, with an old jacket rent at the elbows, and strips
> of the lining hanging down behind; others have an old dirty pina-
> fore; while some have petticoats. They are generally in an unwashed
> and squalid condition; with their hair clustered in wild disorder like
> a mop, or hanging down in dishevelled locks – in some cases cropped
> close to the head.[14]

In Bishopsgate they worked in gangs of five and six, with
several of the boys acting as lookouts to the boy stealing 'wipes'
from gentlemens tails; this boy's movements would be partly
masked by the boy walking by his side who would run off with
the handkerchief if the tail felt it being taken; the tail would
also be pummelled and kicked if he tried to or did make an arrest.
The wipes could be disposed of in Field Lane. This was so well
known that simply mentioning the name in court was almost
enough to secure a conviction. One young man, described as a
'regular out-and-outer', was caught with two silk handkerchiefs
stuffed between his waistcoat and his shirt and was sentenced to
two months' imprisonment. He complained to the Lord Mayor
'I have done nothing; why should I be sent to crib for two months?'
He was asked again where he got the handkerchiefs. He replied
that he had just bought them in Field Lane.

'Policeman, was his back or his face towards Field Lane when
you saw him?' the Lord Mayor asked.

'His face, your Lordship.'

'To be sure. You were going to sell them in Field Lane, my

good fellow. You get things of the kind cheaper than you could buy them there. You shall go to Bridewell for two months.'

As the prisoner went downstairs he was heard to mutter 'It's damned hard that a person can't purchase a rag of a wipe without being charged with stealing it.'[15]

The entrance to Field Lane was at the foot of Holborn Hill. 'You turned down by a projecting grocer's-shop, and found yourself between rows of windowless shops, flouting with ill-matched articles of clothing – coats, bonnets, gowns, though the ground staple was pocket handkerchiefs, especially bandannas, evidently a recent tribute to the light fingered tribe plying in the City.'[16] The wretched creatures living in this foetid rat-infested warren of brothels and slums hated the police and would howl like a pack of wolves to see one brutally treated. When Police Constable 244 William Smith turned into West Street from St John's Court one afternoon in October 1849, he saw a small knot of men standing at the corner of Sharp's Alley. One of them was John Desmond; he was slightly drunk. He was holding a number of twisted sticks in his hands; they were loaded at the ends and covered like life preservers. Desmond handed these sticks to his friends, except for one which he kept hold of the thinner or ferrule end, and swung it against his leg as Smith walked towards them. He struck the wall in a challenging manner. Smith ignored him and walked on past him but turned about suddenly as Desmond attacked him from behind. He parried the blow that was swung at his head and flung the stick into the crowd that suddenly gathered about them. 'You ——,' Desmond raged. 'I don't care for all the —— police together.' Smith caught hold of him and told him that if he tried the same thing again he would be arrested, but that if he went quietly away then he could do so. Desmond sullenly agreed that he would, but as Smith released him he hit the constable in the neck. He was arrested and a violent struggle followed. The crowd of about 120 to 150 persons hooted and yelled and flung stones at the constable. 'All the people were yelling like a parcel of hounds at the officer, and seemed not to care or to have the slightest feeling as to how brutally he was treated.' Desmond had also armed himself with a large clasp-knife and he stabbed Smith in the chest, in the knee and in the left side of the neck above the carotid artery. A constable stationed by the West London Union heard the shouts and hurried to Smith's assistance. Together they overpowered his attacker and brought him to the station in spite of the crowd.[17]

The 'mouchers' used violence in a more constructive way to plunder eating-houses and coffee shops. They would 'enter a public house in a body from three to a dozen persons, call for drink until the landlord will supply no more and then, when payment is demanded, either fight their way out of the house or assume such a threatening attitude as to induce the landlord to let them leave without paying'.[18] However, most beggars prided themselves on their professionalism and scorned such crude methods. A notorious begging-letter writer was quite willing to show to an admiring court before she was sentenced the facile ease with which she could burst into tears. Yet another defended herself by boasting 'that her exertions to support herself deserved any name but that of idleness. On the contrary, mendicancy as she practiced it, required great labour, ingenuity, and memory, and the least slip exposed her to detection, of the consequences of which she was perfectly aware.'[19]

The unions had no way of testing the genuineness of such stories. This favoured the professional mendicants in the indiscriminate scrabble for relief, and many genuinely distressed cases were inevitably shouldered aside by them. Harvey thought it would be less costly to the ratepayers and more kind and less harassing to persons in the workhouse if every person who applied for relief a second time could be detained and employed long enough to enable the guardians to ascertain the veracity of his statement.[20]

Inevitably the conflict of the City of London Union with the West and East London Unions over its failure to provide a workhouse for its casuals made the treatment of the poor of subordinate interest. The poor, finding themselves with nowhere to go came more and more in collision with the police whose efforts to get them relief, were continually frustrated by the unions (see Appendix 6). Eventually, meeting the same pathetic creatures again and again on their beats, they ignored them until, through cold and hunger, they committed some wilful act of vagrancy, or some petty crime, and could be committed to prison.[21]

F2

One of the consequences was a nine-year orgy of window-smashing near the Mansion House. It became so bad that one irate alderman asked for a clause to be introduced into a parliamentary bill 'making the offence, upon repetition twice or thrice, punishable by transportation for seven or fourteen years'. He was supported in this by Sir Peter Laurie who thought 'the practice of non-transportation of delinquents led to much evil to the public. The fact was that the convict prisons were made so comfortable by the humane excesses of some people, that the lazy and vile availed themselves of the facilities which shop windows presented to aid them in getting into prisons where they could maintain comfortable quarters for the year.'[22] There was an element of truth in this. In the Giltspur Street Compter the weekly allowance was 210 ozs of bread, meat and potatoes, whilst the same allowance in the East London Union was 183 ozs, and in the West London Union 148 ozs.[23]

Each alderman had his own way of dealing with them. One was so famous for his animosity to beggars that he was caricatured with a broom in his hand. Another set up a soup kitchen. Some thought criminal reform 'one of the grand humbugs of the day', and others that 'the dirtier was the prison, the heavier the lash, and the longer the incarceration, the better for society and for the offender against its laws'. They often had to deal with would-be suicides who had waded into the water from Blackfriars steps, or flung themselves from the bridge into the river, and who had failed to be swept beneath the barges and rafts. In 1841 the number was so high that Alderman Sir Peter Laurie publicly stated that he would 'put down' suicide. Dickens seized on the phrase and turned him into Alderman Cute in 'The Chimes'. Laurie thought that suicide could be 'put down' with harsh sentences. He sentenced a starving man to the treadmill, and some years later sent a girl who had been seduced and who had tried to poison herself for trial at the Old Bailey where, he told her, he had no doubt that she would be transported. 'He had put an end to persons attempting to drown themselves; he would now try the same cure for attempted poisoning.' *Punch* commented, 'His conquest of suicide by water and poison is, perhaps, among the greatest triumphs of the public mind.'[24]

When he took office Harvey found that the union overseers

were making matters worse still by refusing to give even bread, or money, after eleven o'clock at night. This was being done with the Lord Mayor's approval. Anyone wanting relief had to be lodged overnight in either the police stations or the Compter. Once before, in 1837, the Prison Inspectors had complained of finding in the Compter 'destitute boys, against whom no criminal charge had ever been brought' and who had been left there until either a ship or a situation could be found for them.

Harvey thought it contrary both to law and humanity alike to send persons to prison merely because they were destitute. He could not 'for a moment, think of punishing poor persons by sending them to a prison' and promptly reversed the Lord Mayor's order. Instead he brought a test case against the over-seers to force the unions, particularly the City of London, into finding accommodation. Some was found in Clerkenwell and in some old buildings in Smithfield. Adopting his own suggestion, which in its original form had been thought too penal in character, he arranged for casuals seeking relief after eleven o'clock at night to be taken first to the stations where, if they were found to be known mendicants, they were to be kept and dealt with as rogues and vagabonds. Moving forward on this two-fold front he forced the professional beggars out of the City and into the surrounding areas. Within a few years a member of the Corporation was able to boast that there was 'not one beggar to be seen lurking about for the twenty who used to follow the trade boldly in the streets'.

Only one out of the six police stations was even capable of dealing with them. But not even the words 'Police Station No. 2' on the window and on the lamp over the door could conceal the fact that the building overlooking the cattle pens in Smithfield was nothing more than the former Greyhound public house. It stood on the west side of the market, north of Hosier Lane, opposite the burly figure of Henry VIII that straddles the gate-way into St Bartholomew's Hospital, not far from the spot where his daughters, Mary and Elizabeth, burned martyrs to the Protestant and Catholic faiths. By the side was a covered gateway leading into the yard of the Greyhound Waggon Office. On market days it sheltered horses and jobbers. There were four cells on the ground floor and two in the basement. Inspector Martin wrote to Harvey:

I respectfully beg leave to state that the Lock up Rooms at this
Station, being recently built, and not having been dried in any
way, are so cold and damp, that many of the Prisoners who are
detained in them, sometimes from 15 to 18 hours at a time, are in
such a state with the Cold that when they leave them, they appear
as though they had lost the use of their limbs; as the weather is
likely to be more severe, I trust you will give orders that the said
Lock up Rooms may be warmed in some way, they are likewise
totally dark now, from 5 p.m. to 7 a.m., so that the conveniences
are entirely useless. I also beg leave to state, that most of the
persons, brought in on charges, are penniless, and have no means of
procuring food sometimes before they come in for several hours,
trusting you will be pleased to order that those persons should be
allowed some Bread, or any other refreshment you may deem fit,
as a great many of them commit some trifling offence, for the
purpose of being sent to Prison, in preference to being admitted in
to the Workhouse, which place many of them say, is much worse
than our City Gaols.[25]

Harvey ordered them to be given fourpence worth of bread
and coffee. There were no beds in the cells, and prisoners, even
when they had injured themselves, had to sleep on the floor.
One married couple, in for a family dispute, moaned that they
would have had better treatment in Newgate. Females who had
tried to commit suicide and who were often brought in strapped
to a stretcher, had to be left in their wet clothes.[26]

The landlords of the Greyhound were the governors of St
Bartholomew's hospital who had been most unwilling to let it
be converted into a police station. Eventually they had agreed
to lease it to the Police Committee for 43 years for £140 per
annum and a cash settlement of £80 for the fixtures. At the
same time they had leased to them a piece of land in Moor Lane
for 61 years, from Lady Day 1840, for a ground rent of £40 per
annum and the cost of the insurance.[27] Building was begun in
November 1840 on Station No. 1, and the work was finished by
22 June the following year. The main building was two storeys
high and housed forty men. Because at this time the needs of
the police were so little understood there were many defects in
its construction. There were five cells. But they were separate
from the building and in a yard at the back. During the daytime

the yard gate had to be left open and it was quite easy for friends and relatives to walk in and slip them a bottle of drink; it would have been just as easy to pass them tools or weapons to break out, but there is no record of this having ever been done. The clothing stores were in the basement which was permanently damp – in winter the drains flooded and water bubbled above ground. It was badly ventilated, lit only by gas, and occasionally crackling with vermin.[28]

The Police Committee had already been given notice to quit Station No. 4 at 62 Watling Street. So far they had been unable to find a replacement. The three remaining stations were watch-houses. In 1838 the Clerk of Works had tried to patch them up but without much success. No. 3 Station was in Black Horse Court, Fleet Street. The court was 'narrow and confined' which made the station so dark that candles had to be kept permanently burning in the charge room. The cesspool frequently overflowed and the stench made it impossible for anyone to live there. It was almost as bad as No. 5 Station in Great Tower Street as Harvey found out in a cryptic letter from the next-door neighbour Mr Pereira:

> My vaults run under the 5th Police Station, no. 91 Great Tower Street, the place where the prisoners are confined not being furnished with certain accommodations, in order that they might make themselves comfortable, causes it to come through the floor into my vaults, and being a confined place, you can easily imagine how dreadful must be the smell in it, let alone the idea of being compelled to keep away from one part of my vaults for fear of being covered in it.[29]

No. 6 Station was the old Bishopsgate watch-house overlooking St Botolph's churchyard. Such close proximity to the often-open graves left a 'bittery twang' and 'coppery taste' in the mouth. For a time the station had no cells, and prisoners had to be taken to Moor Lane or Smithfield. The men complained that the charge sheets were often inaccurate as they could not tell the time by the church clock after dark. The rooms were so small and the air so foetid and foul that twenty years later it was still possible for the chairman of the Police Committee to complain

'that the men on duty there were obliged, like fishes rising from
the water, to go into the street to breathe a little fresh air'.

The most pressing need was for a station to house the Reserve.
Besides providing men for the Sessions and Smithfield market
Harvey was also using it to observe and report on the behaviour
of the rest of the force. Naturally this was being resisted by the
men who cold-shouldered and hamstrung the working of the
Reserve whenever they could. This suited Harvey who wanted
the Reserve kept in isolation to maintain its exclusiveness. Some
of the men were detectives.

The exact date of origin of the detective department is uncertain. For many years it was part of the Reserve. The umbilical
cord was not finally cut until 1857. The earliest evidence for its
existence is in a petition from Robert Cousins, subsequently
Harvey's chief clerk, which states that he was promoted to
sergeant of the detective department in December 1841.[30] The
earliest newspaper mention is *The Times* of 8 November 1844
which refers to Joseph Hedington one of the City of London
detective force. Since it was part of the Reserve it was probably
formed at the same time, but again the exact date of origin is
uncertain, as the Reserve was already in existence when the
Court of Common Council gave it its formal approval in November 1841. However, it is apparent from a court report that
neither department was in existence in October 1840, as the
constables were making their own inquiries instead of passing
them, as they were able to later, to the Reserve. According to
The Times report, they had to hire substitutes at their own
expense if they made the inquiries during their hours of duty;
the constables concerned had actually paid two shillings to have
two tours of duty performed by deputy.[31] The alderman told him
that this regulation must have crept in without the Commissioner's knowledge and that the policeman 'was serving the
public as much by endeavouring to discover evidence against a
thief as by patrolling a particular beat, and his pocket was not
to be taxed if he was employed on one duty instead of another'.
Later they passed these inquiries for investigation to twelve
first-class plain-clothes policemen whom Harvey styled the
'Nursery of the detectives'. So between these two dates, October

1840 and December 1841, it is reasonable to assume that the detective department was formed.

Public opinion was hostile to policemen wearing plain-clothes disguises. The men apparently had to wear their uniforms even when they were off duty; this was indicated by the removal of the armband. There were fears that they would be little better than spies or *agents provocateurs*. This had some basis of truth. In 1839 Inspector Todhunter had penetrated the Chartists disguised as a reporter. He wrote seventeen years later:

That at the first Chartist Insurrection, when immense mobs of deluded men, under dangerous and revolutionary leaders, were continually congregated in and around the City, menacing, as you know, the safety of the entire country, Your Petitioner was particularly confided in and selected from the entire force to mix, in private apparel, among them in their open and secret assemblies, to take notes of all their seditious proceedings and intentions, whereby Your Petitioner believes vast mischief was prevented by timely notice of their plans (a transcription of such notes being quickly furnished by him, through the Superintendent, to the highest civic authorities – he believes both to the late Sir Matthew Wood and to the then Lord Mayor). And that in the perilous missions herein referred to, Your Petitioner daily ran the risk of his life may be evidenced from the fact, although he was long believed by the Chartist Leaders and delegates themselves to be a reporter for their own press, his real business there was at length discovered; so that upon one such occasion, being closely hemmed in by a concourse of riotous men, filling almost the entire area of Smithfield, he perceived beside him a man, in the midst probably of many such, with his hand on the handle of a pistol partially concealed in the breast of the blouse he wore, which, in his mad furor, he seemed inclined to use, which Your Petitioner is persuaded he would have done on him in that moment of excitement, had the slightest dismay or trepidation been evinced; but Your Petitioner, mindful alone of his duty and faithfulness to the City, still continued penning his notes, although pointed out as the 'Police Spy' by the well known Arne and other speakers of his class – Your Petitioner can refer to the reports in question for proof of all this.[32]

The only detectives as such in the metropolis were the Bow Street runners and the police officers, the Forrester brothers, John and Daniel, attached to the Marshal's office at the Mansion House. Only they and a few of the runners were left to continue as private investigators when the Bow Street office was merged with the Metropolitan Police force in 1839. One writer said of the runners, 'Neither their numbers nor their organization were calculated to prevent crime, but as a detective police they seldom failed, and we are satisfied that to insure the apprehension of offenders recourse must be had to them again.'[33] Another suggested that the Commissioners should replace them with twenty-five to thirty plain-clothes detectives with pay equal to that of an inspector and with discretionary powers of investigation; the first ten, he went on, should be employed in either the town or the country and they should all be able to call for assistance from any branch of the force.[34]

In 1842, following several brutal murders, a detective department was formed at Scotland Yard consisting of two inspectors and six sergeants. The City Police, of course, was not subject to Home Office control which alone had made it possible for Harvey to form a detective department sooner. Nine men, a third of the Reserve, were detectives. The Reserve was later increased to thirty-two men and the number of detectives to twelve.

At first the detectives were easily recognisable from the police trousers and the unglazed top-hat they wore; they were also frequently seen talking to men on the beats. Some of the aldermen as magistrates condemned them for wearing plain-clothes disguises and some went so far as to urge their prisoners to prosecute them for unlawful arrest.[35] Their future hung very much in the balance. One prisoner was charged with assault by a detective. His evidence was that he stopped the man in Cheapside and asked him what he was carrying in the small leather bag under his arm. Upon which the prisoner called him a 'damned scoundrel' and knocked him down. Both men shouted for assistance and the prisoner was taken. His bag contained only sheets of music. The magistrate complained:

Now, although the police might wear plain clothes to detect crime, yet when they were not dressed as officers they should not act as policemen by themselves, but have the aid of some of the force who were on duty. At least when policemen went about out of uniform their disguise should carry an appearance of respectability about it. If persons were to be stopped by men in the garb of brick-layer's labourers, and submit to be questioned and overhauled, they would be liable to be robbed by thieves. How were the public to distinguish between a real police officer and a bricklayer's labourer? He thought the public were justified in refusing to give any faith to persons in such a garb.

Harvey sent Superintendent Hodgson to court to explain that the men carried warrant cards, expressly for that purpose, to identify themselves, and that if further proof was necessary, they also had their police truncheons with them. Besides which it was customary to administer a form of caution which varied from 'I told him not to say anything particular as it might be used against him' to 'I told him he need not answer any questions but that I was a police officer and would ask him where he got it'. This explanation failed to satisfy the magistrate.

The superintendent was now in plain clothes, but he carried an air of respectability about him that would entitle him to credit if he claimed to be a police officer. Still he must set his face against policemen being dressed up as mechanics and labourers, and claiming to be policemen, stopping the public in the streets, and insisting on knowing what parties had about them. Thus challenged by a man in such a garb, the public could not distinguish between thieves and officers. Sometimes beggars assumed the character of poor mechanics or labourers, and prowled about the streets at night, and the first impression that might strike a person upon being asked to show what property he had about him might easily be that he was assailed by a robber, and he did not think the carrying a card or a truncheon much altered the case. If a constable in such a dress caught a thief, it was all very well, but if he caught a lick instead, he should get no redress from him. If a policeman would take that risk, he must abide by the consequences. For himself, he would protest, as on the part of the public, against policeman assuming such disguises.[36]

There were similar suggestions from the public that the police-men should hunt in pairs, that the uniformed man should be followed by the detective, not only for the one to vouch for the other as the alderman had suggested, but to give each other protection. Because of their plain-clothes disguise the detectives had more arrests but they also took more risks. One of them, John Storey, arrested a particularly violent character George Hackett for assaulting another policeman. Hackett was also wanted on another charge and he was committed to Marlborough Street Court. He broke out from there and went to ground. Storey heard from an informant that he was going to Epsom Races on Derby Day and he positioned himself on London Bridge. His patience was rewarded when he saw Hackett's mistress and a friend crossing the bridge on a cart. Because of the traffic the cart was suddenly forced to stop. At the same time Hackett's head popped up from the bottom of the cart where he was lying. Storey went for him and Hackett leaped out with a life preserver in his hand to meet him. As Storey grappled with him he lashed him several violent blows about the head. He wrenched himself free and ran across London Bridge hotly pursued by Storey with blood pouring across his face. Hackett ran along swinging his life preserver from side to side hitting at anyone who tried to stop him. Somebody wrenched the life preserver from his hand as Storey closed with him and pulled him to the ground. Storey managed to hold on to him in spite of being attacked by Hackett's mistress as well who kicked him on the ground. At the station Hackett asked Hedington, another detective, if he thought he would get 'hookied' (transported) for it; he was – for fifteen years.[37]

The sentences were sometimes unnecessarily harsh because there was no organised system of criminal classification. The scanty criminal records that existed were not produced in court, and magistrates were often not sure whether they had a first offender or a hardened offender before them. They had to rely either on their own memory, or the police officer's, or the gaoler's for a prisoner's past convictions.[38] This was amusingly turned against Charles Dickens when he and Mark Lemon gave evidence against a teenager who had tried to pick Lemon's pocket. Dickens told the Court that he thought he had seen the prisoner at the House of Correction. 'Now, your worship,' the prisoner retorted, 'he must have been in quod there himself or he couldn't have seen me. I know these two gentlemen well; they're no better than swell mobsmen, and get their living by buying stolen goods. That one (pointing to Mr Dickens) keeps a "fence" and I recollect him (to Mr Lemon) at the prison, where he was put in for six months, while I was there for only two.'[39]

In fact, Dickens's dandyism was well suited to the character of a 'swell mobsman' who like him favoured fancy waistcoats, gold rings, chains and studs. They regularly loitered about the banks and clearing-houses. They worked in teams. One of them followed by a boy, would walk into a bank and take up a pen and begin to write. He would watch the movements of customers collecting money at the counters. In case he aroused anyone's suspicions he would have already armed himself beforehand with a cheque on another bank as a 'stall off' or a 'blind'. If he was stopped or questioned he could then plead ignorance to the wrong bank. He would wait to see into which pocket the money was put and then he and the boy would follow their victim into the street where the others were waiting. The boy would give the 'office', the sign, and two accomplices would bear down on the victim 'and with comparative ease effect their object, being assisted by the many facilities which the streets and lanes through which he passes affords them'.[40]

Some of the swell mob were well-educated men and some had been ragged pickpockets who had progressed upwards from the gutter. Most of them were punished at some time or other with several periods of imprisonment. In prison they were further punished with long periods on the treadmill or in solitary confinement, mindlessly cranking for a minimum of ten hours a day a revolving wheel which scooped up and emptied in the same revolution a dredger of sand. Before they were thirty-five the steel had been taken out of them. Their restlessness and anxious looks betrayed them to the trained eye. They spent their money freely, 'lushing' (drinking) in taverns, or betting in the back room of a beershop on the killing skill of some dog whimpering with excitement at the smell, like a hot drain, rising from a heaving mass of sewer rats and water rats huddled together in the bottom of a sawdust pit. Laurie branded the betting mania as being the 'high road to the Old Bailey'. At the height of the craze the gambling-offices included a watchmaker's, a bootmaker's, a tobacconist's and a retailer of wines. One man who had lost his licence as a publican boasted that he did not care for its loss for he had afterwards opened a gambling-office and netted £40,000.

Some of the more daring of the 'swell mob' were burglars also, in spite of a report in 1851 that the 'numbers of fellows who have found burglary an unprofitable and dangerous business are now trying their hands in making spirits for night houses and coffee shops, and that the trade is flourishing wonderfully'.[41] The major problem was making keys to fit locks. This could be done by making wax impressions of the originals or by blackening a key with smoke and, after inserting it into the lock it was to open, filing down the parts wiped clean and indicating the wards into which the key could not go. Because beats had to be patrolled in a fixed time it was quite easy for burglars to know when constables would pass by. The police themselves were well aware of this, but the system was never changed, probably because it was thought that any other method of patrolling would be abused and would expose the men to too many temptations. An ex-City policeman wrote to the *Daily Telegraph*:

Allow me to make a few remarks on the police and burglaries in the City of London. In the year 1856 I was a young hand in that force. I think I was a constable about eleven months – and I must say that I had to keep time with the sergeants and inspectors; for when a man first joins he is well watched. Some sergeants place themselves in doorways, and time the young constable, to see how long he takes to go round his beat; and when a man knows that, he is looking after the sergeant more than the burglars. My beat was College Hill, Dowgate Hill etc. On one occasion I was reported for being five minutes too long, and was fined sixpence. I was allowed about fifteen minutes to go about 1,600 yards. It was at the time that I was in the force that an extensive burglary was committed in Bow Lane. Those clever men called detectives sleep at night, and, of course, the young policeman does not know burglars when he meets them. I had been in the force only a few months when I caught a burglar in Dyers Hall, Dowgate Hill. I received great praise for capturing him; but had the sergeant seen me at the post where I had stood some minutes before I heard the noise, he would have reported me, and I should have been fined 1s.[42]

The most daring example was a robbery in Cornhill on 4 and 5 February 1865. The ground-floor tenant was a jeweller and above his shop were two floors of offices. These were empty by 6.10 pm, Saturday, 4 February. Thomas Caseley and two accomplices slipped unseen into the building and opened the second-floor offices with a key that was habitually left on the gas meter on the staircase. At 7.40 pm two outside accomplices signalled that the jeweller's foreman, the last man on the premises, had locked up and gone home. The burglars went downstairs and amused themselves by opening the first-floor safe. At midnight they began work in earnest. The jeweller's shop was lined on the inside with iron doors and partitions but below it, in the soft underbelly, was a tailor's shop. They broke in and by standing on the cutting-board they managed to force their way through the ceiling and flooring into the jeweller's shop above them. By early Sunday afternoon they had broken through.

The shop was lit even in the daytime by gas. And both the front and rear shutters had observation holes in them for the police to look through. Contrary to what they had expected, the constable on the beat did just that every nine minutes. However, his observation was partly blocked on one side by a partition in front of the safe. Instead the safe had been painted and a mirror hung above it so that anyone looking through the shutter could see not only the safe but anyone standing in front of it. Caseley's task was an almost impossible one.

He and one of his accomplices climbed through the hole with their tools. Almost immediately they had to go back again as the third accomplice, sitting by the window upstairs, watching for the signals of the men outside, signalled with a piece of string that the policeman was coming back. As soon as he had signalled that it was clear again Caseley went back to test the safe by 'lawful' means; it was 'unlawful' in his profession to make a noise. He took hold of a metal wedge about 2 inches long and 1½ inches broad and as sharp as a knife, muffled it with a piece of wood and hammered it in between the door and the frame. If the wedge held then quite clearly something or other was yielding to pressure, and this could be gradually built up to breaking-point. However, if the wedge did not hold this would be impossible. The wedge held.

Caseley was forced to work lying on his chest and kneeling. Instead of being able to get the maximum leverage from the top left-hand corner of the safe he had to work from the bottom. He first of all inserted a small bar to release the wedge, and then another wedge a little larger still to release the bar, then another bar a little bigger still to release the second wedge and so on. Every nine minutes the policemen peered through the observation hole to check that the safe was intact. Every time Caseley had to pull out his wedges and bundle himself and his tools back through the hole. Four minutes in every nine were wasted in this way. At one time, he heard two policemen talking. He could not pull out the wedge and he was forced to strike it sideways to break it.

After nine attempts he tested it with a steel bar and felt the door give about half an inch. This surprised him for the safe was a good one, and he whispered excitedly, 'It's open now'. It was now possible to insert the 'alderman', a jointed iron bar, sometimes five feet in length, and open the safe. Caseley later boasted, 'Once get the alderman in, and the safe must open without the alderman breaks.'

They had broken into the shop at 2.55 p.m. By 3.45 p.m. they were back in the first-floor offices with nearly £7000 worth of jewellery. By 4.40 pm they were miles away on the Guildford road. The safe still looked intact when the owner went to open it the next morning.[43]

Highway robberies were sometimes committed with a life preserver or bludgeon. This was termed 'swinging the stick' or the 'bludgeon business'. Joseph Hedington and Michael Haydon were loitering on London Bridge when they saw Joseph Green, Edward Thomas and Catherine Curtis pass by them under a gas lamp. From the look on their faces they immediately guessed what they were about and followed them. Green and Thomas walked a little way behind the woman and each time she stopped and accosted a passer-by they manoeuvred themselves in position to cover her escape if necessary. One of them, if she was caught, would pretend to be her husband and would beat the unfortunate victim, after he had been robbed, if he attempted to 'accost' his 'wife'. The detectives moved in when she successfully lifted a watch. She ran away while her two accomplices tried to cover her escape. Hedington was struck in the face with the butt end of a whip. But the two men were overpowered and the woman caught before she got very far. The magistrate congratulated the detectives and other members of the force 'who

had heads as well as hands to work with' for bringing to justice
several 'ringleaders of the most desperate gangs of thieves in the
metropolis'. He also issued a warning to the 'swell mob' that
whenever they were brought before him he would send them
for trial or sentence to be dealt with as far as the law could
punish them.[44]

The Reserve still had no permanent home. They were moved
from the Guildhall to Moor Lane and then to the new Station
No. 4 in Bow Lane. The actual address was No. 1 Great St
Thomas Apostle, but because it stood in close proximity to each
it was confusingly known both as Garlick Hill Police Station and
Bow Lane Police Station. The usual complaints soon followed.
Next door was a cow yard supplying fresh milk to the City.
Inspector Spary wrote, 'the manure is kept in a hole close under
the windows of the Mess and Sitting Rooms and which is seldom
if ever properly cleansed. This hole contains from two to three
cart loads, and when it becomes full to overflowing, *then* a cart
load only is taken away merely to make room for fresh manure.
The smell from the above is generally very bad, but whenever
the dung is moved for the purpose of being carted away, this
Station is rendered unbearable.'[45]

Harvey had hoped that Bow Lane would be a permanent base
for the detectives. But the building was too small. The inspector's
bedroom was also the kitchen. There was not even room for an
office for them. Their business had to be conducted in public
where it was often overheard, not only by other constables, but
by casual visitors to the station who often had interested motives
for listening. Idle sightseers lolled about the station door to hear
the prisoners being charged. This state of affairs made it almost
impossible for the detectives to work. Eventually Harvey felt
compelled to bring them to 26 Old Jewry.

Harvey never liked his official residence. He contemptuously
referred to it as 'that great blundering house'.[46] His resentment
stemmed from the time of his appointment when, six months
after he had announced his candidature and his election was
certain, it had been foisted on him by the hostile element of the
Court of Common Council who were resentful of Parliament's
insistence that a Commissioner had to be appointed. In a fit of

pique they had passed a resolution making the Commissioner's residence in the City compulsory. Harvey had been so outraged by their behaviour that he had immediately begun negotiations with his creditors to enable him to withdraw.

The Police Committee asked him to view two private houses in Broad Street and Finsbury Square. The former was the biggest private residence in the City. He rejected both because of the drain either would have imposed on his limited resources. Because of the difficulty of finding a suitable residence the Court of Common Council granted him in lieu for one year, 1840, an allowance of £200. For the next three years he travelled between his house in Brixton and his office in the Court of Requests, Basinghall Street. The latter was without any kind of temporary accommodation for his occasional residence. In a letter to the Lord Mayor in September 1840 he suggested that this might be remedied. His letter was ignored for three months. He was then accused by the Police Committee of not meaning to live in the City. This was no more than a flimsy pretext for the Police Committee not to apply to the whole Court for a renewal of his £200 allowance.

The Police Committee was set on crippling the powers of the Commissioner. The Court of Aldermen was not prepared to intervene on his behalf for fear of upsetting their more than unusually delicate relations with the Court of Common Council. Harvey had believed that the annoyances he had been subjected to were no more than teething troubles inherent in any new post. For the first time he was truly aware of the depth of feeling against him. He should have been warned by a *Times* report, before he was Commissioner, that, whoever was Commissioner 'would have an immensity of trouble, because every gentleman who had anything to do with the old watch would always be bothering and advising to have a finger in the management of the police'.

Early in 1841, the Police Committee heard that the house, warehouse and counting-house of the late Alderman Lea were for sale at 26 Old Jewry. For £6500 they bought them for offices and for the Commissioner's official residence. Harvey was not consulted. He commented bitterly, 'It would seem however quite consistent with the good taste and gentlemanly deportment of the Committee to consult the Commissioner upon the comfort of a Cell and the fit locality of a Station, but whether a house be acceptable to him and his Family in which they are expected to reside is a matter to them of perfect indifference.'

The red-brick buildings were pent up on three sides of a narrow courtyard. There was 'but one entrance for ladies of character and women with none'. The rooms were cold and dark because of the taller buildings blocking them in. At times the house was rendered almost uninhabitable by the smell from the sewers and from a nearby tallow-melting establishment. There were strong rumours that the Police Committee intended to make it even more unacceptable by using part of the buildings as a station house to hold prisoners. The rumours were only stopped by a Police Committee resolution that 26 Old Jewry would only be used for offices and stores and for the Commissioner's official residence. The purchase was completed on 25 May 1841.

It was only after the purchase had been completed that the Police Committee found that the baker's shop by the entrance had built its oven in a cellar under the gateway. It had had possession of the ground for so long that it could not be legally dispossessed. In fact, the baker only gave up the ground after the City Surveyor tunnelled a drain under his oven and altered the level of the courtyard so that the water from the back court was thrown into the street which, since it was without a drain, left it to lie for several months in large pools in front of the baker's shop 'during which period the cellar was twice flooded' and the walls were constantly saturated with water.[47]

Harvey was asked to meet a special deputation of the Police Committee in 26 Old Jewry. The deputation agreed that the house was completely unsuitable for the permanent residence of the Commissioner and his family, and the Sub-committee passed a resolution that it should only be used for his occasional residence. Like another motion that it should be sold, this too was overruled.

The Clerk of Works was told to put the buildings into inhabitable shape. Harvey agreed to meet both him and the deputy chairman to suggest further improvements on the strict understanding that he in no way waived his objections to the house. His suggestions meant that the whole work had to be done over again and the buildings remodelled from the attics to the basements. Offices had to be made for a Superintendent, the clerks and the Secretary, besides storage rooms for the Storekeeper. Floors had to be taken up and relaid, doors rehung, windows blocked up, the room over the library fitted up as a breakfast room, the drawing-room papered with a handsome gold-pattern paper and the kitchen and scullery equipped with dressers, shelves, presses, sink, cisterns, a smoke and range and other fixtures. The original contract was for £606 12s 0d. Harvey's improvements cost a further £1834 13s 0d.[48]

He reluctantly sold his home in Brixton. Perhaps he put too high a price on it, but he complained that he had to lower it by £1200. To furnish his new home he had to sacrifice much of his old furniture and purchase new 'thus creating loss in one direction and outlay in another'. He also had to pay for stabling. He complained that he missed his gardens and his cows. 'My residence here sadly disturbs all this,' he wrote wistfully.[49]

He never ceased to urge, both in committee and out of committee, the unsuitableness of his home in 26 Old Jewry. He had had the Police Committee continually 'wavering, resolving and re-resolving from the effects of the communications' he had made to them from the time they completed the purchase 'to the short and dirty days of December, when they commenced painting, papering and repairing the premises in the Old Jewry'. He had been willing to submit the question of whether it was a suitable house or not to an impartial referee, but the Police Committee would not agree. Eventually they had told him that whatever his objections he had sought the office and he must abide by the consequences.

His handling of the force came in for some equally biting criticism from them. There were sneers at the Commissioner's 'master-mind'. He was compared unfavourably with Whithair who was nominally still the Superintendent. This had begun even before his appointment when *The Times* told its readers, 'The Commissioner would not, as Mr Whithair did, take his horse and ride the whole day through the City, looking after the police.' Harvey had proposed to keep him as his superintendent, but the Police Committee told him that this could only be a temporary measure, until he could be compensated for the service he had rendered in establishing the original force of 500 men. His appointment had been made under the Act of Common Council of 7 November 1838 and was not requisite under the new Act of Parliament which vested the control and management in the Commissioner.[50] But because he was still their officer and he had their support, the Court of Aldermen took the opposing view and implied that they would veto any other choice for superintendent.[51] Harvey played for time. He would neither recognise Whithair's appointment nor would he appoint a superintendent.

He was exasperated still more by the seeming unwillingness of the Police Committee to control the clerks of the civil department, who were appointed by them, and over whom Harvey had no control. The office was split into two opposing factions between Thomas Wood, Harvey's personal secretary, and one of the clerks George Payne. Payne was a favourite with the Police Committee but he was heartily disliked by Harvey. This dislike deepened still more when the Police Committee tried to force him to take Payne as his personal secretary by designating him Clerk No. 1 and Wood Clerk No. 2. Harvey would not recognise the grading. But Payne ignored this and similar rebuffs, and his insolence only increased, as it became more obvious that the Police Committee would do nothing to check the endless 'jarrings and bickerings' between himself and Wood. Eventually Harvey could stand him no more. He stationed a constable outside Payne's office and locked the door on him. He was ordered to take him back. He refused. His letter of explanation is only a partial one:

Shortly after my accession to this office it became necessary – and it was an occasion likely to be of frequent occurrence – to have some business transacted on the Sunday by the clerks, to which Mr Payne demurred upon the ground of religious scruples. Such scruples, honestly entertained, were calculated to elicit my respect, and though I felt their prevalence might be prejudicial to a service, whose weekly work is seven days long, I cheerfully abstained from pressing the business upon him, trusting that the occasional inconvenience would be abundantly compensated by the steady influence of so pure an example.

Subsequently a complaint was made to this office by the Surgeon of the Force, and his wife, that their female servant, a young woman of really unpretending character, had been grossly insulted at the Chief Office, in open day, before a considerable number of officers and men. The complainant and her master appeared before me, from whose evidence it appeared, that the young woman came to the office, daily, with the sick list report, and that, upon one occasion, the most unbecoming remarks and overtures were made to her by an officer on duty, which were followed up by a coarse, personal, and to her very repulsive, salutation by Mr Payne. To soothe the irritation of offended modesty – to assure the master and mistress that their servant would be protected from similar acts of rudeness – and as an example to the force, the officer was allowed to retire from the service. Had Mr Payne been a member of the force he would have shared the fate of the officer; as it was, he was merely reminded of his religious scruples! After this it was found desirable that a book should be kept by the secretary in which every officer of the civil dept., at the Chief Office, should insert his name *over* or *under* a line drawn daily for that purpose, as he might come to the office before or after 9 o'clock, in the morning. In this book Mr Payne thought fit to enter some opinions of his own – conduct under any circumstances to be deprecated but rendered most reprehensible from their impertinent spirit. For this act of conduct Mr Payne was admonished, with an intimation that a repetition of bad conduct would be differently dealt with. Such an act occurred.

Papers were given out with an express direction that they should be signed by the secretary, which order Mr Payne studiously contravened, signing the papers himself under a designation repudiated by the Commissioner; (i.e. secretary) and to conceal the fact, and to effect his purpose, gave directions to a constable to deliver the papers without the knowledge of the Secretary, and when the constable was challenged for his conduct and asked for the papers, he said he had delivered them, having the papers at the time in his pocket. There was reason to believe that this act of evasion was also known to Mr Payne. The constable who so acted was reduced in his pay and Mr Payne was suspended.

I have now complied with the request of the committee by sending a written statement of the particular causes of offence and my opinion remains unchanged – that the appointment of Mr Payne to any office, at least in connection with the Police, was calculated to impair its authority by giving countenance to hypocrisy, indecency, prevarication and official insubordination and to set at naught the judgement of the Commissioner.[52]

Harvey would not take him back. And he insisted on having some control over the clerks of the civil department. The Police Committee would not agree, and eventually the City Solicitor had to intervene to break the deadlock. Meanwhile, Harvey replaced the clerks with policemen. The City Solicitor suggested that, although the Court of Common Council could not give up their rights of 'election' and 'dismissals' of these clerks, they could vest in the Commissioner the power to 'nominate' and 'suspend' them so that his authority over them would be 'as effectively his as if he had the absolute power of appointment in his own right'. He further suggested that this obviously would not end the 'jarrings and bickerings' between Wood and Payne and that a practical step would be to remove the civil department from the police headquarters. The Police Committee acted on this suggestion and ousted the Reserve from the room they were occupying at the time in the Guildhall. It was then converted into an office for Payne who was made the Police Receiver.

Whithair soon followed. In May 1841 he was made Keeper of the Giltspur Street Compter. As a final snub the Court of Aldermen told Harvey that Whithair had given the City better protection with fewer and more disciplined men. Harvey wrote back that as Whithair was still an officer of the Corporation perhaps he would tell him, through the Committee, the means whereby his men were constrained 'to perambulate their Beats singly and vigilantly instead of loitering and gossiping in couples in the Street'; he himself despaired 'of being able to make every Constable patrol his Beat for 9 hours solitary and speechless'.[53]

There were strong rumours that Harvey intended to resign because of the opposition he met with from the Court of Common Council and the Aldermen. The tensions between them were further exacerbated by his publicly repeated statements that the situation of the City Police would not improve until they were controlled by the Home Office. He found his job unpalatable and distasteful to a gentleman, and he made no secret of his wish to re-enter politics. There were strong rumours that he had his eye on the Chief Bailiffship of Southwark which would have made this possible and which was also estimated to be worth £2000 per annum to its possessor.[54]

The Police Committee ignored his repeated requests for stationery, candles and other basic necessities. Harvey warned that unless the relations between them improved 'serious inconveniences must, and indeed do, arise to the prejudice of the Public interests'.[55] He could not pay for cleaners and so he used probationer constables instead – they wore a P on their collar for the first month – to clean Old Jewry. In his spare time the office messenger doubled as Harvey's servant. He wore a plain coat with his police trousers when he was in the house and he waited at table. *Punch* later punned, 'On enquiry it turned out that the fellow cared little for the Harveys, but had an immense attachment to the Whittles.' It was also part of his duties to patrol the courtyard in uniform and chase away those constables who tried to creep down the basement steps to get at the females in the Commissioner's kitchen.

Notwithstanding 'the querulous carpings and ludicrous conceit which ever and anon break out amongst a miserable minority of muttering magistrates',[56] his handling of the force was not openly criticised until December 1845 when he was told that Alderman Copeland was instigating an inquiry into his handling of the police. He was doubly delighted because it told him that the hook which he had 'just cast into the sea of Chancery had caught the Jonah of the "potteries" '.[57] At this time Copeland was a director and Harvey was a shareholder in the Royal North of Spain Railway Company. At the first shareholders' meeting they had recently clashed when Harvey had moved for an adjournment of a few days to test the accuracy of certain statements that had been made by the directors that the scheme was impractical; his motion had been overruled by the 'terror of the threat' that if his amendment was carried the remaining assets would be forthwith transferred to Madrid. Harvey had immediately threatened to file a bill in Chancery if his money was not returned to him; and it was to stop him carrying out this threat, so he alleged in a letter to *The Times*, that had caused Copeland within a week of receiving his solicitor's letter to take the first steps to instigate an enquiry into his handling of the police.

Copeland's charges were partly investigated by the Police Committee in March 1846 and in more detail by the General Purposes Committee in November of the same year. Copeland was not present at the last hearing, having been called away instead to Winchester to the deathbed of his son. He buried him on the same day that the committee made their report dismissing the charges. Copeland was dissatisfied with the committee's findings and he continued to press for a more detailed investigation into his allegations. He kept the issue alive by waging an acrimonious correspondence with Harvey through the columns of *The Times*. He eventually persuaded one of the aldermen that if he would move for a committee of enquiry into the conduct of business at the Chief Office he would prove the truth of his allegations. This deflection of aim away from Harvey and into the workings of the City Police would have a ricochet effect, as Harvey's conduct was still left open to investigation without his accusers having to specify any charges or allege any misconduct on his part. Harvey had heard of no new charges except in 'that vague sort of rumour which constitutes the atmosphere of Guildhall'.

Because there were no tangible charges the chairman of the select committee compared the work of the committee when it was appointed to 'a sort of fishing bill in the Court of Chancery to find out whether there is any ground for a charge.'[58] Copeland was asked to reduce his charges to writing for a basis for the committee to work on. He hurriedly did so and the chairman forwarded a copy of this 'very crude document', as Copeland described his own work, to Harvey without indicating in any way that it was from the committee. Harvey denied that Copeland had any right to send him a list of questions to be answered, and when they met for the first time on 8 February 1847 he told the committee that he considered the paper a 'nullity'. The committee therefore adopted it as their own and loosed Copeland at Harvey.

The fact that the committee was able to investigate the charges at all was only possible with Harvey's consent. If he had insisted he could have confined them to finance, which was all their limited powers empowered them to investigate. But in spite of letting them search his papers and cross-examine whom they like, he clearly feared that he was facing a possible repetition of the Benchers hearing of more than a quarter of a century before. Before he would answer any questions he insisted on being given a copy of the shorthand-writers' notes. He would not let the committee keep the only copy to be used just as it suited individual purposes.

The committee investigated Harvey's use of policemen as his private servants, his plan to redeem pawnbrokers' pledges to provide a fund for the men, his methods of fining, disciplining and the disbursement of gratuities, his railway interests. Inspector Todhunter's marriage (Copeland accused Harvey of condoning immorality), his use of a milk jug from the Lost Property Stores, his similar use of an umbrella when it was raining, his 'plundering' of a supernumerary of part of his wages, and his failure to pay the station women their expenses. Eventually the mover of the enquiry swore that if he had known that he was going to hear this desultory sort of thing he would never have listened to Copeland. Like the rest of the committee he had thought that there was a clear set of charges to be heard and not that the investigation would be a 'vindictive charge setting one man against another for the sake of destroying him'. Harvey with considerable justification accused Copeland of talking up evidence, of 'higgling' with discharged constables, and of going to the stations and throwing out hints that if the policemen's jobs were jeopardised by what they told him then he could find them work. He arrogantly refused to have his character established by the constables of his force and, except for his accuser, he completely swung the committee behind him. When they came to make their report the committee wrote that the result 'entitled the Commissioner to a more favourable consideration than had previously been entertained', and they dismissed the charges as frivolous. Copeland still would not let go, and a few months later he fully justified the remark that had been hurled at him by one of the committee that he had 'a pursuing sort of spirit'[59] when he pressed for an investigation into Harvey's conduct at a Marylebone election. Harvey had discontentedly flung himself back into the political arena and had overwhelmingly been nominated as the Liberal candidate for Marylebone. But instead of resigning his office, as he had promised his supporters, he had to make the humiliating decision to stand down again the same week because of his dependence on his salary and the subsequent shortage of income which would have prevented him from

Constable's uniform before 1865

The changeover to the helmet was in 1865. The style and the shortened tunic indicates that this photograph was taken some years later

201a Bishopsgate (the old watchhouse and original Bishopsgate police station after conversion into a shop), 1867

14. *Execution of the five pirates of the 'Flowery Land' ship, 22 February 1864, with a strong force of City policemen surrounding the scaffold*

15. *The hangman Calcraft's shop sign*

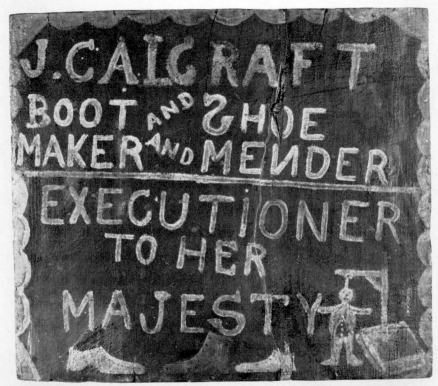

J. CALCRAFT
BOOT AND SHOE
MAKER AND MENDER
EXECUTIONER
TO HER
MAJESTY

taking his seat. Copeland was clearly trying to revive a dead issue, and the Court of Aldermen would not listen to his plea. Finally he was persuaded to let the matter drop by the view that prevailed in the Court of Aldermen that by first offering himself as a parliamentary candidate and then by resigning in favour of his present condition Harvey had merely verified the old adage that 'Brag was a good dog, but Holdfast was a better'.[60]

The committee, besides dismissing the charges, also ratified two earlier reports of the Court of Aldermen that Harvey's salary was too low and should be increased to £1000 per annum; they also recommended that he should be allowed to reside out of the City at a distance not exceeding six miles from the Royal Exchange, and that he should be given a further £200 per annum in lieu of residence. This was so unexpected and so controversial that the Court of Common Council ordered the report to lie on the table. The following year Harvey was given his first and only increase of £200 per annum. Harvey became extremely embittered by this as the years went by, since both he and his legal advisers believed that the Police Committee could have made their recommendations effective without seeking the approval of the Court of Common Council. Although there was nothing he could do about his salary he acted on the remainder of the resolution as if it had been adopted, and lived for long periods outside the City except when he was using Old Jewry as his occasional residence.

Whenever he lived there he did so reluctantly. It was cold, draughty, rat-infested and stank. The constable on duty in Lamb Court was frequently physically sick as a result of the mingled smells from the drains, the cook shop by the entrance, and from the neighbouring tallow-melting establishment. There was also a rapid changeover in outside domestics from the same cause. Harvey complained that he 'paid more for Doctors since I have been crowded in that house than I have ever paid in my life'. His doctors frequently insisted that he and his family leave the house for their health's sake, and it was on one such occasion as this that Harvey's wife slipped as she was crossing a road and broke the neck of the femur. The permanent effects left her crippled. She could not go up or come downstairs, or move about easily without mechanical aid. This embittered Harvey still more.[61]

G

In July 1855 he and his family moved completely out of Old
Jewry except for some rooms which Harvey retained for his
occasional use. He wrote giving his well-known reasons for
leaving to the Court of Aldermen. Both the General Purposes
Committee and the Police Committee to whom his letter was
referred agreed that the house was not a suitable one to live in.
But the final word was with the Court of Common Council and
they still insisted that Harvey should either resign or reside in
the City. They expressed their disapproval at the step he had
taken and in a strongly worded resolution to the Court of Aldermen asked them to enforce the condition of his appointment that
he should live in Old Jewry. The Court of Aldermen would only
agree to forward a copy of this resolution to Harvey and this
impasse was still unbroken the following year when the aldermen's stand was further reinforced by a condemnatory report of
the building from the City Police Surgeon and the City Architect.
By this time Harvey had made his return even more unlikely
by handing over some of his rooms, including his dining-room
and drawing-room, to the detectives for offices.[62]

The detective's *annus mirabilis* was 1857. The retirement of
the Reserve Inspector, Adam Spary, left Harvey free to finalise
the breach between the detectives and the Reserve, and to form
them into separate departments. This was long overdue. His
detectives, he had boasted the previous year, had a 'European
reputation'. Inevitably they specialised in fraud, and earlier that
year, in March, they had brought the legendary 'Jim the
Penman' to trial. In the dock his occupation was insultingly given
as labourer. In fact, besides his talents as a forger or 'shofulman',
James Townsend Saward was also a barrister of the Inner Temple.

His basic materials had been the blank and cancelled cheques
he bought from burglars and thieves. His preliminary move
would be to gauge the worth of the business or the individual
they had been stolen from and to calculate the biggest amount
that could be drawn on their account without the bank becoming
suspicious. He had three accomplices – Henry Attwell, William
Hardwicke and James Anderson. One of these would next hire
some lodgings in a false name. He would also hire a manservant
who would be sent to the bank with the forged cheque. He in
turn would be followed to the bank by one of the remaining

accomplices, who would give the alarm if the cashier's suspicions were aroused and the manservant was detained. If, however, the cheque was cashed, the money was quickly shared out and changed, and the gang dispersed. For years Saward plundered the City banks in this manner. Various dupes were arrested but he was not caught.

Eventually a series of mistakes led to his arrest. A cheque upon a Yarmouth bank came into his hands. He sent Attwell and Hardwicke to Yarmouth where Attwell posed as Mr Attwood and Hardwicke posed as Mr Ralph. There they applied to different solicitors to write to supposed debtors of theirs in London. These letters were sent to an accommodation address and collected by Saward who was now in possession of the solicitors' signatures and could marry them to his stolen cheques. But before this could be done Attwell and Hardwicke had to be extricated without rousing suspicions. He therefore wrote back to the various solicitors complaining of the harshness of his creditor, but promising that the debts would be paid. Attwell and Hardwicke meanwhile joined him in London for a few days before going back to Yarmouth. While they were staying with him Saward remitted the money for his imaginary debts to the solicitors in Yarmouth. He then wrote to tell them that he had paid the money. He then made his first mistake. He bundled the solicitor's letters together and gave them to Attwell, who took them back with him to Yarmouth.

Hardwicke had been anxious to keep up appearances while he was in Yarmouth; while he was in London he had gone to Barclay's bank and paid in £250 to the credit of another of his aliases, Mr Whitney. Unfortunately he had forgotten to pay it in to the credit of his Yarmouth alias, Mr Ralph, and the money was sent down to the credit of Mr Whitney. When Mr Ralph went to receive his money in Yarmouth the bank told him that the only money they had in their hands for that sum had been placed to the credit of Mr Whitney. Hardwicke wrote to Saward in London asking him to intervene to have the matter rectified, but the bank refused to pay the money over except to Mr Whitney. Hardwicke's behaviour in Yarmouth by now had aroused the suspicions of the bank, and both he and Attwell were arrested. In Attwell's lodgings the local police found the bundle of

solicitor's letters. A letter from Saward explaining the incident
at Barclay's bank also fell into their hands but, hearing of the
arrests, he fled. The case was then passed to the City detectives,
two of whom, Moss and Huggett, spent the next three months
in hunting for 'Jim the Penman'. Finally, on Boxing Day, they
tracked him to an Oxford Street public house. Huggett went in
to flush him out while Moss waited outside. Moss presently saw
a door being opened rather gently. He pushed it open and saw
Saward who tried unsuccessfully to bluff his way out.

The main prosecution witnesses against him were Hardwicke
and Attwell, who had already been convicted and sentenced to
transportation for life, and Anderson, who was tried with him.
In spite of a prosecution plea that Anderson had been a mere tool
in Saward's hands, both men were sentenced to transportation
for life.[63]

The long-overdue suppression of the Forrester brothers, John
and Daniel, soon followed. Both had long-established and well-
deserved reputations as thief-takers, but because of their
privileged position as constables attached to the Marshal's office
at the Mansion House they had effectively hamstrung the
workings of the detective department by their ability to select or
reject cases as they pleased. Harvey complained to a parliamentary committee in 1854,

> The practice acts very perniciously; it acts unjustly to the public
> and the police force. If a man goes there, the question is asked, What
> can I do for you? He says, I have lost my watch. You had better go
> down and see the police, is the reply, and he is turned over to our
> men. Supposing it is a forgery of £1000, he is told, Step in sir, and
> he is immediately attended to. These officers are amenable to
> nobody, and the consequence is that the system acts very pre-
> judicially upon the minds of our men, because they fancy that the
> cream of the cases is lapped up by other persons.[64]

In December 1857 the *Morning Advertiser* published a
detailed breakdown of the high fees that Henry Forrester, John
and Daniel's nephew, had charged for a trans-Atlantic chase
lasting 144 days. The item was headed 'A Detective's little bill'.
The *Morning Chronicle* had also picked up the same story. Harvey
forwarded both newspapers to the aldermen with a letter asking

for the suppression of 'the eminent City Firm' of John and Daniel Forrester. The General Purposes Committee was asked to investigate and to report whether they should be placed under the control of the Commissioner or granted a pension. John had been attached to the Mansion House for forty-one years and Daniel for thirty-seven; they were sixty-five and fifty-nine respectively. The Committee recommended that they should be retired on their official salary of £150 a year each 'so long only as they discontinue to be sworn officers of this City'.[65]

The detectives' elation at the sudden upsurge of work that followed their suppression was tempered by the tragedy that ended the year, the murder of one of them, Charles Thain.

Thain had been sent to Hamburg to follow and arrest Christian Sattler an 'ill looking fellow of dark complexion, and with a strong squint in the left eye'. He was a Frenchman who had joined the German Legion and had been stationed at Shorncliffe for nearly two years where he had attained the rank of quarter-master. In 1857 he was committed to Wisbech gaol for stealing a parcel of baby linen. About a week before his discharge he worriedly asked the chief warder how was he to live when he was released, as being a foreigner the English would not give him work. The warder told him that he would not be allowed to starve in a Christian country and that he must ask for relief. This Sattler swore that he would not do. 'He then said he would steal if he could not get employment, and if anyone tried to prevent or to apprehend him he would shoot him like a dog.'

He was discharged from prison on 28 October 1857. Five days later he stole a carpet-bag containing some clothing, brushes, razors, a gold pin, a mackintosh cloak and a considerable sum of bank-notes. He pawned the mackintosh cloak in Cambridge, and with one of his twenty-pound notes he bought a six-guinea watch. The owner of the carpet-bag was a City stockbroker and when it was learned that Sattler had gone to London this information was passed to two City detectives, William Jervis and Charles Thain. They traced the wanted man to the Spread Eagle in Gracechurch Street, only to find that he had fled to Hamburg. Thain went after him and nothing more was heard until 24 November when Harvey received a telegram, 'Send immediately to the ship Caledonia, at St. Katharines Wharf,

London, three men, Sergeant Thain having been shot by the prisoner Christian Sattler'.

Thain with his prisoner had boarded the *Caledonia* on 21 November. As Sattler came on board he complained of the handcuffs which were too tight. Thain had promised him that he would take them off when he was locked up on board but the captain insisted otherwise. Thain had no option to obey, but even though this was explained to Sattler he was furious and swore 'that Thain had broken faith with him – he had not kept his word as a gentleman, and he would shoot him or any other man like a dog who broke faith with him'. Thain adjusted the handcuffs as well as he could and the two men were locked in the same cabin together. On the second day out Thain had to leave his prisoner for about fifteen minutes unguarded. While he was out of the cabin Sattler wrenched a lamp iron from the hull and forced open his chest which, contained, among other things, the pistol he had bought to kill a man in Hamburg who had cheated him of £25. With some difficulty, as he was still handcuffed, he loaded the pistol with a heavy charge of powder and three balls. He then sat down on the folding-stool by his berth and waited. Thain came back about fifteen minutes later, and as he stooped over his bunk to put his cape down Sattler fired into his chest.

A passenger outside heard the shot and burst open the door. He saw that the cabin was full of smoke and that Thain was holding on to his prisoner. Other passengers came to his assistance and held on to Sattler while Thain went to the captain for medical help. Sattler was roughly handled by the passengers. Some American seamen wanted to lynch him. 'Some were for hanging him, some for stretching him and some for throwing him overboard.' The ship was without a doctor; it was two days before it landed and Thain could be hurried to Guy's hospital. He could not be operated on without danger to his life and at 1.30 am on 4 December 1857 he died.

Sattler was tried and sentenced to death. As he stepped on to the scaffold just before eight o'clock on the morning of 9 February 1858 he saw the ring of City policemen, Thain's colleagues, holding back the crowd from the scaffold. He bowed to the crowd, once towards Giltspur Street and once towards Ludgate

Hill, before turning to the hangman and asking that the cap should not be pulled over his eyes. The hangman was William Calcraft whose shop sign reputedly read 'Bootmaker and Executioner to Her Majesty'. He was fond of children, gardening and animals and favoured a short drop. As a rule his victims were still conscious after the drop had fallen and when he climbed on to their backs to strangle them to death. In this instance there was no need. Sattler was lucky. He died almost immediately. 'Very soon after the drop had fallen Calcraft proceeded to pull the cap over the face of the criminal, and the crowd supposing it had been left off in the first instance by carelessness, set up a tremendous yell. The body was cut down at nine o'clock.'[66]

10

The End of an Era

Instead of the old flower-pot tile,
The helmet is a better style.
It has more room and cap-ac-i-ty,
To hold cold mutton or rabbit pie.

Song: 'The Brand New Bobbies'[1]

IN 1859 *The Times* portentously announced that for the first
time within living memory some of the numerous porters and
beadles of the Bank of England had actually been seen sweeping
the filthy footpaths outside. The cause was unknown but it was
rumoured that the reason that they had never been swept before
was to 'prevent respectable men from engaging in designs to
break into the Bank'.[2] There were even bets on the Stock
Exchange that the Mansion House would succeed to the dignity
of having the filthiest footways in the City. Walking was made
more difficult by the combsellers, dogsellers and acrobats who
crowded the pavements, and by the barrows lining the kerbs.
Street vendors jostled the east end of the Royal Exchange with
baskets of fruit, and crippled the shop trade nearby. There were
angry scenes in the streets. Opinion was sharply divided on the
barrow trade. Some of the aldermen thought it would be as
reasonable to complain of a gentleman's carriage standing in the
street. The shopkeepers were supported by the great banking
firms of Lombard Street who memorialized the Lord Mayor, and
the problem was passed to the police. The street sellers were
purged. In one swoop no fewer than forty people were taken up,
most of them young boys 14–20 years of age, and some young
women. They were charged with selling on the footway 'apples
and pears, nuts, children's toys, gutta percha whips, cakes and
other articles, exposed in baskets or in trays, and straps and

sticks'. Some defended themselves by saying that they were only trying to make an honest living, and that having no person to whom they could apply for an honest character, they found it difficult to find other kinds of work; one woman spoke on behalf of her son who, she said, was the sole support of herself and eleven children who were on the verge of starvation, her husband being confined in hospital. He was discharged. The mother of a respectable-looking boy who had been taken up for selling straps, believing he was engaged in an honest living, pleaded hard to have him let off; he was fined. Some were fined, some were cautioned and some were committed to prison for three days; in cases where the prisoner had previously been charged with a similar offence the fine or imprisonment was doubled. The alderman told them that street selling was the worst profession that young boys and girls could follow.

> He did not mean to say that any of them were now dishonest but they would be sure to become so sooner or later. There were plenty of ways of getting an honest living, if they would but try to find them out and conduct themselves properly. To one woman who said in her defence, that she had got six little children to maintain, and that she had no other way of earning a livelihood, the Alderman said she had better go to the union and take her children there, for no one need starve in this country. He then discharged her with a caution.[3]

The streets were similarly obstructed. In most instances, the street widths had not been changed for more than 200 years. In 1866 it was reported that only 168 streets were of sufficient width to admit one line of traffic, only 101 which allowed two, while the remaining 70 afforded room for three lines or more.[4] The situation was aggravated by the monster waggons that crawled through the streets with their ropes and hooks for letting enormous barrels down into tavern cellars, by the draymen quarrelling, by the carters who tried to exact the work of two horses from one, by the omnibuses and by the cabs that had to loiter through the streets because of the infrequency of cab stands. In 1844 Harvey had tried to stop the omnibuses from similarly loitering by stationing a line of policemen from Temple

Bar to Aldgate to hurry them on. This had worked for a time but eventually he had had to abandon it not only because of the manoeuvres of the omnibus proprietors but because of censures from the bench. Stands were provided in various parts of the City but they were always objected to. St Mary at Hill was complained of because it was crowded with carts from the fish market and littered with stinking hampers and boxes. Another complainant objected to the omnibus stand opposite his house in Gracechurch Street and of the Greenwich and Kent Road Omnibuses that were allowed to stand there all day. He wrote to the aldermen, 'They cause me and my patients very great annoyance; at all hours of the day they prevent vehicles from approaching the house; and in wet and cold weather my lobby is filled with passengers with Boxes, carpet-bags and babies waiting for the different omnibuses, and patients have great difficulty in gaining admittance to my surgery. The bawling or "touting" of the Conductors is sometimes almost deafening.'[5] When an attempt had been made on an earlier occasion to remove one of these cart stands one of the aldermen had grumbled that people ought to put up with a little inconvenience instead of wishing to make the City like Berkeley or Grosvenor Square. 'Now, he liked to see carts and waggons crowding after each other through the thoroughfares. It showed that money was stirring as it used to be of old.'[6] The worst blocks were on London Bridge, and in 1855 Harvey undertook to clear the congestion at the request of the Court of Common Council.

Apparently the Court of Common Council was instigated to make the request following a conversation between a doctor and an alderman, who were travelling together, and who missed their train from London Bridge because of a 'block' by a Pickford's van, a costermonger's barrow, a disabled dust-cart and a brewer's dray.[7] The doctor suggested that to solve the problem 'I'd make Pickford follow the donkey, the brewer follow Pickford, keeping close to the left hand kerb, and the right hand kerb kept clear for the slow going traffic from the Surrey side; the midway would then be open for omnibuses and cabs; thus securing four lines of traffic; a luggage train and two express lines in the middle.' Possibly this story is apocryphal but certainly this was the system used. It proved so successful that Harvey was

asked to extend it to King William Street and Gracechurch Street
in 1859. For the first time he went into details of the problems
that arose. The public were warned by advertisements in newspapers and on boards that the scheme was to be extended, and to
ensure that there was a strict observance of the regulations three
sergeants and twenty-one constables were stationed along a 400-
yard stretch of roadway; but by the end of the third week they
found that the drivers of the heavy vehicles had become so
accustomed to their signals that the number of men could be
reduced by a third to two sergeants and fourteen constables.
With practice they found that they could achieve the same result
with six constables only, by stationing them at points where the
most frequent obstructions occurred, and which did not prevent
the omnibuses and cabs from setting down their passengers at
the kerb. These vehicles had been confined to the fast offside lane,
and because it would have seriously interfered with the slower-
moving traffic on the nearside they had been compelled to set
their passengers down in the middle of the road. The hazards for
those getting off were equally as great for those getting on;
women in hooped skirts and top-hatted men had to force their
way through a steady stream of slow-moving waggons and
champing horses. There were complaints from the shopkeepers
that, because of the anxiety of finding and hailing these vehicles,
people had not the leisure to wait in or about their shops and
become customers. They asked for the fast-moving lane to be
switched to the nearside, but Harvey rejected this as impractical.[8]

The scheme slowly involved the police throughout the City.
Some of the street widenings that took place before 1870 eased
some of their problems. The steep climb that the condemned
carts used to make up Holborn Hill disappeared with the building
of the world's first fly-over, Holborn Viaduct. Farringdon Street
below it was linked with New Bridge Street and with Ludgate
Circus, which was built on surplus railway-land, to form part of
the north–south route from King's Cross to Blackfriars Bridge.
In 1865 the Corporation freed Southwark Bridge for more traffic
by buying it and by abolishing the halfpenny tolls. Cannon Street
was widened and extended eastwards to King William Street,
which had been opened in 1835 as part of a north access-route to
London Bridge. Moorgate was widened in 1840. 'Blocks' were

still frequent, often because of the cabs and omnibuses that
meandered through streets like ships without helms in search of
fares. The drivers still clung to the old routes even when the new
routes were open to them because they were more profitable.
Some indication of the problems this caused can be deduced
from a census Harvey took between 12.20 pm and 1.20 pm on
25 March 1862, which showed that 291 omnibuses went through
Cheapside while in the same period only 2 went through New
Cannon Street. Obviously this could not continue. In 1857 the
Court of Aldermen unsuccessfully memorialised the Inland
Revenue Commissioner to make it compulsory upon the face of
their licences that omnibuses and other public vehicles should go
through the new streets.[9] He had no power to order this to be
done and the Court of Common Council were unwilling to give
Harvey any more powers 'little less than despotic' to interfere
with the trade of London. But, as *The Times* pointed, the City was
more or less in a state of siege, and something had to be done.
When they did introduce a bill into Parliament regulating the
routes to be followed, defining the height and breadth of loads,
of the times for loading and unloading waggons, of the breadth
of vehicles between the wheels, and of the hours heavy traffic
would be permitted to pass through the streets, it roused passion-
ate opposition from the trading interests who viewed it as the
destruction of their trade. But the nature of this trade was
changing as well. Some of the City's oldest professions were
being squeezed out with the more familiar of its landmarks like
Temple Bar. Newgate market and Smithfield market in its old
form both disappeared; the latter was replaced by a dead-meat
market. The Giltspur Street compter was closed in 1854 and
demolished in 1855. Holloway Gaol, with its massive feudal
frontage modelled on Warwick Castle, replaced Bridewell as the
City's House of Correction. Newgate still stood, but its days were
numbered. In 1868 the last man was hanged in front of its walls,
and at the end of the century it closed for ever.

Inevitably the rebuilding and the Government-sponsored
schemes like the new route from Blackfriars to the Mansion
House and the extension to the Thames Embankment, while
they improved the City, also drastically reduced the amount of
living-space. The overcrowding became even more acute, and

together with the poor pay Harvey was hard pressed to keep his
men. In a letter to the *Daily Telegraph* an ex-City policeman
offered both an explanation and a solution:

Who can expect a man of real intelligence, smart and active, to join
the force and walk the streets by day or night in all sorts of weather,
and do the disagreeable duty of police, for 20s per week, out of
which he must pay – being compelled to reside in the City – from
3s 6d to 6s a week rent for a back room up some dirty court, where
he and his wife and children are huddled together in a worse plight
than the commonest labourer? He must be content with only one
Sunday to himself out of four or five; he can never have a holiday
at holiday times. He must put up with all this and a thousand and
one other disagreeable matters, and all for 15s per week after the
rent is paid.

The fact is, Sir, an intelligent, active man would rather, if his
trade fails him, go to the docks or wharves, where he may earn from
2s 6d to 3s 6d a day, working less and more regular hours; where he
is more his own master; and where he may, if he sees anything
better, leave at a day's notice. Besides, when a young man joins the
force, should he happen to make a mistake, instead of his fault being
explained, he gets a frown, perhaps a fine, from his inspector, a
good snubbing from the sergeant, and he is laughed at by his
comrades, until he finds his duties very unpleasant, his berth an
unthankful one, his pay not at all equal to his position or expenses.
He gets tired and careless of his duties, and, instead of looking out
for thieves, is dividing his time between glasses of ale, inspectors,
drops of something 'short', sergeants, bits of cold mutton, and
superintendents.

The policeman's pay-night is Friday night in the City, and on
Wednesday or Thursday he finds the money running short, his
children are hungry after dinner, and even he himself cannot keep
his eyes off the cookshop windows. What is the result? Instead of our
worthy aldermen settling a breach of the law, I am afraid a shilling
or a sixpence often settles it. Another great fault in the police
system is, that an officer is never allowed to remain long on any
one beat. I was in the fifth division about two years, and during that
short time I don't think there is a single beat in that division, in all
about thirty, upon which I did not do duty; the result was, I obtained
a first-rate knowledge of the streets, lanes, courts, and alleys, but I
knew nothing of the inhabitants, or of the property left under my
care. Now, let the constable be paid 30s per week, and permit him

to reside where he may think proper; this will induce those who are in the force to try their utmost to keep in, and will also attract a better class of men to apply for the situation. Let the inspectors and sergeants receive a rise in proportion; we should then have inspectors more gentlemanly and sergeants better educated. Place the constable on a beat and tell him that so long as he conducts himself properly, and the property under his care is safely kept, he shall keep his beat, and on no account change him. He will then in a few months become acquainted with all persons residing on his beat, with those premises which are the weakest, those which contain the most valuable property, and those which contain property the most dangerous in case of fire. He will know at what time the house and places of business open and close, and who are the proper persons to open and close them. He will also know what places are left unoccupied at night, and where lights are left burning; and should he see a stranger hanging about, he will at once, without the slightest hesitation, be able to challenge him, and demand his business.

With good pay as an inducement, and a beat of his own, it would be a policeman's pride and endeavour to keep all things in proper order, and thereby keep his situation. He would scorn to take a bribe, and, instead of his time being occupied in looking after his superiors and what he can make, it would be entirely taken up in the careful performance of his duties.[10]

In 1853, the City Police and two divisions of the Metropolitan police, 'D' and 'T', took the previously unprecedented step of petitioning their respective Commissioners for an increase of pay.[11] The men of 'D' and 'T' divisions sent round robins to Sir Richard Mayne. Except for the men who were either sick or on duty, the City police publicly met in the Temperance Hall, Blackfriars, and sent twelve delegates, two from each division, to see Harvey. He listened to them sympathetically. He promised to present their claim to the Court of Aldermen and the Court of Common Council and touched on some of the other points that had been raised at the meeting, notably his alleged preference for promoting military men. He confessed that so far from military men finding favour with him, he feared he sometimes yielded to an adverse prejudice for he was far from considering mere military discipline and stolid obedience to orders, never looking to the right nor left, suitable qualifications for promotion. He unflatteringly concluded 'Soldiers were expected to act; constables were expected to think as well as act. Soldiers were expected to be sober on duty; constables were expected to be sober at all times.'[12] The increases the Police Committee granted were small,* but the men were pleased and proposed buying Harvey a piece of plate. He was touched, but firmly rejected the suggestion when he considered that he might, and most probably would, have to punish or even dismiss at some future date some of the contributors.

However, the increase quickly proved inadequate, and within a few years Harvey was complaining yet again that his experienced men were resigning and, worse, he was having to replace them with men 'of inferior capacity, and whose first object, after the trouble of their training, is to quit the service'. The other reason why this was so, besides pay, was bad housing. Some police lodgings had been provided in Huggin Lane but the majority of the force was still living in slum tenements like St Anne's Blackfriars, where 134 families, with 283 children between them, only 76 of whom were over 10 years of age, lived in forty houses. In the week these children played in the courts, knocking doors, ringing bells and strewing the ground with rubbish; but on Sundays they relinquished them to the betting men from St Bride's Lane for gaming and who, before they began, always

*	Previous pay			From 1 Jan. 1854		
Inspectors of Reserve	£2	10s	0d	£2	15s	0d
Inspectors of Divisions	2	4	6	2	10	0
Sergeants	1	4	0	1	8	0
Detectives	1	5	0	1	10	0
1st class constables	1	2	0	1	3	0
2nd class constables	1	0	0	1	2	0

after a probation of one month

3rd class constables		19s	0d	£1	0s	0d
4th class constables		18	0	1	0	0
5th class constables		17	0	1	0	0

Future increases were always at a higher rate than the Home Office increases to the metropolitan police. This was always a source of grievance until the police rate was split between the Corporation and the Home Office in 1919. The higher rate attracted more recruits and eventually led to the height qualification being lifted to 5 feet 11 inches, the tallest in the country.

timed the constable over his beat so that they would know when to break off. Any woman who passed by was insulted.[13]

Outside the City small houses could be had for the rent that the men were now paying for one or two rooms. They asked for the restriction compelling them to live in the City to be lifted. The Police Committee warmly approved of the idea, but Harvey objected. His main objection was that if this request was granted indiscriminately to all the married men he would lose nearly five-sixths of the force and would have no reserve to call on in emergencies. Basically the problem was one of communication. The stations had only just been equipped in 1860 with the telegraph. The anxious Vestry Clerk of the Parish of Allhallows, Lombard Street, had insisted on a written undertaking that at any time after notice the police would remove their telegraph wires from his steeple. Each man if he was outside the City could only be contacted by another constable on foot. But Harvey also seems to have felt that off duty the men could not be trusted and that once free of his iron grip discipline would slacken. He proposed instead that the six existing stations should be replaced with three new station-houses, two of them at each end of the City, east and west of Old Jewry, and one not far from Guildhall, and having accommodation for the single men. He proposed also that a square of model houses should be built to house the married men and their families where they would have 'all the advantages of cheap residence, with good ventilation, water, gas, washing and drying conveniences, and a large central area as a playground for their children' and which would also give the force 'a never-failing reserve of men to meet serious emergencies'.[14]

Because of the difficulties of finding suitable sites, only a part of the plan was acted upon in his lifetime. The station that was built upon the east side of Bishopsgate was completed after his death. It had three floors, two rooms on the roof flats, a library and some accommodation for the married sergeants and single men. At the back was an infirmary with a dispensary, a surgeon's room, a waiting-room and four wards for fifty patients. The police surgeon was George Borlase Childs. He was married to an ex-London actress, Julia Hibbert, and the secret was well concealed from their children that she had once been on the stage — her only known role is Polly Peachum in *The Beggar's Opera*.[15]

She was five years older than him and they had been married for a similar period when he had been appointed surgeon in 1844. He was then twenty-eight years old and his youthful inexperience had contrasted sharply with his predecessor, Samuel Brand, who had been the surgeon to a mining company in South America before being appointed the surgeon to the Day Police in 1832. There had been unpleasant allegations that Childs had owed his appointment to parental influence and several of the other unsuccessful candidates had petitioned to have him removed. He was too sensitive, and ten years later he complained to a Parliamentary Select Committee that it was still being rumoured that he had only received his appointment because he was the son of one of the partners of an alderman.

In October 1861 he was asked to report generally upon the dress of the force.[16] He strongly recommended the substitution of the Britannia helmet for the top hat which let in water round the brim, easily became shapeless, and had a dirty greasy appearance from the perspiration that oozed through the soft porous material; the elastic chin-strap soon broke and the glazed-leather

tops either rose up or sunk in. He discarded the idea of using the cap which had already been substituted in some counties, in Kent and Hampshire, as not being 'handsome; it wants elevation, gives a mean slouching air to the wearer and affords no protection from external violence'. In spite of the strong feeling for change hats continued to be worn until 1865 when they were replaced by the broad-brimmed combed helmet that was then being worn by the Metropolitan Police. In 1864 a new-style black felt hat was tried and fitted with a helmet plate of a bronze garter with

the constable's number in the middle surmounted by the
City's dragon-wing crest. Eventually this was replaced by the
dragon crest that is worn today.[17] He condemned the coat as the
'relict' of a past age and again, referring to the counties, recommended the substitution of a tunic. Trousers, he suggested,
should be double-lined at the knee to ward off rheumatism and
the men issued with waterproof leggings. He also recommended
that each man on joining should be compelled to provide himself
with two flannel shirts, two pair of flannel drawers and two
jerseys, one of each to be produced at a monthly kit-inspection.
Childs's most damning remarks were reserved for the boot, as it
was then frequently made in London, and had a straight
inflexible sole and little or no instep. He wrote that this double
pressure from the unyielding sole and the lowness of the instep
not only destroyed the arch of the foot but threw an extra strain
on the muscles of the leg particularly on the Achilles tendon.

Besides crippled feet the main complaints were acute catarrh,
rheumatism, and stomach and bowel complaints. The average
length of service was four years. From 1852 to 1856 the number

of men who left the force from all causes amounted to 594, this
being about 54 more than the average strength of the entire
force for that period. The average length of service of those who
retired on pensions or gratuities in this period, as being unfit for
further service (injuries excluded), was 10 years 176 days. Of
those injured on duty and pensioned 7 years 182 days, and of
those who resigned without compensation 1 year 218 days. Childs
treated on average about thirty patients a day, and out of his
salary of £200 per annum he had to provide them with medicine,
strappings, lint, bandages and all other surgical and medical

necessities. This in effect meant that for his attendance and medicine he was remunerated less than eightpence per head.[18]

Harvey had found, on his appointment, 'many men already engaged, more or less undesirable from age and disorders, but who it would have been harsh to remove without some provision being made for them.' In 1848 some of these men still remained and 'after struggling many years with their growing infirmities' were 'no longer of any service whatever'. But, by the terms of the City Police Act, under no circumstances could a constable be superannuated, however long his service, who was under sixty years of age, unless he was physically incapacitated from discharging his duties, and then only if he had served with diligence and fidelity for fifteen years. Since the Act was only in the tenth year of its operation it was quite clear that none of these men were entitled to any allowance whatsoever unless they had been injured in the execution of their duty. The City Solicitor confirmed Harvey's interpretation, and only seven out of the twenty-two Childs had returned as unfit were entitled to any allowance. This was particularly harsh, as some of them had been in the Day Police as well almost from its inception and had served in the police from ten to fifteen years. Ironically, however, this situation had been foreseen by one of the marshalmen.

The marshalmen had always been privileged to serve all the City's summons and warrants; for each one they had served they had charged the public two shillings. As they had died off their places had been abolished and by 1839 there had only been one surviving marshalman, Henry Foster. In 1839 he had claimed the serving of all the police summonses as well, but Harvey had strongly challenged this, as the Metropolitan police everywhere served their own summonses and Harvey had wished to standardise his procedure with theirs. Foster's right to these fees had been undeniable, but eventually he had given way on condition that the fees were not paid over to Harvey or applied to the maintenance of the force but were formed into a new fund, under the control of the Court of Aldermen, and used for the relief of those policemen who became incapable from doing their duty, whether through violence, accident or sickness, over the next fifteen years, during which time the superannuation fund was to grow untouched.[19]

The Police Committee offered them either a lump sum of money to establish themselves in a business or in a trade or a small weekly allowance for a limited period of three years. The allowances were between 3s 6d and 7s 6d a week, and by themselves made living in the City impossible. Most of the men compounded for a lump sum and several of them, those whom Childs had diagnosed as having afflicted lungs, consumption and chest diseases, did so in the firm belief that they would be dead before the last weekly allowance was paid. William Oakley had cancer of the stomach and his chances of living were slight, but he was still alive fifteen years later, when he was sixty-five, and had struggled through as a watchman, though by then he was incapable of doing anything for himself. The others tried to open small businesses, most of them favouring either a greengrocer's or a chandler's shop, with varying degrees of success. In some cases they tried to fall back on their old trades such as leather-work or baking, but most of them were too old or too ill to be successful.[20]

The phrase Childs commonly used to describe them was 'Worn Out'. 'By the term "Worn Out" made use of in my certificates, I would wish to imply that such Officers and Constables are prematurely aged, and suffer from defective physical strength and other bodily infirmities. . . .'[21] These were the same men who, when they entered the force possessed, 'a high standard of health, and capable of undergoing a more than ordinary amount of physical exertion'. This premature ageing was largely blamed on the houses they were forced to live in and

on the stations. This was so generally understood that it was
widely believed by outsiders that the men's allowances were
given to them as compensation. There was ample justification for
such belief. In 1849, Station Sergeant John Mitchell petitioned:

I joined the City Police in February 1841, was promoted to Sergeant
in March 1845, and in May 1845 I commenced the duty of Station
Sergeant at Bishopsgate Street, where I continued 'till January
1848, when you was kind enough to give an order for me to be
transferred to Fleet Street Station, from my having complained to
the Superintendent that my health was seriously injured by the
very unhealthy situation of the Charge Room at Bishopsgate Street,
for besides being obliged to inhale the foul air, caused by the Gas
and want of ventilation, there was a water closet in the cellar
directly under the stool where I sat, and there being no ceiling to the
cellar, the most offensive smell used to come up between the boards,
also there were two more water closets in the cells within a few feet
of the desk I was obliged to write at, and the smell was frequently
most intolerable, from persons using them that were brought in
drunk, and if the window was opened to admit fresh air, there was
the Church Yard, and several graves just under the window, and
I sincerely believe that the above causes combined with my confined
position when on duty for 24 hours, with the loss of every other
night, during the last four years, has been the means of producing
such a general debility and weakness of my constitution, that I am
unfit to undertake any kind of employment to enable me to obtain
a living.[22]

This was no exaggeration. Most of them knew that when they
left they faced only poverty and misery in some cases aggravated
by debt. The fact that they did face this and were not compelled
to retire only serves to underline the truth of Child's phrase
'Worn Out'. Inspector Todhunter wrote,

With no trade nor profession nor business habits on which I can now
fall back what alas have I to look forward to to make up for any
deficiency of income? with a large and increasing family compelled
hitherto to reside in the City where rent is high and health is
vitiated I have been wholly unable out of my small salary to lay by
one penny towards what is hastening upon me and you will, Sir,
I am very confident plainly perceive that my confession in no sense

argues improvidence for my family, now, after three deaths, consisting of six young children with the daily expectation of a seventh, is and has been invariably depending on me for support nor is this all for I have an account for medical expenses to that family amounting to nearly £20 to which is to be added another on my own account for £19.–17–0 of which I have by monthly instalments cleared off £9 though how I am now to liquidate the first or the large balance of the other as God is my judge I know not and foresee in at least the latter case what will inevitably happen for I have a hard creditor to deal with who has from the first shown he will not forgo one shilling of his charges. [23]

He had to relinquish his literary pursuits and the sedentary life he had planned, to stave off this catastrophe. His sufferings grew worse and, five years after he had retired, he died on Christmas Eve 1862, aged fifty. His wife petitioned the Police Committee to grant her the allowance that had automatically stopped with his death as the creditors intended to seize the furniture and books if it was not paid.

The size of the allowances depended entirely on the recommendation Harvey made to the Police Committee. It was based on the number of reports that a man had against his name and was frequently grossly unfair as most of these were of a trivial nature and extended over the whole of his service. His remarks against each man's name were generally brief and to the point:

221 George Wardle. This man has a wife and three children. He has been a most useful member of the Detective force, the duties of which have seriously damaged his physical powers, as also his moral character. A weekly payment will alone be of any real benefit to him.

224 John Bunce. This man has a wife and five children; two are on his hands. His age is 58 and he unfit for work. The number of reports against him sadly weakens his claim to consideration. A small weekly payment is all that can be recommended.

261 John Townsend. The services of this man have been long and exemplary. His family relations are very unfortunate and such as render a weekly payment the only mode of compensation.

340 William Bowles. This man is 61 years old, and incapable of labour. His services have been long but not satisfactory. He has a sickly child and wife. A small weekly payment will alone be of service to him.

550 John Pickard. This man is a widower with one child. He stands very bad in the books; still the length of his services may perhaps induce the Committee to give him a trifle of money.[24]

Harvey soon disabused them of the belief that his recommendation was only a formality and that their long service and weekly contribution entitled them either to the allowance or to the return of their money. The first incident involved Cornelius Dolohunty. In 1857 Harvey sacked him after repeated warnings for drunkenness. His dismissal automatically lost him the allowance his seventeen years' service would have entitled him to. He was a popular man, and Harvey was petitioned by both the constables and the local tradesmen to reinstate him. The Police Committee also asked him to reconsider his decision but he refused presumably because it would have created a precedent and would have been bad for discipline. Dolohunty tried to find work but failed. He struggled through the winter living on charity. He begged Harvey to reinstate him or at least to recommend the Committee either to return his contributions or to give him an allowance. He ended his petition,

To avert this calamity and to save us from the horrors of absolute want, I earnestly entreat for the sake of my heart broken and afflicted wife, whose health has entirely given way under our heavy trials – for the sake of our innocent and helpless children, even now the objects of hunger and want – and for the sake of an aged and infirm parent, wholly dependent on me for support, that you will have compassion on us; and by doing what I am seeking at your hand (recommending my case specially to the Committee) save us from the evils which threaten to overwhelm us.[25]

The lesson was quickly rammed home. He forwarded with the petitions of two long-serving constables, Crocker and Spring, both of whom had nearly twenty years' service, a note that 'It is certainly most desirable, with a view to the efficient working of the force, that the officers and constables should understand that in the consideration of their claims good conduct has a guiding influence.' The Police Committee ignored the hint as the reports against them extended over a long time and were mainly trivial. Crocker had not had a report against him for the last six years. They were both awarded pensions, but the Court of Common Council refused to ratify them and made them payable for one year only. The whole force was thrown into a 'very serious gloom' and Harvey was only persuaded to change his mind after sixty or seventy of them had publicly protested at his harsh treatment.[26]

Injury payments were automatic but the amounts were too small to compensate the victims either for their injuries or their inability to work. Richard Gaul's injuries left him partially paralysed down the left side, deaf, suffering from violent head-aches, blinded in the left eye and with defective sight in the right. He was given fifteen shillings a week. John Hassett had been attacked by a mob on Fish Street Hill. He was beaten and left unconscious with fractured ribs and internal injuries. The permanent effects were convulsions and partial paralysis. He was given ten shillings a week.[27] The payments were equally small to police widows and only given out of charity. Small sums of five shillings and three shillings a week for widows with seven and five children were only meant to assist them until they could find more regular work charring, washing and needlework. Few of them, including the men, were spared 'the painful humiliating necessity of resorting for assistance to the last refuge, namely the Workhouse'.[28]

Conclusion

HARVEY died on 27 February 1863. He had retained much of his youthful vigour to the last. Little more than a fortnight before he had given a public reading of Addison's tragedy *Cato*. He became ill on Friday, 23 February. His symptoms from a carbuncle on the mouth were not alarming, but on the Sunday night his condition rapidly worsened. Within a short time erysipelas supervened. Scarlet patches and innumerable small blisters flowered over his face and scalp. His features became distorted, and the eyes had to close beneath the weight of the thickened lids. His body became weakened still more by a high temperature. Feverishly he struggled with the pain until the Tuesday morning. He died at 6.30 am. He was seventy-seven years old.

'The deceased gentleman', wrote the *Daily Telegraph*,

had held the post of Chief Commissioner of the City Police since the establishment of the force in 1839, and his appointment to that office, whatever truth may be in the assertion that he owed it to his formidable power of oratory in the House of Commons, and his antagonism to the government of the day, was soon justified by the admirable discipline which he enforced and maintained in his control of this large body of men, and still more by his organisation of their numbers.

The City press was critical but more frank. Their assessment came nearer the truth.

When a man is compelled to leave his chosen path, but takes with him the same singleness of purpose, which he would have shown in a career of his own choosing, he becomes entitled to the approbation of all who are concerned in the issue, and we can say of the late Mr Harvey that he laboured earnestly in an occupation that was never exactly suited to his temperament and inclinations.

The Court of Aldermen and the Court of Common Council felt only relief according to Sir Henry Smith, the third Commissioner. He wrote,

> Harvey, no longer able to fight in the Westminster arena, devoted the remainder of his life to fighting, socially and professionally, his masters, the Court of Aldermen. He cared for nobody, no, not one; would leave the City when he chose – on one occasion he absented himself for three weeks, without even leaving his address. He lived in the Old Jewry, and died there, at enmity, I may say, with everyone.

His iron pride would not permit anything else, not even in his later years when much of the initial ill-will towards the police force had been dispelled. For over half a century his life had been spent in opposition, and by then he had become too old and too suspicious to change. His pride was a mask for his frustrated ambitions; from these there was no release, not even in age. He always hoped that some day events would somehow make it possible for him to re-enter political life. Only his threatened bankruptcy had severed him from the House of Commons and had forced him to stoop to pick up a pittance which in his younger days he would not have hesitated to have thrown before the electors of Colchester. Of his humiliating dependence on his £800 salary he does not seem to have been aware. Not, at least, until 1847, when it forced him to withdraw his nomination as one of the prospective Liberal candidates for Marylebone, a humbling experience for such a proud man after he had publicly accepted the nomination that same week and at the same time had promised that he would resign the office of Commissioner. It was this withdrawal and final realisation of his dependence on his salary that at last condemned him to, thought not to accept uncomplainingly, the 'uncongenial occupation in which his peculiar abilities found no fitting sphere . . .'.

Initially much of the hostility was for the office and not for the man. Parliament's insistence that a Commissioner had to be

appointed meant that a great deal of opposition had to be overcome. Possibly much of this opposition would have disappeared
if Harvey had allowed the wards to retain the influence over the
police that they had once had over the watch. Though this would
have placed his successors, if not Harvey himself, in a position
similar to that in which some police chiefs are placed in some
states of America today:

> Sometimes, a mayor appoints a Commissioner or Director of Public
> Safety. Sometimes, one is elected by local inhabitants. Frequently,
> he is given power to appoint a chief of police under him, although
> he is usually a man with no knowledge of police requirements.
> Irrespective of the manner of their appointment, Chiefs of Police
> have little or no security of office and are frequently discharged or
> disgraced and dismissed as innocent victims of the vicissitudes of
> party politics. To maintain themselves in office, they require the
> qualities of a political party tactician far more than ability as a leader
> of police. Appointments of men under him, disciplinary action, and
> promotions are often all firmly in the hands of the mayor or
> Director of Public Safety to whom he is indebted for his own
> appointment. Both he and all the members of his force are often
> obliged to be aware that their careers and continued employment
> depend wholly on loyalty to 'bosses', of the political machine and
> other kinds, and not on good service to the public.[1]

This point is worth stressing. Nowadays we assume that the
police force is an impartial body. In Harvey's day this was not so.
Nor was there any guarantee that the police would be impartial.
Harvey's success lay in the fact that he successfully achieved this
impartiality by breaking the City of London police out of the

mould and away from the old system of patronage and political control. But he achieved his success, not because of his understanding of the problem, but for the wrong reasons. At no point in his letters does he show that he was aware of the motives activating the wards to behave as they did. Obviously he realised that he was involved in a power struggle, but he could only see the issues involved – Payne, his salary and Old Jewry – as personal issues dictated by dislike towards him. This is not really surprising since his career had been warped by similar personal issues. Andrew was always to be a bitter memory. Probably the wards could have obtained the degree of control they sought if they had dealt with Harvey as the equal he rightly considered himself to be. Mistakenly they dealt with him as paid employee and insulted his pride. No deadlier insult to such a proud man could have been devised than when they gave their support to his clerk and openly urged him on to challenge the Commissioner's authority. From this point on the final breach in their relationship was inevitable. After it had become a fact, Harvey insisted always on a rigid demarcation of authority and strict adherence to the terms of the Police Act. His inflexibility, in fact, was a means of protecting himself, but sometimes it was no more than an extension of his injured pride.

He was equally inflexible in his handling of the force. In his judgements he sometimes has an almost Olympian detachment. Each man's behaviour – even when he was off duty – was strictly controlled and scrutinised. On duty the discipline became even tighter. The resignations and frequent dismissals, particularly in the early years, for often trivial offences, sometimes seem unnecessarily harsh, but clearly a new standard had to be set if the break with the past was to be complete. Total obedience was guaranteed by the constant threat of instant relegation to a lower class of pay for misbehaviour as well as the damaging effect that such a report would later have on pension rights. The cumulative effects of these minor offences could be, and often were, financially disastrous. This policy, though admirable for discipline, made for total inflexibility. The men were afraid to use their initiative. Rather than lose financially they rigorously kept to the time of their beats, even if this did mean losing arrests. He maintained this rigidity to the end. Even when the Police Committee showed that it was willing to let the men live outside the City, Harvey never released his grip on them. He did not believe that they could be trusted. His insistence that he should always have the men nearby in case of possible rioting showed how little he understood how social conditions in the City had changed from the time of the Gordon Riots six years before his birth. By the time of his death, there were very few of his old enemies left to oppose him. He was only making new ones by fighting ghosts. His death meant that the force could advance.

His successor, Sir James Fraser, was immediately granted what Harvey had first been denied – permission to live outside the City. The City was rapidly making the transition to a purely commercial centre, and the residential areas were being pushed to its boundaries. Within a few years there was a mass emigration of policemen to the suburbs. Gradually the remaining residential population dwindled. In this century it was Hitler's bombs that dispersed the remainder. Only since the rebuilding have they begun to come back.

APPENDIX 1

THE NUMBERS AND DISTRIBUTION OF WATCHMEN

(a) Watch Acts of 1663 and 1705

	No. of watch-men fixed by Act of 1663	No. actually hired prior to Act of 1705	No. confirmed by Act of 1705
Aldgate Ward	34	25	25
Bishopsgate Ward	80	28	31
Broad Street Ward	30	23	24
Billingsgate Ward	30	14	21
Bridge Ward Within	25	20	20
Bassishaw Ward	12	5	6
Cornhill Ward	16	10	10
Candlewick Ward	24	12	12
Cordwainer Ward	24	10	14
Cheap Ward	25	18	20
Cripplegate Ward Without	90	21	28
Coleman Street Ward	32	18	18
Castle Baynard Ward	40	17	24
Dowgate Ward	36	11	14
Farringdon Ward Within	50	28	36
Lime Street Ward	11	8	8
Langborn Ward	34	22	23
Portsoken Ward	60	27	26
Queenhithe Ward	40	11	10
Vintry Ward	34	11	14
Walbrook Ward	20	14	14

This is not a complete documentation of the City Watch. Figures are not available for some wards and precincts for a comparison to be made.

(b) Watch Act 1775–4

	No. of Beadles hired	No. of Watchmen hired	Each Watchman paid yearly
Aldersgate	2	33	£13
Aldgate	1	25	£26
Bassishaw	1	6	£13
Billingsgate	1	26	£13
Bishopsgate	2	40	£26
Bread Street	1	13	£20
Bridge	1	28	£13
Broadstreet	1	32 watchmen	£18
		6 watchmen	£23
		2 superintendent watchmen	£25
Candlewick	1	20	£13
Castle Baynard	2	17	£26
Cheap	1	28	£20
Coleman Street	1	33	£13
Cordwainer	1	24	£13
Cornhill	1	20	£13
Cripplegate Within	1	27	£13
Cripplegate Without	2	22 watchmen	£26
		4 patrolling watchmen	£36
Dowgate	1	18	£13
Farringdon Within	2	55	£13
Farringdon Without	4	78	£21 7s 0d
Langborn	1	40	£13
Lime Street	1	14	£13
Portsoken	1	20 watchmen	£26
		10 watchmen	£13
Queenhithe	1	14	£21
Tower	2	40	£13
Vintry	1	20	£13
Walbrook	1	19 watchmen	£21
		2 patrolling watchmen	£30

Number of Beadles hired: 35
Number of Watchmen hired: 736

APPENDIX 2

A HIGHWAYMAN'S LAWS*

THE highwayman William Holliday – he was hanged in 1695 – drew up the following 'laws':

Art. I directs – That none of his company should presume to wear shirts, upon pain of being cashiered.

II. – That none should lie in any other places than stables, empty houses, or other bulks.

III. – That they should eat nothing but what they begged, and that they should give away all the money they got by cleaning boots among one another, for the good of the fraternity.

IV. – That they should neither learn to read nor write, that he may have them better under command.

V. – That they should appear every morning by nine, on the parade, to receive necessary orders.

VI. – That none should presume to follow the scent but such as he ordered on that party.

VII. – That if anyone gave them shoes or stockings he should convert them into money to play.

VIII. – That they should steal nothing that they could not come at for fear of bringing a scandal upon the company.

IX. – That they should not endeavour to clear themselves of vermin, by killing or eating them.

X. – That they should cant better than the Newgate birds, pick pockets without bungling, outlive a Quaker, outswear a lord at a gaming-table, and brazen out all their villainies beyond an Irishman.

Patrick Pringle, *Stand and Deliver, The Story of the Highwayman* (1951).

* See Chapter 3.

APPENDIX 3

THE CITY MARSHALS' SALARY AND PROFITS

Osmond Cooke's salary and profits as given to the City Lands Committee in 1762.[1]

	£	s	d
Salary	135	0	0
By Chance Freedoms	8	8	0
Bartholomew Fair	18	0	0
By attending Hospitals	5	5	0
By attending Welch feast		15	0
By attending Anniversary Charity Children		15	0
By attending Merchants etc.	16	16	0
By attending Lady Mayoress Rout	3	3	0
By attending Post Office	3	3	0
Election of Members of Parliament	2	2	0
Sheriffs sworn – 3 Ells of Holland and		10	6
Perquisites	12	0	0
Xmas Box sent by the Brewers	12	12	0
A Scarfe on Lord Mayor's Day			
	£218	9	6

The following is an extract from the City Lands Committee report to the Court of Common Council on 23 March 1775: The Upper Marshal is allowed a Salary of £100 and the Under Marshal £60 a year as also £10 a year to each for keeping a horse and the Court of Aldermen usually give each of them a freedom yearly as a Gratuity. . . .'[2]

* See Chapter 4.

APPENDIX 4

SCALE OF ALLOWANCES
FOR WATCHMEN AND POLICE

Note: Many of the watchmen had been employed for a short time only
and pensions were not given to those that had been employed for
less than five years.

Scale of allowances

From	5 to 10 years service a donation of from	£1 to £5		
	10	15	£2	£8
	15	20	a weekly allowance 3s	5s
	20	25	4s	6s
	25	30	5s	7s
	30	35	6s	8s
	35	40	10s	

Abstract of donations and weekly allowances

		£	s	d
To 81 men a donation of £1 each amounting to		81	0	0
109	2	218	0	0
40	3	120	0	0
7	4	28	0	0
6	5	30	0	0
1	6	6	0	0
244 men Donations amounting to		£483	0	0

		£	s	d
To 3 men a weekly allowance of 2s 6d per week each		19	10	0
36	3s	280	16	0
32	4s	332	16	0
34	5s	442	0	0
1	5s 6d	14	6	0
13	6s	202	16	0
6	7s	109	4	0
3	8s	62	8	0
3	10s	78	0	0
131 men. Weekly allowances amounting to for the year		£1541	16	0

* See Chapter 6.

APPENDIX 5

WAGES FOR THE POLICE 1840

	£	s	d
Constables			
1st class constable against whom no charge had been recorded during the preceding 12 months	1	2	6
2nd class	1	0	6
3rd class		19	6
4th class		18	6
5th class		17	6
Probationer 1st class		14	0
Probationer 2nd class		12	0
Sergeant	1	4	6
Station sergeant	1	5	6
Inspector	2	5	6

APPENDIX 6

COMMISSIONER'S ANNUAL REPORTS

Summary, for the Year 1847

Number of Persons taken into Custody

	Men	Women	Children	Total
Number of persons taken before Magistrates	3859	1525	—	5384
Number of Vagrants	152	106	64	322
Number of Destitute persons	367	339	129	835
Number of Charges not taken, for the reasons assigned on the Occurrence sheets	2784	1023	—	3807
Number of Drunken persons, discharged when capable of self protection	1733	1230	—	2963
Total number taken to the various Stations	8895	4223	193	13311

Summary, for the Year 1848

Number of Persons taken into Custody

	Men	Women	Children	Total
Number of persons taken before Magistrates	3941	1866	—	5807
Number of Vagrants	402	307	228	937
Number of Destitute persons	583	460	226	1269
Number of Charges not taken, for the reasons assigned on the Occurrence sheets	2862	1003	—	3865
Number of Drunken persons, discharged when capable of self protection	1621	1189	—	2810
Total number taken to the various Stations	9409	4825	454	14688

Summary, for the Year 1849

Number of Persons taken into Custody

	Men	Women	Children	Total
Number of persons taken before Magistrates	3446	1680	—	5126
Number of Vagrants	204	215	140	559
Number of Destitute persons	479	381	253	1113
Number of Charges not taken, for the reasons assigned on the Occurrence sheets	2787	1033	—	3820
Number of Drunken persons, discharged when capable of self protection	1599	1132	—	2731
Total number taken to the various Stations	8515	4441	393	13349

APPENDIX 7

THE COMMISSIONERS SINCE HARVEY

Colonel Sir James Fraser, K.C.B.	1863–90
Lieutenant-Colonel Sir Henry Smith, K.C.M.	1890–1
Sir William Nott-Bower, K.C.V.O.	1902–25
Lieutenant-Colonel Sir Hugh S. Turnbull, K.C.V.O., K.B.E.	1925–50
Sir Arthur Young, C.M.G., C.V.O., K.P.M.	1950–71

NOTES

Abbreviations

Calendar 1298–1307   *Calendar of the Early Mayors' Court Rolls of the City of London A.D. 1298–1307*, ed. A. H. Thomas

Calendar 1323–64   *Calendar of the Plea and Memoranda Rolls of the City of London A.D. 1323–64*, ed. A. H. Thomas

Calendar 1364–81   *Calendar of Plea and Memoranda Rolls of the City of London A.D. 1364–81*, ed. A. H. Thomas

Calendar 1413–37   *Calendar of Plea and Memoranda Rolls of the City of London A.D. 1413–37*, ed. A. H. Thomas

Chronicles   *Chronicles of the Mayors and Sheriffs of London A.D. 1188–1274 and the French Chronicle of London A.D. 1259–1343*, trans. H. T. Riley

Elizabethan Underworld   *The Elizabethan Underworld*, ed. A. V. Judges

GL   Guildhall Library

GRO   Guildhall Records Office

JOR   Journal of the Court of Common Council

Liber Albus   *Liber Albus: the White Book of the City of London*, ed. H. T. Riley

Memorials 1276–1419   *Memorials of London and London Life in the XIIIth XIVth and XVth Centuries A.D. 1276–1419*, ed. H. T. Riley

PCP   Police Committee Papers

Rep.   Repertories of the Court of Aldermen

Chapter 1. Watch and Ward

1. John Stow, *Survey of London*, Everyman Library, p. 91.
2. Ibid. p. 10.
3. *Memorials 1276–1419*, pp. 92 and 95.
4. Ibid. pp. 34–5.
5. *Liber Albus*, p. 240.
6. Stow, *Survey of London*, p. 92.
7. *Chronicles*.
8. *Calendar 1413–37*, p. xxxvi. Detailed reference in Rolls for 1323–64 (see n. 13) p. 189.
9. *Liber Albus*, p. 247.
10. Walter de Gray Birch, *The Historical Charters and Constitutional Documents of the City of London*, p. 144.
11. *The Corporation of London. Its Origin, Constitution, Powers and Duties*, pp. 125–6.
12. Ibid. p. 125.
13. *Calendar 1323–64*, p. 133.

14. Quoted in L. F. Salzman, *England in Tudor Times*, p. 64.

15. See (1) the King against Mason, Indictment for refusing to serve the office of constable, (2) the King against Samuel Rogers. Cases in point with Samuel Rogers Esq., elected Constable of Cornhill Ward, (3) Extract from Register for Choice of Officers in Aldgate Ward 1638. Small MS. Box 29 No. 22 GRO.

16. See Rep. 8, fo. 145; Rep. 16, fo. 255; and Rep. 18, fo. 326 GRO.

17. Rep. 31, pt 1, fo. 26.

18. Quoted in T. A. Critchley, *A History of the Police in England and Wales 900–1966*, p. 18.

19. The Humble Petition of William Brown, Citizen and Barber. Small MS. Box 29 No. 22 GRO.

20. Stow, *Survey of London*, p. 93n.

21. JOR 5, fo. 29 GRO.

22. *Memorials 1276–1419*, pp. 34–5.

23. Ibid. p. 561. Also *Calendar 1413–37*, pp. xxvi, xxviii–xxix, xxxvii.

24. *Calendar 1298–1307*, p. 57.

25. Ibid. pp. 124–5.

26. Ibid. pp. 218–19.

27. *Calendar 1364–81*, p. 57.

28. *Calendar 1298–1307*, p. 70.

29. See JOR 45, fos 425–8, 'An Act of Co.Co. for the better ordering of the Night Watches within ye City of London and liberties thereof', 10 October 1663. Also Nightly Watch Committee Minutes November–December 1704 – Abstract of Newlands Bill – Misc. MSS. Box 245.1, and Stow, *Survey of London*, ed. J. Strype, 6th ed., 2 vols (1755) p. 490.

30. *Notes and Queries*, 8th series, vol. 4, p. 86.

31. William Bullein, *A Dialogue against the Pestilence*, 1573 (first published 1564). Quoted in J. Dover Wilson, *Life in Shakespeare's England*, p. 96.

32. *Analytical Index to Remembrancia A.D. 1579–1664* (1878) p. 395.

33. William Bullein, quoted in Dover Wilson, *Life in Shakespeare's England*, p. 97.

Chapter 2. The City Marshals

1. William Bullein, quoted in Dover Wilson, *Life in Shakespeare's England; Notes and Queries*, 7th series, vol. 1, p. 465.

2. Norman G. Brett-James, *The Growth of Stuart London*; Stow, *Survey of London*, ed. Strype, II 536.

3. *Elizabethan Underworld*, pp. xlix–l

4. Walter Bell, *Fleet Street in Seven Centuries*; E. Beresford Chancellor, *The Annals of Fleet Street*.

5. Rep. 80, fos. 100, 106, 111 and 112b.

6. Bell, *Fleet Street in Seven Centuries*; and *Elizabethan Underworld*, p. li, n. 2.

7. *Elizabethan Underworld*, p. xv, n. 2.

8. Quoted in Christopher Hibbert, *The Roots of Evil*, p. 25.

9. Rep. 3, fo. 164.

10. Rep. 4, fo. 76b.

11. Ibid. fo. 215.

12. Quoted in R. H. Tawney and Eileen Power, *Tudor Economic Documents*, II 337–9.

13. Robert Copland, *The Highway to the Spital House* (1535–6). Reprinted in *Elizabethan Underworld*, pp. 1–25.

14. Tawney and Power, *Tudor Economic Documents*, II 306–12; *Elizabethan Underworld*, p. xxix.

15. Quoted in Bell, *Fleet Street in Seven Centuries*.

16. E. G. O'Donoghue, *Bridewell Hospital – Palace, Prison, Schools*, p. 156; *Elizabethan Underworld*, p. lxii.

17. Bell, *Fleet Street in Seven Centuries*.

18. Rep. 10, fo. 204b; Rep. 12, no. 2, fo. 292b; Rep. 11, fos. 384b and 460b; Rep. 15, fos. 288, 367 and 450. See also Thomas Allen, *The History and Antiquities of London, Westminster and Southwark and Parts Adjacent*, pp. 277–80.

19. Rep. 17, fo. 378b.

20. *Elizabethan Underworld*, p. xviii.

21. Thomas Harman, *A Caveat or Warning for Common Cursitors, vulgarly called Vagabonds* (1566). Reprinted in *Elizabethan Underworld*, pp. 61–118.

22. Ibid. p. 117.

23. Ibid. p. 92.

24. Allen, *History and Antiquities*, pp. 277–80; Stow, *Survey of London*, ed. Strype, II 537.

25. Allen, *History and Antiquities*, p. 310; Stow, *Survey of London*, ed. Strype, II 547.

26. JOR 24, fos. 38–40.

27. Allen, *History and Antiquities*, p. 202.

28. Bell, *Fleet Street in Seven Centuries*,

29. Quoted in *Elizabethan Underworld*, pp. xxxviii–xxxix.

30. Stow, *Survey of London*, ed. Strype, II 541.

31. Rep. 23, fo. 548.

32. 26, fo. 179.

33. Stow, *Survey of London*, ed. Strype, II 548.

34. See Rep. 34, fo. 125.

35. Rep. 40, fo. 183.

36. *Court and Times of James I*, 2 vols (1849) II 245–9. Also *Calendar of State Papers Domestic* (1619–23) p. 244.

37. Eric Maple, *The Dark World of Witches*, pp. 76–7.

38. Rep. 42, fo. 213b.

39. Proclamation 'An Act for the Reformation of the Negligence of Constables, and of the Abuses and Misdemeanours of Apprentices, Carmen, and others, and for the better Apprehension of the Offenders'. PD 10.48 GL.

40. Ibid.

41. Lord Mayor's Proclamation. PD 10.49 GL.

42. Lord Mayor's Proclamation. PD 10.73 GL.

43. Lord Mayor's Proclamation. PD 10.71 GL.

44. Ned Ward, *The London Spy Revived* (n.d.) p. 37.

45. Rep. 41, fo. 350.

46. Rep. 43, fo. 282.

47. Rep. 44, fo. 184; and Rep. 45, fo. 444.

48. Rep. 46, fos 70, 98 and 177.

49. Ibid. fos 265, 342; Rep. 47, fos 133, 175; Rep. 51, fos 132, 269 and 303; JOR 40, fo. 48.

50. 'An Act of Common Council for the better ordering of the Night Watches within ye City of London and liberties thereof,' 10 October 1663. JOR 45, fos 425–8.

51. Extract from a speech by the Lord Mayor of London in the year 1667 when he rejected the applications of a number of men who had applied for the position of Borough Constables. City of London Police Museum.

52. 'The humble petition of Robert Wilkins abt. Miscariages of Watching.' Watch and Ward Misc. MSS. 10.13 GRO.

53. Stow, *Survey of London*, ed. Strype, II 490.

54. See Abstract of Newlands Bill and Nightly Watch Committee Minutes, November–December 1704. Misc. MSS. Box 245.1 GRO.

55. Rep. 55, fo. 381; Rep. 59, fos 184b and 324b.

56. 'A True account of a Bloudy and Barbarous Murder, committed on the body of John Sparks, Waterman, by John Hutchins in Fleet Street near Serjeants Inn, London, on Wednesday the 3rd of December, 1684.' Broadside 25.38 GL.

57. Bell, *Fleet Street in Seven Centuries*.

58. *The Devils Cabinet Broke Open: or a new discovery of the Highway Thieves*, London, 1658. A.3.3. no. 43 GL.

59. Ibid.

60. John Pearson, *The London Charleys of the 18th Century; or half-past twelve o'clock, and a Very Cloudy Sort of a Morning*, 1827.

Chapter 3. The Marshal and the Bucklemaker

1. James Whiston, 'England's Calamities Discover'd' (1696) fo. 19. A.7.7. no. 58. GL.

2. John R. Kellett, 'Some Late Seventeenth Century Schemes for the Improvement of the Corporation of London's Revenues', *Guildhall Miscellany*, vol. 1, no. 9 (July 1958) pp. 27–34, and 'The Financial Crisis of the Corporation of London and the Orphans' Act, 1694', *Guildhall Miscellany*, vol. 2, no. 5 (October 1963) pp. 220–7.

3. Whiston, 'England's Calamities Discover'd', fo. 15.

4. B.S. 8.109 (1696) GL. See also R. R. Sharpe, *London and the Kingdom*, 3 vols (1894) II 320, 321 and 326. Also JOR 53, fo. 714.

5. Lewen to Williams. JOR 57, fo. 207b (1717–36). Petition of Elizabeth Hitchen.

6. *An Answer to a Late Insolent Libel entitled A Discovery of the Conduct of Receivers and Thief-Takers in London*, 1718. Pam. A.1.2.65s GL.

7. Evidence against Charles Hitchen, Under Marshal. MSS. 105.8 GRO.

8. Rep. 117, fo. 281.

9. Sir John Fielding, *An Account of the Origin and Effects of a Police*, 1758.

10. Gerald Howson, *Thief-taker General. The Rise and Fall of Jonathan Wild*, p. 20.

11. Quoted in ibid. p. 46.

12. *Tyburn Chronicle*, 2 vols (1768) II 145.
13. Ibid. II 159.
14. *Elizabethan Underworld*.
15. Quoted in Howson, *Thief-taker General*, pp. 40–1.
16. Reprinted in *Tyburn Chronicle*, II 156–78
17. *Select Trials at the Sessions House in the Old Bailey 1720–1741*, 4 vols (1742) III 74–5. Ref. AN 33.1 GL.
18. Howson, *Thief-taker General*, p. 288.

Chapter 4. Riot and Reform

1. Henry Fielding, *An Enquiry into the Causes of the late Increase of Robbers* (1751) p. xxix.
2. 'The humble Petition of Richard Pearse Executioner.' Court of Aldermen Reports and Papers 1705–6.
3. *Daily Post*, 5 February 1726. Quoted in Howson, *Thief-taker General*, p. 280.
4. Fielding, *Enquiry into the Causes of the late Increase of Robbers*, pp. 4 and 145–6.
5. Rep. 179, fo. 190; and Rep. 180, fo. 329.
6. Leon Radzinowicz, *A History of English Criminal Law and its Administration from 1750*, vol. 2 (1948) pp. 326–32 and 338–9.
7. Howson, *Thief-taker General*, p. 65; JOR 60, fo. 26.
8. *A Descriptive Account of the Old House, West Street, Smithfield* (n.d.). Pam. 5428 GL.
9. 'The Petition of the Marshals Men, John Brook, Joseph Norman, Thomas Deming, Mark Bushell, John Sharpe and Robert Jackson.' Court of Aldermen Reports and Papers September 1737–February 1738.
10. *Gentleman's Magazine*, vol. xxxv (1765) p. 145. Quoted in John Ashton, *The Fleet. Its Rivers, Prison and Marriages*, pp. 165–6.
11. M. Dorothy George, *London Life in the Eighteenth Century*, pp. 76, 348.
12. Rep. 110, fo. 140b.
13. Rep. 128, fo. 418.
14. JOR 70, fo. 233b.
15. Rep. 183, fo. 173.
16. Rep. 174, fo. 128; and 'The humble Petition of the Inhabitants from St. Pauls Churchyard to Temple Bar.' Court of Aldermen Reports and Papers January–March 1770.
17. Quoted in Rosamond Bayne-Powell, *Eighteenth Century London Life*, p. 203.
18. Rep. 142, fo. 145; Rep. 163, fo. 433; and Journal of the Committee for City Lands, vol. 79, fo. 72.
19. Hugh Phillips, *The Thames about 1750*, pp. 39–40.
20. See JOR 56, fos 237b and 246; Rep. 166, fos 14 and 29, together with 'Petition of several persons desiring to be admitted constables'. Court of Aldermen Reports and Papers July–December 1761.
21. Bayne-Powell, *Eighteenth Century London Life*, pp. 101–2.
22. 10 George II, cap. 22.
23. Rep. 16, fo. 439; and P.A.R. Book 8, fo. 23 GRO.
24. Report of Commissioners of Streets etc. re Nightly Watch 1774/5. Small MS. Box 12, no. 10 GRO.

25. JOR 66, fos 134–8 and 262–9.

26. Ibid. fo. 195b.

27. *The Complete Newgate Calendar*, ed. G. T. Crook, 5 vols (privately printed for the Navarre Society, 1926) IV 77–86.

28. JOR 66, fos 208–31b.

29. 'The humble petition of James Stoakes Citizen and Wheelwright of London.' Court of Aldermen Reports and Papers January–March 1758.

30. Rep. 153, fos 88, 111 and 134. See also 'The humble petition of the Churchwardens and Overseers of the poor of the Parish of St. Botolph without Aldgate London', Mr Morgan Vaughan's affidavit and Richardson's petition. Court of Aldermen Reports and Papers January–April 1749.

31. Rep. 153, fos 316, 329, 354, 391 and 493; Rep. 154, fo. 117; Rep. 155, fos 389, 390–2, 395–7; JOR 59, fos 276b–279, 318–20b and 339–41.

32. JOR 66, fos 208–31b.

33. JOR 65, fo. 295b.

34. JOR 66, fo. 45b.

35. Ibid. fos 84b, 106b and 119b.

36. Ibid. fo. 195b.

37. JOR 67, fos 135b and 159.

38. Rep. 183, fo. 332.

39. See Rep. 171, fo. 174; Rep. 177, fo. 63.

40. George F. E. Rudé, 'The Gordon Riots: a Study of the Rioters and Their Victims', *Transactions of the Royal Historical Society*, 5th series, vol. 6 (1956) pp. 93–114.

41. See Rep. 164, fos 88 and 197; Rep. 169, fos 223 and 227.

42. I have based this summary on several accounts: (1) *Memoirs of Thomas Holcroft*, ed. W. Hazlitt, 3 vols (1816); (2) *Reminiscences of Henry Angelo*, 2 vols (1904); (3) J. P. De Castro, *The Gordon Riots*; (4) Christopher Hibbert, *King Mob*; (4) Rudé, 'The Gordon Riots'.

Chapter 5. The New Police

1. *Report on the Nightly Watch and Police of the Metropolis. Ordered, by the House of Commons, to be Printed, 24 March 1812*, p. 2.

2. Horace Bleackley, *The Hangmen of England*, pp. 113–32.

3. State Papers 37, no. 21, fo. 225. See also fos 243 and 247. PRO.

4. *Parliamentary History*, vol. 21 (1780–1) col. 1314.

5. Ibid. See complete debate, 5 March 1781.

6. *Parliamentary History*, vol. 25 (1785–6), debate in the Commons on the London and Westminster Police Bill, 23, 27, 28 and 29 June, cols 888–913.

7. Radzinowicz, *English Criminal Law*, II 173–7.

8. B.M's miscellaneous pamphlets, 816.1.5 (43).

9. *Parliamentary History*, vol. 25, col. 891.

10. Ibid. vol. 25, col. 910.

11. Rep. 189, fos 239–44.

12. *Parliamentary History*, vol. 25, col. 901.

13. G. D. H. Cole and Raymond Postgate, *The Common People 1746–1946*, p. 92.

14. Radzinowicz, *English Criminal Law*, III 117.

15. *Parliamentary History*, vol. 25, col. 902.

16. Ibid. vol. 25, cols 912–13.

17. Radzinowicz, *English Criminal Law*, III 117–21.

18. *Report from the Committee on the State of the Metropolis: with the Minutes of Evidence taken before the Committee, and an Appendix of Sundry Papers. Ordered, by the House of Commons, to be Printed, 1 July 1816*, p. 143.

19. Journal Committee City Lands, vol. 78 (1786–7) fo. 316b.

20. *Report from the Select Committee on the Police of the Metropolis. Ordered, by the House of Commons, to be Printed, 11 July 1828*, pp. 51–5, evidence of John Wontner. From 1816 to 1822, when he was thrown from his horse and badly injured, Wontner was City Marshal. Subsequently he became the Keeper of Newgate.

21. *Report from the Committee on the State of the Metropolis* (1816) p. 231.

22. *Report from the Select Committee on Metropolis Police Offices; with the Minutes of Evidence, Appendix and Index. Ordered, by the House of Commons, to be Printed, 29 June 1837*, p. 121.

23. Radzinowicz, *English Criminal Law*, II 298–306.

24. William Blizard, *Desultory Reflections on Police: with an Essay on the Means of Preventing Crimes and Amending Criminals* (1785) p. 18. A.8.7. No. 59 GL.

25. Place Papers, vol. XL, BM. Add. MSS. 27,828 fo. 128, cutting City Police.

26. *Report from Select Committee on Metropolis Police Offices* (1837) pp. 176 and 179.

27. JOR 69, fos 148b and 257.

28. *Parliamentary History*, vol. 25, col. 891.

29. Rep. 195, fos 97 and 130; Rep. 205, fos 243–4 and 366.

30. Rep. 224, fos 148–51.

31. *Report from the Select Committee on Metropolis Police Offices; with the Minutes of Evidence, Appendix and Index. Ordered, by the House of Commons, to be Printed, 11 July 1838*, p. 140.

32. Rep. 216, fos 402–4.

33. *Report from the Committee on the State of the Metropolis* (1816) p. 260.

34. Rep. 195, fo. 125; Rep. 205, fos 436 and 612.

35. Rep. 233, fos 41–7.

36. *Rules, Orders and Regulations for the Police of the City of London*, 1824.

37. Rep. 228, fos 460–6 and 517–18.

38. *Report from the Select Committee on the Police of the Metropolis. Ordered, by the House of Commons, to be Printed, 17 June 1822*, pp. 92–3.

39. Ibid.

40. *The Times*, 27 September 1843.

41. *Report from the Committee on the State of the Metropolis* (1816) pp. 263–4.

42. *The Times*, 3 December 1816.

43. Rep. 221, fos 180–4.

44. *Report from the Select Committee on Metropolis Police Offices* (1837) p. 144.

45. Minutes of the Court of Common Council, 5 April, 20 September, 4 and 11 October, 1 and 7 November 1827.

46. *Report from the Select Committee on the Police of the Metropolis* (1828) p. 36.

47. Norman Gash, *Mr Secretary Peel*, pp. 492–6.

48. *Hansard*, new series, vol. 21, cols 867–84.

49. Charles Hindley, *The Life and Times of James Catnach* (*Late of Seven Dials*), *Ballad Monger* (1878) pp. 205–6.

Chapter 6. The Last of the Charleys

1. *The Times*, 6 June 1829.

2. Charles Reith, *A New Study of Police History*, p. 124.

3. *Hansard*, 3rd series, vol. 49.

4. *Report from Select Committee on Metropolis Police Offices* (1837) pp. 145–8, paper 'Nightly Watch and Police' delivered in by Mr Alderman Venables.

5. Ibid. p. 110.

6. *Report from the Select Committee on the Police of the Metropolis; with the Minutes of Evidence. Ordered, by the House of Commons, to be Printed, 13 August 1834*, pp. 202 and 205.

7. *Report from the Select Committee on Metropolis Police Offices* (1838) p. 141; also *Report from the Select Committee appointed to inquire into the State of the Police of the Metropolis within the Metropolitan District, and the State of Crime therein* (1833) pp. 197–8; and *The Times*, 27 June 1832.

8. *Report from the Select Committee on Police of the Metropolis* (1833) pp. 204–6.

9. *The Times*, 21 June 1830.

10. Minutes of the Court of Common Council, 21 October 1830.

11. *Report from the Select Committee on Metropolis Police Offices* (1837) p. 143.

12. Ibid. p. 144.

13. Police Committee of Aldermen, 3 February 1832; and Rep. 236, fos 369–73.

14. Rep. 236, fos 343–5.

15. *Report from the Select Committee on Police of the Metropolis* (1833) pp. 195–7.

16. JOR 107, fos 34–5; and Sir Peter Laurie's evidence to Select Committee, 1838 (*Report*, pp. 125–7).

17. *The Times*, 27 July 1832.

18. Rep. 236, fo. 535; and JOR 107, fos 59b–61.

19. *The Times*, 11 May 1833.

20. JOR 107, fo. 394; JOR 108, 10 and 21 May 1833. *The Times*, 10 May 1833.

21. JOR 109, fos 264b–266.

22. Rep. 242, fos 172–4.

23. Ibid. fos 184–7.

24. Minutes of the Court of Common Council, 6 November 1838, 'Nightly Watch and Police Bill 1838–1839'.

25. Charles Hindley, *Life and Times of James Catnach*.

26. Police Committee Ward Returns 1839 (Pension Recommendations). Also Police Committee 1839 Ward Returns of Watchmen discharged.

27. Minutes of the Court of Common Council, 25 March 1839.
28. Ibid. 12 April 1839.
29. Mepol. 2/22 PRO.
30. *Hansard*, 3rd series, vol. 13 (1833) cols 648–714.
Inns of Court – Case of Mr D. W. Harvey. *Second Report from the Select Committee on the Inns of Court with Minutes of Evidence and Appendix. Ordered, by the House of Commons, to be Printed, 4 August 1834. Parliamentary Papers* (1834) vol. 18, *Reports from the Committees.*
Documents relating to the Application of Daniel Whittle Harvey Esq. To be called to the Bar and his rejection by the Benchers of the Inner Temple. Ordered, by the House of Commons, to be Printed, 3 June 1834. Parliamentary Papers (1834) vol. 48, *Accounts and Papers.*
31. *The Times*, 28 February 1839.
32. Ibid. 10 March 1819.
33. Ibid. 31 October, 10 and 21 November 1823.
34. Ibid. 16 February 1839.
35. *Hansard*, 3rd series, vol. 49, cols 331–44. London Police – Riders to Bills.
36. 2 and 3 Victoria, c. xciv (a Local Act, 1839).

Chapter 7. The Early Victorian City of London

1. *The Groans of the Gallows, or the Past and Present Life of William Calcraft, the Living Hangman of Newgate.* PAM 1490 GL.
2. Peter Cunningham, *Handbook for London.*
3. 'Aleph,' *London Scenes and London People.*
4. *Report of the Commissioners appointed to inquire into the existing state of the Corporation of London* (1854) pp. 336 and 337.
5. Report to the Court of Common Council from the Coal and Corn and Finance Committee. Presented 28th November 1839. P.A.R. 13, fo. 199, pp. 20–1.
6. Ibid. p. 21.
7. *Report of the Select Committee appointed to inquire into the State of Smithfield Market, and the slaughtering of cattle in the Metropolis. Ordered, by the House of Commons, to be Printed, 19th July 1828*, p. 4.
8. *First Annual Report, 1848–9*, in John Simon, *Reports relating to the Sanitary Condition of the City of London*, 1854.
9. *Report of the Select Committee appointed to inquire into the State of Smithfield Market*, p. 21.
10. Ibid. p. 107.
11. *First Report of the Commissioners for inquiring into the state of large towns and Populous Districts* (1844) p. 204.
12. Ibid. p. 209.
13. John Simon, *First Annual Report, 1848–9.*
14. R. A. Lewis, *Edwin Chadwick and the Public Health Movement 1832–1854*, p. 150.
15. *Report from the Select Committee on Improvement of the Health of Towns, together with the Minutes of Evidence, Appendix and Index* (1842) p. 91.
16. Ibid. p. 161.

17. *London Journal* (1853) and miscellaneous cuttings. Noble Collection 48.5 GL.

18. C. E. R. Sherrington, *A Hundred Years of Inland Transport 1830–1933*, pp. 72–5.

19. Cunningham, *Handbook for London*, p. 98.

20. Sherrington, *Inland Transport*, pp. 51–6.

21. *Report of the Commissioners appointed to inquire into the existing state of the Corporation of the City of London* (1854) p. 21.

22. Rep. 241, fo. 295–7. The humble petition of the Inhabitants near London Bridge.

23. J. Timbs, *Curiosities of London*, pp. 688–91.

24. Rep. 227, fo. 511–18.

25. Cunningham, *Handbook for London*, p. 119.

26. *Report of the Commissioners appointed to inquire into the existing State of the Corporation of the City of London* (1854) p. 257.

27. *The Times*, 4 May 1829.

28. *First Report from the Committee on the State of the Police of the Metropolis* (1817) p. 456.

29. H. Morley, *Memoirs of Bartholomew Fair*, p. 384.

30. *The Times*, 27 March 1840.

31. *Report of the Commissioners appointed to inquire into the existing State of the Corporation of the City of London* (1854) p. 51.

32. *The Times*, 17 December 1839.

Chapter 8. The Guinea-a-week Men

1. *The Croker Papers*, ed. Louis J. Jennings, 3 vols (1884) II 18–19.

2. Harvey to Police Committee, 24 April 1861. PCP April 1861.

3. Harvey to General Purposes Committee of Aldermen, 7 February 1861. PCP January 1861.

4. Quoted by Mrs C. S. Peel in *Early Victorian England*, ed. G. M. Young, I 131–2.

5. Rep. 245 (1840–1) pp. 144–9.

6. Petition to Harvey from the inspectors, sergeants and constables. PCP January 1861.

7. *The Times*, 5 January 1850.

8. Ibid. 13 July 1852.

9. Ibid. 2 July 1849.

10. Harvey to Police Committee, 24 October 1853. PCP October 1853.

11. Report of the Commissioners appointed to inquire into the regulations affecting the Sanitary condition of the Army, the organization of hospitals and the treatment of the sick and wounded with Evidence and Appendix (1858), *Papers of the House of Commons (1857–8)*, vol. 18, pp. 239–42, evidence of the City Police surgeon, George Borlase Childs.

12. Surgeon's report. Childs was asked 'to report upon the probable duration of life of the men in the Police Force – of the peculiar diseases to which they are liable – with general observations upon the Medical history of the Police Force'. PCP March 1862.

13. George Payne, Police Receiver, to Police Committee, 29 April 1846. PCP April 1846.

14. Rep. 246, pp. 76–110. Rules and Regulations.
15. Superintendent Hodgson to Harvey, 2 November 1849. PCP November 1849.
16. *The Times*, 11 September 1852.
17. Ibid. 11 March 1840.
18. Harvey to Thomas Wood, Alderman, 21 May 1845. PCP May 1845. See also 'Draft letter to the Bankers, Merchants and Traders in the City of London' (PCP February 1846), and Report of the Police Committee to Court of Common Council, 24 September 1845 (PCP September 1845). Also Minutes of Court of Common Council.
19. Harvey to Police Committee, 24 April 1861. PCP April 1861.
20. Surgeon's report to Police Committee re clothing, 18 November 1861. PCP November 1861.
21. Surgeon's report on accommodation for constables and prisoners at different stations. PCP October 1848.
22. Minutes of enquiry, instituted by order of the Commissioner, into a Complaint preferred by Mr Wakefield of No. 8 Sun Street, Bishopsgate, and also by Mrs Bird of No. 12 Princes Street, Barbican, against Inspector T. Hunter. There are two variants of the inspector's name – Tod Hunter and Todhunter – the latter is more commonly used. PCP February 1847.
23. Minutes of evidence before the (Select) Police Committee of the Common Council re the Commissioner of Police and the conduct of business at the Chief Office. February–March 1847, vol. 5, p. 203. 562B GRO.
24. Ibid. vol. 5, p. 264.
25. Ibid. vol. 2, p. 93. See also pp. 68–9 and 95.
26. *The Times*, 12 and 14 September 1842.
27. *The Times*, 1 August 1850.

Chapter 9. Beggars, Swell Mobsters and Shofulmen

1. Report '1842 February 26th 9.30 p.m.'. PCP March 1842.
2. *The Times*, 27 January 1848.
3. 'The humble petition of the Board of Guardians of the West of London Union.' PCP January 1842.
4. Rep. 252, fos 554–7.
5. *Mayhew's Characters*, ed. Peter Quennell, p. 137.
6. *Mayhew's Characters*, p. 134.
7. *The Times*, 11 January 1849.
8. Quoted in J. J. Tobias, *Crime and Industrial Society in the Nineteenth Century*, p. 76.
9. Thomas Beames, *The Rookeries of London*, pp. 53–5.
10. *The Times*, 28 October 1862.
11. Ibid. 27 and 28 October 1840.
12. *Mayhew's Characters*, p. 122.
13. *The Times*, 20 December 1849.
14. *London's Underworld*, ed. Peter Quennell, p. 137.
15. *The Times*, 26 October 1843.
16. 'Aleph', *London Scenes and London People*.
17. *The Times*, 9 October 1849.
18. Ibid. 12 April 1847.

19. Ibid. 8 April 1847.

20. Ibid. 8 April 1844.

21. Ibid. 18 February 1840, 25 and 27 February 1841. Also newspaper cuttings PCP February 1841.

22. *The Times*, 8 March 1848.

23. Ibid. 9 February 1843.

24. Philip Collins, *Dickens and Crime*, pp. 184–8.

25. Inspector Martin to Harvey, 17 November 1840. PCP November 1840.

26. Inspector Martin to Harvey, 20 June 1843. PCP June 1843.

27. Printed report 'Police Committee report on the state of the Police Stations of the City of London 11th May 1859'. GRO.

28. John Morris, Storekeeper, to Harvey, 4 October 1848. PCP October 1848.

29. S. F. L. Pereira to Harvey, 19 November 1840. PCP November 1840.

30. Petition of Robert Cousins. PCP May 1856.

31. *The Times*, 21 October 1840.

32. Petition of Joseph Todhunter, Inspector of Police. PCP December 1856. Chartist meetings took place in Smithfield in April and May 1839. In a meeting between the Lord Mayor and the Secretary of the London Chartists Committee *The Times*, 7 May 1839, quotes the former by saying 'The Lord Mayor said that calling upon the people to attend the meeting armed, and arms having been brought into and deposited in Smithfield, *as he knew was the case. . . .*' He was seemingly alluding to Todhunter's reports.

33. *The Times*, 8 May 1840.

34. Ibid. 30 May 1840.

35. Ibid. 28 March 1850.

36. Ibid. 7 and 9 February 1850.

37. Ibid. 30 May and 14 June 1850.

38. Ibid. 16 May 1849.

39. Ibid. 21 March 1849. See also *The Times*, 3 August 1849, when he, Cornelius Hearne, was sent for trial for stealing a silk handkerchief.

40. *The Times*, 8 December 1845 and 15 February 1847.

41. Ibid. 16 June 1851.

42. *Daily Telegraph*, 14 February 1865.

43. Two good summaries are in the *Morning Star*, 15 February 1866, and *The Times*, 16 February 1866.

44. *The Times*, 5 November 1847.

45. Inspector Adam Spary to Harvey, 23 May 1850. PCP May 1850.

46. This subject is one of the main themes of Harvey's correspondence for the next twenty years. For this part of the story the two main quarries are Harvey's letter of 16 February 1842 (PCP February 1842) to the Lord Mayor, and the Police Committee printed report, 16 December 1841. A,90/L. Other reports are referred to in the next chapter.

47. City Solicitor to Police Committee, 27 July 1842 (PCP July 1842) and letter, n.d., G. Bracher to Police Committee, March and April 1843.

48. Clerk of City's Works to Police Committee, 28 February 1843. PCP February 1843.

49. Harvey to Police Committee, 29 March 1843. PCP March 1843.

50. *The Times*, 28 April 1840.

51. Harvey to Town Clerk, 26 January 1841. Police Committee of Aldermen, Misc. papers 1841.

52. Harvey to Police Committee, 5 November 1841. PCP November 1841.

53· Harvey to Police Committee of Aldermen, 7 December 1841. Police Committee of Aldermen, Misc. papers 1841.

54. *The Times*, 23 February 1841.

55. Harvey to Lord Mayor, 19 April 1842. PCP April 1842.

56. Harvey to H. Woodthorpe, Esq., 11 January 1841. Police Committee of Aldermen Misc. papers 1841.

57. *The Times*, 2 and 6 January 1847.

58. Minutes of Evidence before the Select Police Committee of the Common Council re the Commissioner of Police and the conduct of business at the Chief Office. February and March 1847. 8 vols. Shelf 540E GRO.

59. *The Times*, 17 July 1847.

60. Ibid. 30 September 1847.

61. Harvey to Police Committee, 11 September 1846. PCP September 1846.

62. Memorandum (n.d.) Superintendent Hodgson to Harvey. PCP June 1860.

63. *The Times*, 6 and 7 March 1857.

64. *Report of the Commissioner appointed to Inquire into the existing state of the City of London and to collect information respecting its constitution, order and government etc. Together with the Minutes of Evidence and Appendix*, 1854.

65. Rep. 262, fos 112–14, 164 and 208–10.

66. *The Times*, 25 November, 5 and 14 December 1857, 7 January and 10 February 1858.

Chapter 10. The End of an Era

1. M. Willson Disher, *Victorian Song* (1955) p. 133.

2. *The Times*, 24 February 1859.

3. Ibid. 5 November 1860.

4. Ibid. 16 February 1866.

5. Rep. 165, fos 85–6.

6. *The Times*, 21 February 1844.

7. *Notes and Queries*, 11th series, vol. 7, p. 257.

8. Rep. 263, fos 183–93.

9. *The Times*, 30 October 1857.

10. *Daily Telegraph*, 14 February 1865.

11. *The Times*, 29 July 1853.

12. Ibid. 12 August and 23 December 1853.

13. Report Inspector Howard and Acting Inspector Knight. PCP January/February 1860.

14. Harvey to Police Committee, 28 January 1861. And Superintendent Hodgson to Harvey, 24 January 1861. PCP January 1861.

15. Private information from Childs's great-granddaughter Mrs S. M. Kemsley.

16. Report Mr Childs, Surgeon Police Force re clothing, 18 November 1861. PCP November 1861. Superintendent Hodgson to Harvey, 2 November 1849. PCP November 1849. Also PCP January 1863.

17. Messrs Ellwoods to Colonel Fraser. Colonel Fraser to Sub Police Committee, 21 September 1864. PCP September 1864.

18. Surgeon's Report. PCP March 1862.

19. Report. Police Fund. PCP January 1862.

20. Harvey to Police Committee, 28 February 1863. PCP January 1863. Individual petitions and Harvey to Police Committee, 28 March 1848. PCP March 1848.

21. Childs to Harvey, 23 September 1856. PCP September 1856.

22. John Mitchell, Station Sergeant, to Harvey, 7 June 1849. PCP November 1849.

23. Petition of Inspector Joseph Todhunter. PCP January 1857. And the humble petition of Margaret Todhunter. PCP January 1863.

24. Individual petitions. PCP December 1851.

25. Petition of Cornelius Dolohunty. PCP March 1857.

26. Petition to Harvey, 26 July 1859. PCP July 1859. Petitions of Thomas Crocker and John Spring; and Harvey to Police Committee, 23 February 1859. PCP February 1859.

27. Petitions of Richard Gaul and John Hassett. PCP January 1861.

28. Petition of William Bowles. PCP December 1851.

Chapter 11. Conclusion

1. Charles Reith, *The Blind Eye of History*, p. 106.

Appendix 3. The City Marshals' Salary and Profits

1. See JOR 66, fos 208–31b.
2. Ibid. fo. 195b.

SELECT BIBLIOGRAPHY

Joseph Adshead, *Prisons and Prisoners* (1845).

'Aleph', *London Scenes and London People* (1863).

Thomas Allen, *The History and Antiquities of London, Westminster and Southwark and Parts Adjacent* (1827).

John Ashton, *The Fleet. Its Rivers, Prison and Marriages* (1889).

Rosamond Bayne-Powell, *Eighteenth Century London Life* (1937).

Thomas Beames, *The Rookeries of London* (1857).

Walter Bell, *Fleet Street in Seven Centuries* (1912).

Walter de Gray Birch, *The Historical Charters and Constitutional Documents of the City of London* (1887).

Horace Bleackley, *The Hangmen of England* (1929).

Norman G. Brett-James, *The Growth of Stuart London* (1935).

Calendar of Early Mayors' Court Rolls of the City of London A.D. 1298–1307, ed. A. H. Thomas (1924).

Calendar of Plea and Memoranda Rolls of the City of London A.D. 1323–64, ed. A. H. Thomas (1926).

Calendar of Plea and Memoranda Rolls of the City of London A.D. 1364–1381, ed. A. H. Thomas (1929).

Calendar of Plea and Memoranda Rolls of the City of London A.D. 1413–37, ed. A. H. Thomas (1943).

E. Beresford Chancellor, *The Annals of Fleet Street* (1912).

Chronicles of the Mayors and Sheriffs of London. A.D. 1188–A.D. 1274 and the French Chronicle of London A.D. 1259–A.D. 1343, ed. H. T. Riley (1863).

G. D. H. Cole and Raymond Postgate, *The Common People 1746–1946*, 4th ed. (1964).

Philip Collins, *Dickens and Crime* (1962).

The Corporation of London. Its Origin, Constitution, Powers and Duties (1950).

T. A. Critchley, *A History of Police in England and Wales 900–1966* (1967).

Peter Cunningham, *Handbook for London*, 2 vols (1849).

J. P. de Castro, *The Gordon Riots* (1926).

Early Victorian England, ed. G. M. Young, 2 vols (1963).

The Elizabethan Underworld, ed. A. V. Judges (1965).

Norman Gash, *Mr Secretary Peel* (1964).

M. Dorothy George, *London Life in the Eighteenth Century* (1930).

Christopher Hibbert, *King Mob* (1958).

—, *The Roots of Evil* (1963).

Gerald Howson, *Thief-taker General* (1970).

R. A. Lewis, *Edwin Chadwick and the Public Health Movement 1832–1854* (1952).

Liber Albus: the White Book of the City of London, ed. H. T. Riley (1861).

Eric Maple, *The Dark World of Witches* (1965).

Henry Mayhew, *Mayhew's Characters,* ed. Peter Quennell (n.d.). Selected from *London Labour and the London Poor.*

—, *London's Underworld,* ed. Peter Quennell (n.d.). Selected from *London Labour and the London Poor.*

Henry Mayhew and John Binny, *The Criminal Prisons of London and Scenes of Prison Life* (1862).

Memorials of London and London Life in the XIIIth, XIVth and XVth Centuries. A.D. 1276–1419, ed. H. T. Riley (1868).

R. J. Mitchell and M. D. R. Leys, *A History of the English People* (1967).

H. Morley, *Memoirs of Bartholomew Fair* (n.d.).

E. G. O'Donoghue, *Bridewell Hospital – Palace, Prison, Schools* (1923).

Hugh Phillips, *The Thames about 1750* (1951).

Leon Radzinowicz, *A History of English Criminal Law and Its Administration from 1750,* vols 1–4 (1948–68).

Charles Reith, *The Blind Eye of History* (1952).

—, *A New Study of Police History* (1956).

L. F. Satzman, *England in Tudor Times* (1933).

G. A. Sekon, *Locomotion in Victorian London* (1938).

C. E. R. Sherrington, *A Hundred Years of Inland Transport 1830–1933* (1969).

Lieutenant-Colonel Sir Henry Smith, *From Constable to Commissioner* (1910).

John Stow, *Survey of London,* Everyman Library (1956).

R. H. Tawney and Eileen Power, *Tudor Economic Documents,* 3 vols (1951).

A. G. Temple, *Guildhall Memories* (1918).

J. Timbs, *Curiosities of London* (1867).

J. J. Tobias, *Crime and Industrial Society in the Nineteenth Century* (1967).

John Dover Wilson, *Life in Shakespeare's England* (1920).

Index

Index

Index